HIDDEN HEROISM

HIDDEN HEROISM

BLACK SOLDIERS IN AMERICA'S WARS

ROBERT B. EDGERTON

Westview
PRESS

A Member of the Perseus Books Group

Published in 2001 in the United States of America by Westview Press, 5500 Central Avenue, Boulder, Colorado 80301-2877, and in the United Kingdom by Westview Press, 12 Hid's Copse Road, Cumnor Hill, Oxford OX2 9JJ

Find us on the World Wide Web at www.westviewpress.com

Library of Congress Cataloging-in-Publication Data
Edgerton, Robert B., 1931–
    Hidden heroism : Blacks in America's wars / by Robert b. Edgerton.
       p.   cm.
    Includes bibiliographical references and index.
    ISBN 0-8133-3858-1
    1. Afro-American soldiers—History.   2. United States—History, Military.
3. United States—Armed Forces—Afro-Americans—History.   4. United States—
Race relations.   5. Race discrimination—United States—History.   I. Title.

E185.63 .E34   2000
355'.009'96073—dc2

The paper used in this publication meets the requirements of the American National Standard for Permanence of Paper for Printed Library Materials Z39.48-1984.

Text design by Cynthia Young
Set in 11-point Adobe Berthold Garamond by the Perseus Books Group

10   9   8   7   6   5   4   3   2   1

Contents

Acknowledgments

Many fine books and articles listed in the footnotes and bibliography examine the participation of blacks in one of America's wars, and several previous works have described the entire history of blacks in America's military services. J. D. Foner wrote *Blacks and the Military in American History* in 1974, followed by *Strength for the Fight* by Bernard C. Nalty in 1986, *The History of African-Americans in the Military* by Gary Donaldson in 1991, and *The African-American Soldier* by Lt. Col. (Ret.) Michael Lee Lanning in 1997, and most recently, George Astor wrote *The Right to Fight* in 1998. All of these books provide accurate, insightful overviews of this history. These authors are highly qualified and I recommend their books to any interested reader. However, these books differ from *Hidden Heroism* because with very few exceptions they do not examine the many factors that gave rise to the "natural coward" stereotype, helped to maintain it for so many years, and created the racial division that still troubles American life. Also, these books do little to place American military history in the larger social and cultural context of race relations, nor do they examine the experiences of soldiers of African ancestry in the military forces of other slave-owning countries. Except for Nalty's, these books also do not provide endnotes that would permit interested readers to pursue matters of interest further.

Because *Hidden Heroism* spans more than two centuries of warfare under changing social and cultural conditions, it proved impossible for me to consult all the primary documents in any systematic fashion. There is a vast store of rich information in letters and diaries, newspaper and magazine stories, records of the War Department, the historical offices of the five military services, the Manuscript Division of the Library of

Congress, regimental histories, ships' logs, unit disciplinary records, promotions, medals, transfers, and the like. With the help of three dedicated graduate student research assistants—Paula Wilkinson, Patricia Tilburg, and especially R. Jean Cadigan—I have been able to access all of these sources on a selective basis, focusing either on limited historical periods such as times of military combat, or on the need to examine particular primary sources mentioned in secondary documents. Thanks to the resources of the Inter-Library Loan Department of the Charles A. Young Research Library at UCLA, I have been able to obtain published sources from libraries throughout the country, and thanks to the rapidly expanding resources available on-line, I have been able to consult obscure archival materials from collections that I had not previously known existed. I have no doubt that I have missed much that is relevant, but thanks to the primary sources I have mentioned along with a host of secondary books and articles, I believe that the events and patterns I describe are accurate. I am also most grateful to Rob Williams at Westview Press for his keen editorial eye, as well as Carol Jones and Michelle Trader for their astute editorial assistance. Once again, Margaret Ritchie did a superb job of copyediting.

My own military service in the United States Air Force from January 1951 to October 1954 introduced me to a racially integrated world that I had not previously experienced. It also painfully introduced me to Jim Crow and police brutality when two Air Force friends and I, one of them an African American lieutenant, refused to move to the back of a bus in San Antonio, Texas.

Introduction

This book is about the heroism of African Americans throughout the history of America's armed forces, and white America's refusal to recognize their many achievements, insisting until very recently that they were "natural cowards" unsuited for military combat. In America's military forces, as in all aspects of American life, black men and women have faced profound racial discrimination, even hatred. Like other members of their race throughout history, blacks in our military had to struggle against Jim Crow laws in the South that affected almost every aspect of public life, including military bases. The North usually lacked Jim Crow laws but maintained racial discrimination that was at times even more rabid than the racism that existed in the South. Until recently, America's military forces were dominated by southern beliefs and values that degraded blacks despite their military achievements.

Although black men fought valiantly in all but one of America's wars—they were not permitted to fight in the war against Mexico—the U.S. government was often opposed to the use of blacks in the armed forces, and the War Department was openly hostile to the idea. Blacks were suitable for menial labor but because they were "natural cowards"—their typical description by white southern officers and some northerners—combat was out of the question. Both within the military and in civilian life, there was also the ever-present threat of white violence. Black soldiers were murdered, and many black civilians, including women and children, were killed in riots; others were hanged, beaten to death, or burned alive. Racial integration of the military did not begin until the 1950s, but soon after, the civil rights movement of the 1960s would accelerate social changes that benefited blacks in military as well as civilian life. Overt racial discrimination slowly lessened, and more African American men and women achieved success in business, the academic world, medicine, law, and even the judiciary. In 1982, Alice Walker won the Pulitzer Prize for fiction for *The Color Purple,* and in 1993, Toni Morrison won the Nobel Prize for contributions to literature.

Today, black newscasters appear on television in virtually every national news broadcast seen in this country, Ed Bradley has been seen on *60 Minutes* for twenty years, television "personalities" such as Oprah Winfrey and Bill Cosby are household names, and black actors and actresses play a wide variety of sympathetic roles in motion pictures, including heroic ones where black characters played by actors such as Sidney Poitier and Denzel Washington triumph over weak, corrupt, or evil white antagonists. In *Shaft,* Samuel L. Jackson breaks all the rules—heroically. And all kinds of black entertainers have achieved public acclaim and fortune, including vocalists as different as Nancy Wilson, Lauryn Hill, and Nat "King" Cole, all of whom proved immensely popular with white listeners. A black woman, Mae C. Jemison, M.D., Ph.D., became an astronaut, police departments have slowly desegregated, and increasing numbers of African Americans have been elected or appointed to governmental posts at the local, state and federal levels. Long-segregated collegiate and professional sports have opened to blacks as well, with baseball stars from Jackie Robinson to Sammy Sosa capturing America's hearts; today, Michael Jordan and Tiger Woods are two of America's best-known and most popular public figures, as reflected in their many lucrative product endorsements and television commercials. Even in the Deep South, high school and college football and basketball teams have become dominated by black athletes, to the growing acceptance of white fans. Large white crowds cheer while football games between schools such as Georgia and Georgia Tech, Alabama and Auburn, and Mississippi and Mississippi State are played by teams with a majority of black players, while some black assistant coaches pace the sidelines and other blacks serve as officials.

On June 7, 1999, *Newsweek* ran a cover story entitled "The Good News About Black America (And Why Blacks Aren't Celebrating)." It went on to conclude, "It's the best time ever to be black in America. Crime is down; jobs and income are up. White kids choose African-Americans as their heroes. But not everyone's celebrating." Based on a *Newsweek* poll as well as polls by scholars at Harvard and William and Mary, *Newsweek* reported:

Black employment and home ownership are up. Murders and other violent crimes are down. Reading and math proficiency are climbing. Out-of-
wedlock births are at their lowest rate in four decades. Fewer blacks are on
welfare than at any point in recent memory. More are in college than at
any point in history. And the percentage of black families living below the
poverty line is the lowest it has been since the Census Bureau began keeping separate black poverty statistics in 1967.[1]

What is more, blacks are moving into positions of power in corporate
America and the number of blacks elected to public office has increased
sixfold since 1970. Although more black men than ever before are in
prison, black academic achievement remains lower than that of whites,
and the suicide rate among young black men has risen—hardly a sign of
renewed hope—many black inner-city neighborhoods have been renewed and almost as many blacks as whites respond positively when
asked about their expectations for the future. Even the police, so long
seen by many blacks as racist and brutal, have begun to receive higher
approval ratings. In a U.S. Justice Department poll released on June 3,
1999, blacks were as satisfied as whites with police in several cities—97
percent of both blacks and whites approving in Madison, Wisconsin; 89
percent of blacks compared to 95 percent of whites in San Diego; and
81 percent of blacks versus 88 percent of whites in Savannah, Georgia.
Black approval ratings were less favorable in some other cities, including large ones like Chicago (69 percent of blacks, 89 percent of whites)
and New York (77 percent of blacks, 90 percent of whites). In Los Angeles, a city long associated with black accusations of police brutality, 82
percent of blacks were satisfied with the police compared to 89 percent
of whites. All of these percentages are in response to a question about
satisfaction with police in one's own neighborhood. Satisfaction with
the police in general may be lower. For example, a *Los Angeles Times* poll
released a few months earlier than the *Newsweek* story found that black
satisfaction with the police in the Los Angeles Police Department in
general was only 48 percent.[2]
And the media need not search far for angry accusations of police
misconduct against blacks. As this is written in the first year of the "new
millennium," black activists in Riverside, California, were continuing to
demand a federal investigation of the repeated shooting of nineteen-
year-old Tyisha Miller by four white police officers, and citizens of both
races expressed concern about police misconduct in the shooting death

of a small, mentally ill, homeless black woman, fifty-four-year-old Margaret Mitchell, in Los Angeles. In New York, a white police officer plead guilty to sodomizing a Haitian immigrant, Abner Louima, with a broom handle. The officer apologized to his own family but not to Louima before receiving a thirty-year prison sentence.[3]

As we enter the twenty-first century, racial hatred and discrimination have not vanished from America; they continue to pervade this society in both subtle and overt forms. The NAACP challenged the four major television networks to correct their near-exclusion of minorities in their fall 1999 prime-time programs. Web sites promoting racial hatred, much of it directed against African Americans, have proliferated on the Internet, as witness the murderous rampages of self-proclaimed white supremacist Benjamin Nathaniel Smith in Illinois and Indiana, in July 1999. Smith was a member of the white supremacist "World Church of the Creator," with forty-six chapters and a Web site, including one for children. Newspapers and television sets regularly report accusations of police brutality directed against blacks. An incident in New York City in February 1999, in which four white police officers fired forty-one shots at an unarmed, twenty-two-year-old African, killing him, created a public and media firestorm of protest, as did the NYPD shooting of an unarmed black man, Patrick Dorismond, in March 2000. The trial of John W. King for dragging a black man to a hideous death behind a pickup truck horrified the nation, including the small East Texas town where it took place in 1999. A jury of eleven white citizens and one black found King, a self-proclaimed racist, guilty of murder, sentencing him to death. King expressed no remorse during the trial and spat racial epithets as he left the courtroom. A second defendant was also convicted and sentenced to death. A third man was found guilty and sentenced to a life term.

Over the past half century, America's armed forces have hardly been immune from racial hostilities, but since the end of the Vietnam War, such attitudes and incidents have proven to be increasingly rare. In his autobiography, General Colin Powell, former chairman of the Joint Chiefs of Staff, wrote, "The army was living the democratic ideal ahead of the rest of America. Beginning in the fifties, less discrimination, a truer merit system, and leveler playing fields existed inside the gates of our military posts than in any Southern city or Northern corporation."[4] Today, although blacks constitute about 12 percent of the American population, they represent over 20 percent of America's enlisted personnel in the armed forces, and blacks make up close to 10 percent of the officer corps, many of them graduates of one of the military academies. Numerous African Americans have attained the rank of general or admiral, and recent military confrontations in Grenada, Panama, the Persian Gulf, Bosnia, and Kosovo have made the presence of African American men and women, including officers, in our military operations seem perfectly natural when seen on CNN or elsewhere. So it is in the film industry, where more and more popular films such as *Three Kings* and *Rules of Engagement* cast African Americans as senior military officers. Military recruiting posters shown on television almost invariably show at least one African American.

However, until well into the Korean War, the presence of African Americans in the armed forces was anything but natural. And even after the Korean War ended in 1953, many prominent American military men and politicians firmly believed that blacks lacked the courage to serve in combat or the intelligence and moral character to become officers. Why these beliefs arose and how they persisted for so long is a complex story that begins even before black African slaves reached North America, and one that has continued throughout the history of this country. Few Americans today appear to be aware that black men, and sometimes women, fought in combat even before the Revolutionary War and have been intrepid warriors in all but one of this country's wars since then. This lack of awareness is not surprising given the extent to which the history books used in our schools have ignored these achievements. What is more, until quite recently there was a concerted effort by many, including highly placed military men and political leaders, to portray black soldiers as fools and cowards. The accomplishments of black Americans in military service not only play a pivotal role in black history but deserve a place of respect in the history of all Americans.

ONE

"The Average Negro Is Naturally Cowardly"

From the earliest days of the British colonies in America, a few military men and civilians argued that black Americans, free or slave, should be allowed to fight against whatever pressing threat was at hand—by Indians, French, or Spaniards—and some of them did so. Even southern colonies like North Carolina and Virginia used blacks in their militias during the French and Indian War, and blacks served in the militias of most northern colonies, especially New York.[1] After the fighting ended, a few of these African Americans were praised for their service, with their courage and devotion to duty sometimes noted. But there were many more voices, often influential, that opposed arming such men, arguing that whatever military service they might provide was useless because blacks were far too undisciplined, unintelligent, childlike, and downright cowardly ever to be entrusted with arms. Sometimes, a more forthright reason was given. In 1703, the South Carolina law granting slaves the right to fight Indians was revoked: "There must be great caution used, lest our slaves, when arm'd, become our masters."[2]

As time passed, evidence that black Americans had fought courageously in America's earlier wars was not only ignored but was also systematically denied by influential military officers and government officials. Although some blacks were praised for their service as warriors during the time of the Revolutionary War, "authorities" were quick to dismiss them as useless cowards. Many leaders during the Revolution, including George Washington, who often said that he favored the abolition of slaves, considered blacks "cowardly, servile and distinctly inferior by nature."[3] This conviction continued for almost 200 years thereafter until the conflict in Vietnam finally convinced most Americans—but still not all—that blacks could fight every bit as courageously and as well as other Americans.

Although this rejection of blacks as soldiers was by no means confined to the American South, it received its most strident support there, typically taking the form of assertions that Africans were by nature inferior in all ways. It was widely said, and apparently actually believed by many, that in the course of history, the very few men in Africa who had been relatively courageous and intelligent had never been enslaved but instead had done the enslaving of others. Moreover, it was said, the most manly and intelligent of those who had been taken into slavery had been sold in the West Indies with only the childlike and cowardly dregs being sold in the United States. Arguments like these were made so consistently and so confidently that they seem to have convinced many Americans that Africans were, in fact, naturally cowardly and that only the most craven of these docile, timid, childlike, "subhuman" people had been brought to slavery in America.

There were powerful self-protective factors at work in creating this image of cowardice, as anyone possessing even a passing acquaintance with slavery in the American South can readily understand. The specter of armed slaves taking their revenge against white slave owners was an unceasing nightmare that grew in urgency for slave masters as word of the Haitian revolution of 1791 reached America, stunning many southerners with the news that black slaves had killed hundreds of French slave owners before setting themselves free. Haiti, then known as Saint-Domingue, was by far the richest island in the West Indies, and its takeover by some 500,000 slaves, two-thirds of them African-born, was unthinkable to American slave masters, not to mention their counterparts in the West Indies. When Napoleon sent thousands of French soldiers with orders to defeat the rebels and reimpose slavery, the U.S. South rejoiced only to despair again when the ingenuity and courage of the black rebels led by Toussaint L'Ouverture, Henri Christophe, and Jean J. Dessalines—with help from tropical diseases—decimated the French, setting Haiti free.[4]

This successful slave rebellion was made only slightly less fearsome to U.S. slave owners because of their increased insistence that slaves in the United States were so meek and cowardly that they need not be feared.

One slave owner freely admitted that his slaves could easily kill him and his family, "Yet we all feel so secure, and are so free from suspicion of such danger, that no care is taken for self-protection—and in many cases, as in mine, not even the outer door is locked."[5] At the start of the U.S. Civil War, a Virginian rose in the Confederate Congress to boast that "the slaves" loyalty was never more conspicuous, their obedience never more childlike."[6] At this same time, British lawyer and famed Crimean War correspondent William "Billy" Russell toured the South, everywhere being told about the childlike docility of the slaves. But if the slaves were so docile and cowardly, he wondered, why did he everywhere encounter such elaborate police precautions, night patrols, curfews, and the like? Russell concluded, "There is something suspicious in the constant never-ending statement that 'we are not afraid of our slaves.'"[7] Charles Olmstead, a northern visitor to Alabama in 1860, also commented on the constant vigilance of southerners over possible slave rebellion, the slightest rumor often sparking a major military response. He came to the conclusion that Alabama farmers were "terrified" of their slaves.[8]

As Russell and Olmstead suspected, the slightest sign of aggression by a slave would usually bring brutally harsh punishment. Even so, there were approximately 250 armed slave uprisings in the South, and a few in the North, most of them leading to the loss of white lives. An example occurred in 1712 in New York City, where black and Indian slaves joined in revolt killing 9 whites and wounding others. In response, 18 slaves were captured, tortured, and hanged or burned to death. One was sentenced to be "burned with a slow fire that he may continue in torment for eight to ten hours."[9] In Louisiana, in 1811, some 500 slaves armed themselves and rebelled, marching on New Orleans in military formation. They were met by troops who shot 60 to death and later executed another 16. In 1822, a slave in Charleston, South Carolina, divulged an alleged plan of rebellion to be led by a former slave named Denmark Vesey, who had won $1,500 in a lottery and purchased his freedom. He had lived a respectable life for some years in Charleston before conceiving a plan to raise an army of 9,000 slaves, kill every white man, woman, and child in the city, then sail to Africa and freedom.[10] Vesey and 36 slaves were hanged.

Nat Turner's 1831 rebellion in Virginia left fifty whites dead, fourteen of them women and thirty-one of them children. Although it was the last major armed slave rebellion in the United States, it was the bloodiest and the longest remembered, with those who participated in it branded as madmen, not human beings with legitimate grievances.[11] Still, neither this rebellion nor any other in U.S. history came close to success. All were small in the numbers of rebels involved, local in scope, and of short duration. The largest, Nat Turner's insurrection, lasted only two days. This should not be surprising because except in South Carolina, Mississippi, and Louisiana, slaves were badly outnumbered by whites, who were not only heavily armed but could also call upon their state and local militias and even the federal army for support. What is more, the slaves often had paid informants among them. Conversely, in the West Indies, where slaves greatly outnumbered whites, revolts often came close to the success seen in Haiti, and several led to the establishment of free colonies. A similar pattern was seen in Brazil, and even a relatively small number of African slaves in Mexico staged larger revolts against their Spanish masters than any seen in the United States.[12]

Even before the slaves arrived in the New World, aboard the heavily guarded ships of various European nations, African men and women and children often joined together and despite their chains, debilitating illnesses, and near starvation overcame their heavily armed and usually vigilant guards, taking over the ships and sailing some of them back to Africa and others to parts of South America or the Caribbean, where these Africans set up free villages, some of which survived well past the time of emancipation in the United States. All told, there were many hundreds of shipboard slave rebellions, about one for every eight to ten voyages, according to one historian.[13] Another historian found that despite the incredible odds against the slaves, some 20 percent of the more than 400 shipboard insurrections he studied succeeded in freeing all or some of the captives.[14] Although the great majority of these rebellions failed, they did not do so because the men, women, and even children who fought to regain their freedom lacked courage

African slaves landed in Florida as part of a Spanish expedition as early as 1526, and many soon after escaped to take up life with Indians, but the first African slaves to reach the English colonies in America arrived at Jamestown, Virginia, in 1619 aboard a Dutch privateer. By the following year, slaves had reached New York, and in 1641, Massachusetts became the first state to give statutory recognition to slavery. Still, the flow of slaves to the northern east coast of the American colonies was a trickle compared to the flood of African men and women sold along the rice and tobacco areas near the coast farther south. What is more, the death rates of slaves in cold Massachusetts were twice those of whites, whereas whites in South Carolina died twice as often as African slaves, usually as victims of malaria.[15] Transatlantic slave ships occasionally sailed directly to Charleston, but most of the slaves who were shipped to the American colonies came from the West Indies, relatively few coming to the colonies directly from Africa, reinforcing the southern belief that they were discards unwanted by West Indian planters.[16]

In reality, there were few enough West Indian plantations that could afford to sell any of their slaves, except, perhaps, those who were the most intractable, not the most docile. The death rate among these dreadfully overworked, badly underfed, and disease-prone slaves was so great that until well into the nineteenth century, the West Indian slave population could not reproduce itself.[17] In 1789, for example, two-thirds of the West Indies slaves were African-born.[18] Unruly West Indian slaves could be flogged savagely, some even killed, but given the shortage of slaves, sublethal punishment was much preferred. For example, an English Jamaican plantation owner named Tom Thistelwood recorded in his diary that after a slave ate some sugar cane he should have been harvesting, he ordered the man flogged, then bound in a prone position while another slave was ordered to "shit in his mouth."[19] And as far as a senior student of West Indian slavery could judge from Thistelwood's diary, the man did not appear to have been a sadist.[20] Similar forms of brutal and degrading punishment were common throughout the Caribbean from Danish to Spanish territory.

While slaves were trickling into the North American colonies early in the seventeenth century, larger numbers of white indentured servants were arriving from jails and workhouses throughout Britain and elsewhere in Europe. Among them were thousands of Scottish soldiers taken prisoner by Oliver Cromwell, but the majority were common people described as "dirty, lazy, rough, ignorant, lewd, and often criminal."[21] So many hardened criminals were indentured to North American colonists that Benjamin Franklin sarcastically declared that the colonies should repay the mother country for her generosity in sending over every criminal short of murderers by "return shipments of rattlesnakes."[22] These white indentured servants either quickly worked off their period of indenture or simply moved on, often to become productive citizens in another colony, but many others barely managed to eke out a living on the vacant but infertile hill country to the west.

Their departures left the colonies' needs for labor largely unmet. One solution was the enslavement of Native Americans. By 1704, South Carolina had almost half as many Indian slaves as adult white residents, but like indentured Europeans, these Indians had a tendency to vanish or to fall ill. In response, some were sold to the West Indies, where they were easier to control.[23] African slaves, on the other hand, endured the southern climate and local diseases reasonably well, and due to their skin color it was far more difficult for them to "disappear." Unbeknownst to their owners, these slaves brought with them hookworm, deadly *falciparum* malaria, yellow fever, and smallpox, all of which would plague whites in the South for many years to come—partial retribution, some educated blacks would later say, for their enslavement.

During the early years of slavery, most slaves in northern states, and even some in the South, were treated as if they were indentured servants who, after some years of labor for a white "master," could become free to go their own way, buy land, or take up jobs in towns. A. P. Upsher, a member of President John Tyler's cabinet, left this clause in his will:

> I emancipate, and set free, my servant, DAVID RICH, and direct my executors to give him one hundred dollars. I recommend him, in the strongest manner, to the respect, esteem and confidence of any community in which he may happen to live. He has been my slave for twenty-four years, during which time he has been trusted to every extent, and in every respect. My confidence in him has been unbounded; his relation to myself and family has always been such as to afford him daily opportunities to deceive and injure us, and yet he has never been detected in a serious fault, nor even in an intentional breach of the decorums of his station. His intelligence is of a high order, his integrity above all suspicion, and his sense of right and propriety always correct, and even delicate and refined. I feel that he is justly entitled to carry this certificate from me into the new relations which he now must form. It is due to his long and most faithful services, and to the sincere and steady friendship which I bear him. In the uninterrupted and confidential intercourse of twenty-four years, I have never given nor had occasion to give him, an unpleasant word. I know no man who has fewer faults, or more excellencies, than he.[24]

When the Cavaliers from the south and west of England arrived in the Chesapeake region, they at first attempted to create a culture for their African slaves that would re-create the relationships between their ancestors and the rural proletariat that worked on their large English estates. Slaves were rarely referred to as anything but "my people," "my hands," or "my workers," and "they were made to dress like English farm workers, to play English folk games, to speak an English country dialect, and to observe the ordinary rituals of English life in a charade that Virginia planters organized with great care."[25] As one student of the times wrote, "The South was not founded to create slavery; slavery was recruited to perpetuate the South."[26] The speech forms that would come to dominate much of the southern "accent" also came from regional dialects spoken in the south and west of England. *Yaller* for *yellow*, *ah be* for *I am*, and *chimbly* for *chimney* are a few examples among hundreds. What is more, the so-called black dialect, with its *dis* and *dat*, *leastways, fust, his'n*, and the like, owed its origin to this same source. Africanisms were added later.[27]

Attitudes would change as the years passed. This cultural charade ended and chattel slavery took over, but during the mid-eighteenth century, and lasting for many years thereafter, not only were slaves in the North as well as the South reasonably well treated, but many northern towns celebrated what was known as "Negro Election Day," an annual festival that attracted blacks from the countryside to towns for the election of black "judges" and "kings" who would "rule" the town for a day, dressed in their masters' clothes, riding their horses, and feasting on "tribute" given to them. Along with great feasting there was parading—in grand costumes—and much dancing, and no small amount of alcohol was downed. In addition to the pleasures of this one-day role reversal, this annual ritual gave northern slaves an opportunity to choose leaders who could resolve disputes and present complaints to white masters during the ensuing year.[28]

So it was in the British West Indies, where slaves enjoyed a "noisy, unrestrained, and orgiastic" Saturnalia for two or three days at Christmas. As in the Saturnalia of slaves in ancient Rome, West Indian slaves not only abandoned all work, but they dropped any hint of subservience, becoming disrespectful toward their owners and overseers, and sometimes verbally aggressive as well. The mood during this Saturnalia was largely relaxed and celebratory, but the usual markers of inequality were set aside, and slave owners permitted excesses that would ordinarily be punished severely. But after Christmas ended, slave owners once again issued orders and slaves meekly obeyed.[29] This pattern of annual ceremonial license did not spread throughout the Caribbean or to the U.S. South although slave owners on most plantations did tend to relax their control somewhat on Sundays and Christmas.

The numbers of slaves in the colonies grew to represent over 19 percent of the entire population in 1790, but whereas the numbers of slaves in the South increased dramatically, those in the North fell from 60,000 in 1775, to 36,000 in 1800, to only 3,568 in 1830, most of them in New Jersey.[30] Owners of the 450,000 slaves held in the South in 1775 improved their techniques of control, adding subtle psychological mechanisms to the threat—but infrequent actuality at that time—of deadly physical force. Slave owners encouraged ties of loyalty between slaves and their owners' families by, among other things, having slave women suckle white children, and by making house slaves so much a part of the family that they often developed great affection for their masters.[31] It was also a common practice for slave masters to be unfailingly kind to slave children, leaving the need for discipline entirely to their parents.[32] They also encouraged strong emotional bonds among slaves themselves so that a man's escape from a plantation and his slave family would seem less desirable. At the same time, however, although slave owners repeatedly insisted that they rarely separated slave family members by sales to other slave owners, from 1820 to 1860 every decade saw 10 percent of all slaves in the northern tier of slaveholding states sold to new masters in the Deep South, where slavery was growing in profitability.[33] Even much earlier, it was common for slave families to be sold apart from one another. For example, James T. Woodbury, a British visitor to Washington, D.C., who wished to visit George Washington's tomb, was guided there by an elderly black man who had long served travelers in this way:

> This old man was formerly the slave of General Washington. Mr. Woodbury asked him if he had any children. "I have had a large family," he replied. "And are they living?" inquired the gentleman. The voice of the aged father trembled with emotion, and the tears started to his eyes, as he answered: "I don't know whether they are alive or dead. They were all sold away from me, and I don't know what became of them. I am alone in the world, without a child to bring me a cup of water in my old age." Mr. Woodbury looked on the infirm and solitary being with feelings of

deep compassion. "And this," thought he, "is the fate of slaves, even when owned by so good a man as General Washington! Who would not be an Abolitionist?"[34]

While slave owners consistently inculcated the idea that male slaves were "happy-go-lucky," meek, and passive creatures who were quite incapable of martial spirit, they also went out of their way to reward slaves for their docility when, as so often happened, they deceptively portrayed themselves as docile.[35] Many whites knew better—some slaves killed themselves rather than endure the horrors of their lives—but their image of a compliant, nonaggressive population of slaves may have allowed slave-owning families to feel safer on their isolated plantations. This tradition continued well into the twentieth century. For example, sociologist U. G. Weatherly wrote in 1923 in the *American Journal of Sociology*—the leading journal in that field—that "the Negro belongs to perhaps the most docile and modifiable of all races."[36] How this could have been written after the bloody "red summer" of 1919, which we will discuss later, is difficult to explain.

Some of the slaves who were taken to the New World came from African societies with a history of practicing such a benign form of slavery that second or third generations of slaves' descendants could become free, esteemed, and even wealthy men and women, their slave origins never to be mentioned. The Kingdom of Asante was such a place. But elsewhere in Africa, slavery could be every bit as brutal as it was in the West Indies or Brazil. People taken into slavery by such societies can hardly have been expected to accept their fate passively, and most fought valiantly until overwhelmed. What is more, although few southern slave owners appear to have known much, if anything at all, about African history, most African societies placed great value on martial ability, and for many, bravery in battle was a man's highest virtue, one that women fervently encouraged, even demanded. Courage in battle was inseparably linked to wealth, spiritual values, esthetics, and sexuality. Africans captured in battle and sold into slavery may have been on the losing side of a battle, but many were every bit as imbued with a warrior ethos as those who captured them.[37]

Some black Americans, both slave and free, fought well in the various wars against Indians and the French that preceded the Revolutionary War, but their first publicly acknowledged service as soldiers came in the War for Independence. It is widely asserted today that the first American to die in this war was a powerful, six-foot-two-inch, light-skinned forty-seven-year-old runaway slave from Framingham, Massachusetts, named Crispus Attucks. A sailor for nearly twenty years, his ship was in port in March, 1770, when he led a group of white Bostonians in shouting insults, throwing snowballs, and brandishing clubs against a unit of British troops whose history of drunken brawling and explosive violence appalled some of their own officers and incensed many Americans.[38] Apparently without orders from their commander, the British soldiers opened fire and Attucks was the first to die, followed by several white Americans.[39] This "Boston Massacre" became famous, but later research has shown that a black youngster, Christopher Snyder, had been killed by British soldiers a few days earlier.[40]

At the Battle of Bunker Hill, it was often written that an African American named Peter Salem—also from Framingham—shot and killed British major John Pitcairn, but the accuracy of this claim is in doubt. However, another African American named Salem Poor received a citation for unquestioned bravery during this battle; it was signed by fourteen white officers: "We only beg leave to say, in the person of this said negro centers a brave and gallant soldier. The reward due to so great and distinguished a character, we submit to Congress."[41] Another slave, named Saul Matthews, received high praise from Baron von Steuben, General Lafayette, and General Nathaniel Greene. Despite growing protest from the southern colonies, many African American slaves and freedmen alike joined Washington's army in the early stages of the war, enduring the frostbite and the frequent near starvation of his troops, only to be sent away when southern objections grew too shrill.

In response, other runaway slaves joined British loyalist forces, where they were used primarily as laborers, guides, spies, and pilots in the Chesapeake waters in return for the promise of freedom after the war. Perhaps 100,000 slaves joined the British in search of their freedom, and some fought bravely against Washington's men.[42] Most notable among those who fought were men in the Royal Governor of Virginia, Lord Dunmore's, so-called Ethiopian Regiment, each of whom wore a sash across his British uniform with "Liberty to Slaves" written on it.[43] Few of these men or others who fought in British units found freedom. Instead, most died of smallpox while crowded onto British ships. So common was smallpox among them that British officers actually planted infected men on "Rebel Plantations" hoping to create chaos and death.[44] Over 1,000 of these runaway slaves eventually found freedom in Africa, others settled in Canada and Britain, and a few even settled in Central Europe after visiting there as a drum corps. Others found refuge in the West Indies as freedmen, but some were resold into slavery.[45]

Only in 1775, after tens of thousands of blacks had joined the British, and Washington's beleaguered army had become dangerously depleted, did he again accept black enlistments. At least three blacks are known to have crossed the Delaware with Washington on the way to his victory at Trenton, New Jersey. One of these was "Prince Whipple," sent to this country by his royal parents to be educated, only to be sold into slavery to a general named Whipple. Another bore the impressive name of Oliver Cromwell.[46] Cromwell served directly under General Washington for six years and nine months. He lived to be 100.[47] Most of the 5,000 or so blacks who eventually served in the Continental Army fought in racially integrated infantry regiments. They also ate together with whites in the same mess. Other runaway slaves served as laborers. The growing shortage of white manpower led Rhode Island to recruit a nearly all-black regiment of 226 men commanded by a white colonel, Christopher Greene. The unit fought bravely, once preventing a Continental Army defeat by holding its line against three attacks by 1,500 Hessians under Count Donop. A German nobleman who served with Washington's men and saw the black Rhode Island troops in action wrote that of all the American units, "that regiment is the most neatly dressed, and best under arms, and the most precise in its maneuvers."[48]

French troops under Count D'Estaing who aided Washington included 545 black men from Santo Domingo who fought well in the siege of Savannah in 1779. Among them was a young teenager named Henri Christophe, who after the Haitian revolution would become that country's king.[49] Another all-black unit, known as the "Bucks of America," was commanded by a black colonel named Middleton. After the war, John C. Hancock presented the unit with a silk banner bearing his initials as a tribute to their courage and devotion.[50] Blacks also served on many naval vessels for the Americans and British alike, again doing so bravely while living in fully integrated shipboard conditions. They fought in every major naval battle in the war. Blacks also fought in the naval war against France from 1798 to 1800, and others fought for Spain in its attempt to dislodge the British from the Mississippi River Valley, with six black officers receiving medals from the king of Spain.[51]

After the end of the Revolutionary War, there was some public praise for the courageous service of black troops in Washington's army, and several received commendations for heroism. But it was not until well into 1863, when the Union was attempting to justify its use of former slaves as soldiers in that terrible conflict, that anything like "official" praise for their Revolutionary War service came to them. On September 26, 1863, the *Army and Navy Journal* published an article entitled "Negro Soldiers in the Revolution":

> The record is clear, that from the beginning to the conclusion of the war of the Revolution, Negroes served in the Continental armies with intelligence, courage, and steadfastness; and that important results in several instances are directly traceable to their good conduct.

If these "intelligent, courageous, and steadfast" men expected American society to reward them with better jobs or improved civil rights after their military service, most were disappointed. A few did receive freedom, but most did not. Despite his plaudits, Saul Matthews returned from his military service to slavery in Virginia and was not set free as a reward for his exploits until 1792.[52] Some others like the steadfast William Flora were eventually given land grants, but most white Americans were quick to forget the wartime service of blacks, continuing to employ them in menial jobs or hold them as slaves. At the end of the War for Independence, the new United States Congress passed a militia act that created an all-white military. The Navy continued to accept blacks because most white seamen preferred to work on civilian fishing boats or merchant ships, where the pay was better and conditions were less "disciplined." Few white Americans knew that black and white sailors lived fully integrated and surprisingly amicable lives aboard U.S. Navy ships.[53]

Soon after the Revolutionary War, large numbers of European immigrants poured into northern cities, taking the unskilled jobs previously held by blacks. Between 1830 and 1860, almost five million Irish, German, and Scandinavian immigrants arrived. Most of the Germans and Scandinavians took up midwestern farming lands, but the Irish competed directly with free blacks (who by 1860 numbered nearly 500,000), forcing large numbers of them into poorly paid service or menial work.[54] Racial discrimination and segregation grew in the North throughout this period, and southern control of its growing slave population became more and more strict.

Assured that neither the Army nor the Marine Corps would enlist any African Americans who might, southerners feared, lead a Haitian-like insurrection by armed black men, southern cotton planters relied on their slaves for ever-higher profits thanks to Whitney's cotton gin. So matters remained until the onset of the War of 1812. Unlike their American counterparts, who now scorned black military recruits, British Royal Marines on Tangier Island in Chesapeake Bay trained 200 run-away slaves in marksmanship and precise close-order drill before deploying them in several attacks on the Maryland and Virginia coasts, including an advance on Washington, D.C., and an attack on Baltimore. These black Royal Marines fought so well that they were later incorporated into a regular battalion of the British army.

Despite the British success in training former slaves for combat during the War of 1812, the Americans refused to permit recruiting of black slaves or freedmen until late in 1814, after fighting in the American northeast had ended. But as British forces, including 1,000 black troops, were massing in Jamaica to attack New Orleans, General Andrew Jackson, the commander of U.S. forces on the Gulf Coast, called for free black Louisiana volunteers to join the colors, promising equal pay, rations, and bounty rights with whites, even though blacks would serve in segregated units. Two black battalions, each of about 300 men, were quickly organized and armed, each unit commanded by a black major, one of whom, Francis E. Dumas, was actually a slave owner himself.[55] The black volunteers contributed to the great American victory at New Orleans by holding their ground and shooting down many of the British regulars, who attacked gallantly but futilely. Among the British units were black soldiers from the West India Regiment who tried but failed to turn the American flank right.[56] In this final battle of the war, after twenty-five minutes of combat, 700 British officers and men lay dead, with another 1,400 wounded.[57] Neither side realized that a peace treaty had been signed two weeks before this deadly battle took place.[58]

General Jackson commended the American blacks for their "courage and perseverance in the performance of their duty," giving special praise to one of their black commanders, Joseph Savory, but the volunteers would not be allowed to remain in the army, nor was there any public acclaim for their service.[59] Instead, a War Department memorandum in 1815 once again insisted, "A Negro is deemed unfit to associate with the American soldier," and in 1820, the U.S. Army reiterated that "no Negro or mulatto would be accepted as recruits."[60] State militias followed the same policy. African Americans did continue to serve in the Navy, but increasingly rabid southerners refused to recognize the right of black men to serve there. South Carolina actually threatened to arrest any black sailor who came ashore in that state, and a U.S. senator from that state, John C. Calhoun, authored a bill excluding blacks from naval service except as cooks or servants. The Senate passed the bill but it died in the House after Secretary of the Navy Abel P. Upshur glibly assured the Congress that it was unnecessary because blacks never made up more than 5 percent of the crew of any ship.[61]

Perhaps the secretary was unaware that one-fourth of Commodore Matthew Perry's crew that had defeated the British in a bloody three-hour battle on Lake Erie in 1813 was African American. Perry later reported that his black sailors seemed to be "absolutely insensible to danger," citing three men for special heroism.[62] Whites and blacks ate together on Perry's ships, where there was no apparent racial discrimination. They fought and died together, too. So it was during a battle in this same war between the armed U.S. Navy brig *General Thompson* and a British frigate. According to the U.S. ship's commander, Captain Shaler:

> The name of one of my poor fellows, who was killed, ought to be registered in the book of fame, and remembered as long as bravery is a virtue. He was a black man, by name John Johnson. A twenty-four pound shot struck him in the hip, and took away all the lower part of his body. In this state the poor brave fellow lay on the deck, and several times exclaimed to his shipmates: "Fire away, my boys; no haul a color down!" Another black man, by the name of John Davis, who was struck in much the same manner, repeatedly requested to be thrown overboard, saying that he was only in the way of others.[63]

Although African Americans were no longer permitted to fight in the U.S. Army, they fought against it courageously and ferociously during what became known as the Seminole Wars. During and after the War of 1812, substantial numbers of black slaves fled to Florida, then a Spanish territory, where they took refuge with the Seminoles and other Indians. Many of these blacks were enslaved by the Seminoles, but their "enslavement" bore little resemblance to the slave conditions they had fled. Although they were required to pay a modest annual tribute in the form of a small percentage of the crops they grew, they lived the rest of the year together in their own villages, carried their own firearms, and behaved as free men.[64] There was also extensive intermarriage with the Seminoles, and many blacks achieved positions of prominence. Several U.S. military expeditions, including one led by Andrew Jackson, invaded Florida to recapture runaway slaves, killing many of them as well as Seminoles in the process. Florida was soon purchased by the United States but the fighting continued as more escaped slaves and Indians alike took up arms.

In 1835, a major U.S. military expedition was launched against them, but the blacks and Seminoles held out for seven murderous years, killing 1,800 American troops and costing the United States the huge sum for that time of $40 million. Throughout this protracted, vicious warfare, runaway slaves fought with courage so desperate that American soldiers came to respect and fear them.[65] General Rufus Saxton wrote admiringly, "The Negroes would stand and fight back, even with bare hands."[66] The blacks did not fight in these wars as vassals of the Seminoles, they fought as equals. As U.S. General Thomas S. Jesup noted, "Throughout my operations I found the Negroes the most active and determined warriors; and during the conference with the Indian chiefs I ascertained that they exercized an almost controlling influence over them."[67] A United States colonel added that although the Seminoles fought bravely, the "Negroes. . . were their best soldiers."[68] Nevertheless, blacks were excluded from the all-white U.S. army that served in the Mexican War of 1846–1848, a war that cost 13,000 American lives, two-thirds of them white southerners, the men most eager to volunteer for combat. A thousand or so blacks served on U.S. Navy warships that blockaded Mexican ports but saw virtually no combat.

When the American Civil War began in 1861, few Americans appear to have had any knowledge about the past military exploits of African Americans, but most Northerners and virtually all Southerners were vehemently opposed to their enlistment as soldiers, although a few may have served in howitzer batteries outside Richmond. However, the South did not hesitate to use many thousands of slaves to build fortifications and gun batteries, repair bridges and roads, and perform other forms of agricultural and military labor, including marching to war with their owners as menservants, a role in which many came under Union fire. Other slaves cut timber, dug coal, made iron, and hauled supplies to the front. They also made valuable contributions to the Confederate war effort by their work in arms factories. Half the workers in the Trede-

gar Ironworks in Richmond, the most important weapons factory in
the South, were black and so were three-quarters of the men in a major
naval ordinance plant in Selma, Alabama.[69] Black women also made
valuable contributions as nurses, cooks, and laundresses in hospitals—
all this despite Southern insistence that both black men and women
were "irresponsible, childlike, and racially inferior."[70]

The doctrine of black racial inferiority became so deeply entrenched
that it encompassed physical abilities as well as mental ones. Leading
southern physicians agreed that blacks could only properly perform
certain basic physiological functions when under the control of white
men, as Dr. Thomas Cooper declared in 1828. Dr. S. C. Cartwright of
the University of Louisiana explained that only under "the compulsive
power of white men" who force blacks to "labor or excercize," are the
lungs able to "perform the duty of vitalizing the blood more perfectly
than is done when they are left free to indulge in idleness. It is the red,
vital blood sent to the brain that liberates their mind when under the
white man's control; and it is the want of a sufficiency of red, vital
blood that chains their mind to ignorance and barbarism when in freedom."[71] That men of any degree of education could sincerely believe
that the "idleness" of slaves was natural to them rather than a response
to slavery is as remarkable as the belief that they were natural cowards.
In some parts of West Africa, such as Dahomey, African people worked
so hard that European visitors were amazed.[72]

Surprisingly, despite growing racial tensions during the pre–Civil War
years, southern towns and cities at this time did not impose rigid racial
segregation in housing, most streets housing both races side by side.
Nothing comparable existed in the North, where blacks were residen-
tially segregated in all cities. What is more,

> Every Southern city had its demimonde, and regardless of the law and the
> pillars of society, the two races on that level foregathered more or less
> openly in grog ships, mixed balls, and religious meetings. Less visibly
> there thrived "a world of greater conviviality and equality." Under cover
> of night, "in this nether world blacks and whites mingled freely, the con-
> ventions of slavery were discarded," and "not only did the men find fel-
> lowship without regard to color in the tippling shops, back rooms, and se-
> cluded sheds, but the women of both races joined in." The police blotters
> of the period are cluttered with evidence of this, but they bear witness
> only of the sinners who were caught.[73]

In these same southern cities, there was a preponderance of white men over white women and a shortage of black men because so many had been sold off as slaves to rural plantations. The result was considerable racial mixing, with 12 percent of all African Americans in the South being listed as "mulatto" in the census of 1860, and the proportions of mulattos among blacks in cities running from 35 to 50 percent.[74] Moreover, these lighter-skinned African Americans often received preferential treatment in the South. Matters were different in the North.

During his visit to the United States in 1831, the year of a bloody race riot in Providence, Rhode Island, a state where Quakers, including William Penn, owned many slaves before 1800, when Quakers abolished slaveholding, Count Alexis de Tocqueville was startled by the depth of racial hatred he found in the North: "The prejudice of race appears to be stronger in the states that have abolished slavery than in those where it still exists; and nowhere is it so intolerant as in those states where servitude has never been known."[75] As de Tocqueville discovered, the rigid racial segregation in all public arenas of life that became known as "Jim Crow" was actually far more strict in the North than the South at that time. Only in Massachusetts among the northern states could blacks serve as jurors, and several northern states, including Illinois and Indiana, passed constitutional provisions restricting the entry of blacks altogether.

As wealthy freed slaves learned when they attempted to visit Europe, they were not entitled to passports because officially they were not U.S. citizens.[76] Nevertheless, quite a few northern free blacks, many of them mulattos, had achieved success in a variety of occupations such as medicine, law, and the ministry. More middle-class occupations that were open to them included small businesses, carpentry, absentee farming, and work as mechanics, barbers, and undertakers. A few free blacks even owned slaves and sent their children to school in France.[77] But the great majority of blacks in the North lived impoverished lives as common laborers or household servants.[78]

Education, which was virtually nonexistent for blacks in the South before the Civil War, was only marginally better in the North. Although Boston's schools were integrated by 1860, they were a rare exception. Racial segregation was imposed on northern trains, even in Massachusetts, an otherwise unusually tolerant state. White churches, including the Quakers, were so intolerant of blacks that they were compelled to form their own churches, and these places of worship became central to black social life. In 1840, 93 percent of the free blacks in the North were denied voting rights. What is more, terrible mob violence against blacks took place in several northern cities, such as Philadelphia and Cincinnati. The attacks in Cincinnati were so brutal that half of the city's 2,200 black inhabitants emigrated to Canada, where they founded the town of Wilberforce, Ontario.[79] While all of this racial separation and hatred was taking place in the North, blacks' staunchest advocates, the so-called abolitionists, surprisingly continued to accept the racist stereotype that people of African descent were mild, gentle, and tranquil—"the mildest and gentlest of men"—not at all like the whites who oppressed them.[80] And few white northerners advocated racial equality.

During the famous Lincoln-Douglas debates of 1858, Lincoln forthrightly reflected the northern public's mood, and probably his true feelings, when he declared:

> I will say then that I am not, nor ever have been in favor of bringing about in any way the social and political equality of the white and black races [applause]—that I am not nor ever have been in favor of making voters or jurors of negroes, nor of qualifying them to hold office, nor to intermarry with white people, and I will say in addition to this that there is a physical difference between the black and white races which I believe will forever forbid the two races living together on terms of social and political equality. And inasmuch as they cannot so live, while they do remain together there must be the position of superior and inferior, and I as much as any other man am in favor of having the superior position assigned to the white race.[81]

It is no surprise that when war came, most people in the North were opposed to the use of blacks, whether freedmen or fugitive slaves, in the Union Army. The following song, composed by a Union Army colonel, Charles G. Halpine, but attributed to "Private Miles O'Reilly," was a popular Irish parody of Irish soldiers of the time:

> *Some say it is a burning shame to make the Naygurs fight,*
> *An' that the trade o' being kilt belongs to but the white:*
> *But as for me, upon me sowl, so liberal are we here,*
> *I'll let Sambo be murthered, in place of meself, on every day of the year.*

On every day of the year, boys, and every hour in the day,
The right to be kilt I'll divide wid him, and divil a work I'll say.
In battles wild commotion I shouldn't at all object,
If Sambo's body should stop a ball that was coming for me direct,
An' the prod of a southern bayonet, so liberal are we here,
I'll resign and let Sambo take it, on every day in the year,
On every day in the year, boys, an' wid none of your nasty pride,
All right in a southern baynet prod, wid Sambo I'll divide.
The men who object to Sambo, should take his place and fight,
An' it is better to have Naygur's hue, than a liver that's weak and white,
Though Sambo's black as the ace of spades, his finger a thryger can pull,
An' his eye runs straight on the barrel sight from under its thatch of wool,
So hear me all, boys, darlin, don't think I'm tipping you chaff,
The right to be kilt, I'll divide with him, An' give him the largest half.[82]

Some Irishmen took this message to extremes. Union efforts to draft more white men into service led to the "Draft Riots" in New York City in 1863, when Irish immigrants who had replaced blacks in all manner of jobs such as longshoremen, barbers, waiters, brick-makers, and domestic servants were forced to face a military draft. Fearful that their jobs would be taken by blacks and furious that wealthy whites could avoid the draft by paying $300, they rioted, smashing prominent stores and assaulting the police, along with any blacks who could be found. The army fired on them with canister and grapeshot, but before the violence ended, perhaps 1,300 men, women, and children lay dead, most of them black. Many other blacks fled the city in terror.[83]

Despite Northern opposition to the use of blacks in their army, thanks to an order by Secretary of the Navy Gideon Welles in September 1861, the Union Navy greatly increased the numbers of African Americans it recruited. Approximately 30,000 of its 120,000 wartime enlistees were black. Out of sight and apparently out of mind, these black sailors served in virtual anonymity. Still, four of them earned the Congressional Medal of Honor. One runaway slave, Robert Smalls, who, in a daring exploit, hijacked into Union hands the *Planter*, an armed 300-ton, side-wheel Confederate steamer filled with military hardware, was actually commissioned as an officer in the United States Colored Troops (USCT) and served as commander of the ship for the duration of the war.[84] After the war, he was repeatedly elected to South Carolina's Congress.[85]

Fearful of the reaction of whites in border states, Lincoln refused to call for the arming of freed slaves, much less the emancipation of slaves, until January 1863. However, much earlier than this, members of Lincoln's cabinet, led by Secretary of War Simon Cameron pressed him to arm blacks whether free or slave. Not only did Lincoln not agree with Cameron, but in January 1862, he sent him packing, literally, as ambassador to Russia. Early in 1862, some Union military leaders followed Cameron's lead by actually enlisting blacks into their forces in South Carolina, Louisiana, and Kansas, but until late August 1862, Lincoln continued to oppose the arming of black men.[86] Lincoln was not only still concerned about the reaction in border states but fearful that black men lacked both the intelligence and the courage necessary to become soldiers. He had so little confidence in them that in September 1862 he said, "If we were to arm them, I fear that in a few weeks the arms would be in the hands of the rebels."[87] Lincoln would eventually endorse emancipation and even limited suffrage, but he also held many racist views.[88]

After Lincoln reluctantly made his Emancipation Proclamation and it was finally implemented, 180,000 black volunteers would serve in racially segregated combat units of the Federal Army known as "United States Colored Troops." Over 144,000 of these men came from slave states.[89] Others had varied backgrounds. Nicholas Said, who was born in Sudan of princely parents, amazed officers and men of the Fifty-fifth Massachusetts USCT by his ability to speak Arabic, Turkish, Mandra, and Russian in addition to his native Kanouri. He was also able to speak and write fluently in English, French, German, and Italian.[90] The use of blacks as soldiers, whether former slaves or not, was not without Northern resistance, especially on the part of many white officers who believed that accepting command of such "inferior" troops—who they feared would prove to be nothing more than laborers—would deprive them of glory and promotion. Nevertheless, some did so in search of money and rank, and others did so because they believed in black rights, even knowing that the Confederates were sworn to execute any white officer captured in command of black soldiers and on at least four occasions were known to have done so.[91]

Many blacks would serve in USCT labor battalions, but before the war ended there would also be 120 black infantry regiments, 12 heavy artillery regiments, 10 companies of light artillery, 7 cavalry regiments, and 5 regiments of engineers. In all, by the war's end, blacks made up

10 percent of the Union forces. When the Union army betrayed its promise to pay them the same $13.50 per month received by white soldiers, some of the black troops mutinied and were actually executed. All were outraged by this blatant discrimination, but most continued to serve, and almost all of these men were so determined to erase their "natural coward" stereotype that they fought gallantly.[92] At least 3,000 African Americans died in combat, and it is estimated that another 40,000 to 70,000 died of wounds or disease. Their death rate was proportionately much higher than that of white soldiers in the Union Army, in part because they were so often used as assault troops and in part because their medical care was usually even worse than that given white troops.

The first black soldiers to engage in battle were South Carolina Sea Island men during the first week of November 1862, when they successfully raided Confederate lines, killing 9, taking 3 prisoners, destroying valuable Confederate property, and returning with 150 slaves. Their commander reported, "The colored men fought with astonishing coolness and bravery. For alacrity in effecting landings, for determination, and for bush fighting I found them all I could desire, more than I had hoped for. They behaved bravely, gloriously, and deserve all praise."[93] These men were the 1st South Carolina Volunteers, later to be led by Colonel Higginson.

Other blacks soon after displayed their courage in battle. Louisiana men led by General Godfrey Weitzel attacked Port Hudson, Louisiana, on May 27, 1863. These raw recruits, almost all of them former slaves on Louisiana plantations, stormed the entrenched city of Port Hudson, fighting hand-to-hand against Confederate soldiers who probably included some of their former masters and brutal overseers. Word of their uncommon bravery spread among Union troops as it probably did among Confederates. Union General John C. Palfrey described their valiant attack against well-entrenched, hard-fighting Confederates, concluding that the blacks "fought without panic, and suffered severely before falling back in good order. Their conduct and its indication of character and manliness made a profound impression on the army."[94]

A Union officer who was with them at the battle wrote that they

made six or seven charges over this ground against the enemy's works. They were exposed to a terrible fire and were dreadfully slaughtered. While it may be doubted whether it was wise to so expose them, all who witnessed these charges agree that their conduct was such as would do honor to any soldiers . . . the conduct of these regiments on this occasion wrought a marvelous change in the opinion of many former sneerers.[95]

Another officer told a newspaper reporter:

You have no idea how my prejudices with regard to negro troops have been dispelled by the battle the other day. The brigade of negroes behaved magnificently and fought splendidly; could not have done better. They are far superior in discipline to the white troops, and just as brave.[96]

Not long after, a Confederate officer reported that when his troops attacked a Union force at Milliken's Bend, "This charge was resisted by the negro portion of the enemy's force with considerable obstinacy, while the white or true Yankee portion ran like whipped curs almost as soon as the charge was ordered."[97] But black soldiers' heroism was slow to become known to the general public, either North or South.[98]

One of the first regiments of former slaves actually to be mustered into the Federal Army, and, as we have seen, the first one to see combat, was the 1st South Carolina Volunteers, all of whom were illiterate and only one in ten of whom showed any sign of white ancestry. Soon after their first battle, they came under the command of white Colonel Thomas Wentworth Higginson, a staunch abolitionist and former friend of John Brown, who had spent ten years at Harvard, where he excelled in mathematics, mastered five languages, and became a clergyman before entering the army, originally commanding white recruits. When these men from South Carolina's remote Sea Islands had been properly uniformed, they were formally welcomed into the Union Army by several officials, one of whom read them the Emancipation Proclamation and dramatically declared them free men. They spontaneously responded by singing "My Country, 'Tis of Thee." Higginson was so profoundly moved by this beautifully rendered declaration of patriotism that he soon after wrote, "I never saw anything so electric; it made all other words cheap; it seemed the choked voice of a race at last unloosed."[99]

Higginson later wrote about what it was like to train these men, then go into battle with them. He first noted that when they were in the company of strangers, they adopted a mask of "stupidity"—just as they had done with their slave owners and overseers—but when they relaxed, they proved to be clever and delightfully funny.[100] A Federal prisoner in a Southern prison also noted that black field hands who worked there at first appeared to be docile and stupid but later revealed not only intelligence but courage in helping the Northerners to escape.[101] To Higginson's surprise, these untutored former slaves learned to master army drills, as well as to load their muskets and fire them, faster than the white recruits he had previously commanded.[102] They also learned rules of sanitation faster than their white counterparts.[103] The same surprising ability to learn rapidly was also noted by white officers of other USCT units.[104]

Many of Higginson's former slave soldiers had been whipped by their masters when they sang with joy after Lincoln's election, but now they were free to sing what they liked every night after training and many did so with gusto. While some of them sang and danced at night, most sat sedately talking, smoking, and cleaning their weapons. Others attended a school organized by the regiment's chaplain, and some men who sought out education proved to be truly gifted.[105] Many soldiers probably enjoyed gambling but Higginson did not report it. When it came time for these black soldiers to go into battle, they proved themselves to be remarkably alert sentries as well as brave, clever soldiers who used deception well and ignored minor wounds.[106] Higginson found them more excitable than white troops but equally brave, concluding, "It was their demeanor under arms that shamed the nation into recognizing them as men."[107] Higginson can be excused for his hyperbole given his fondness and respect for these men, but although some Americans accepted them as men, many in the North and all but a few in the South emphatically still did not.

Confederate President Jefferson Davis vehemently opposed the use of slaves as soldiers. His reasons had to do with the Confederacy's declared inequality of the races, a position well stated by Southern General Clement H. Stevens: "I do not want independence if it is to be won by the help of the Negro. . . . The justification of slavery in the South is the inferiority of the Negro. If we make him a soldier, we concede the whole question."[108] The issue of their "natural cowardice" also arose, but less often after black Union troops fought valiantly against Confederates. Although the gallant attack of the black 54th Massachusetts Regiment was beaten back with the loss of over half its men by well-entrenched Confederate forces at Fort Wagner, South Carolina, on July 18, 1863, it removed any doubts in anyone's mind who was there about the fighting prowess of black soldiers.[109] William H. Carney, an African American sergeant who carried the flag throughout the attack, became the first man of his race to receive the Medal of Honor, his nation's highest award for valor in combat. Although severely wounded, he proudly carried the colors well above the ground throughout the battle.[110] In 1989, the background of the 54th Massachusetts and its heroics at Fort Wagner were dramatized in *Glory*, a large-budget Hollywood motion picture starring Denzel Washington, Matthew Broderick, and Morgan Freeman.

Asked before the battle how he intended to organize his attack on Fort Wagner, Union Major-General Truman Seymour replied that he would "put those damned niggers from Massachusetts in the advance; we may as well get rid of them one time as another."[111] Seymour was one of many who, before this battle took place, did not believe that blacks could fight.. The black troops' gallantry changed many minds, including his. When New York black volunteers of the 20th USCT soon after marched through New York City, the *New York Times* noted the "revolution" in Northern attitudes:

> Eight months ago the African race in this city were literally hunted down like wild beasts. They were shot down in cold blood, or stoned to death, or hung to trees or to lamp posts. . . . How astonishingly has all this been changed! The same men who could not have shown themselves in the most obscure street in the City without peril of instant death, even though in the most suppliant attitude, now march in solid platoons, with shouldered muskets, slung knapsacks, and buckled cartridge boxes down through the gravest avenues and busiest thoroughfares to the pealing strains of martial music, and everywhere are saluted with waving handkerchiefs, with descending flowers, and with the acclamations and plaudits of countless beholders.[112]

Even before the courage of black troops was so conspicuously demonstrated in battle, Union Major-General David Hunter sent this favorable report to Secretary of War William Stanton:

> I find the colored regiments hardy, generous, temperate, strictly obedient, possessing remarkable aptitude for military training, and deeply imbued with that religious sentiment (call it fanaticism, such as like) which made the soldiers of Oliver Cromwell invincible. . . . They accept with

patience the slights and sneers occasionally thrown upon them by thoughtless or malignant hands, assured that in the day of trial or conflict they possess and stand ready to evince those qualities of true manhood and soldiership which must redeem, in the eyes of all just and generous men, however prejudiced, the misfortune of their darker skins and that condition of utter degradation out of which they feel themselves but now emerging.

And in this connection I am also happy to announce to you that the prejudices of certain of our white soldiers against these indispensable allies are rapidly softening or fading out.[113]

Southerners, too, learned about the valor of black soldiers and they were not pleased, treating some fifty black prisoners taken from the 54th Massachusetts cruelly, murdering some. When word of this brutality spread, blacks in the Union Army and their white officers feared that they could expect no quarter, and on April 12, 1864, at a place called Fort Pillow in Tennessee, their fears were borne out. Led by Confederate Cavalry General Nathan Bedford Forrest, who would later become the leader of the postwar Ku Klux Klan, Confederates took advantage of a flag of truce to move into assault positions close to the weakly fortified and defended position. After interviewing twenty-one black survivors of the battle, a member of the U.S. Congress and a Northern senator jointly wrote the following report to a House Joint Select Committee a few weeks after the fort's capture:

Immediately after the second flag of truce retired, the rebels made a rush from the positions they had so treacherously gained and obtained possession of the fort, raising the cry of "No quarter!" But little opportunity was allowed for resistance. Our troops, black and white, threw down their arms, and sought to escape by running down the steep bluff near the fort, and secreting themselves behind trees and logs, in the bushes, and under the brush—some even jumping into the river, leaving only their heads above the water, as they crouched down under the bank.

Then followed a scene of cruelty and murder without a parallel in civilized warfare, which needed but the tomahawk and scalping knife to exceed the worst atrocities ever committed by savages. The rebels commenced an indiscriminate slaughter, sparing neither age nor sex, white or black, soldier or civilian. The officers and men seemed to vie with each other in the devilish work; men, women, and even children, wherever found, were deliberately shot down, beaten, and hacked by sabers; some of the children not more than ten years old were forced to stand up and face their murderers while being shot; the sick and the wounded were butchered without mercy, the rebels even entering the hospital building and dragging them out to be shot, or killing them as they lay there unable to offer the least resistance. All over the hillside the work of murder was going on; numbers of our men were collected together in lines or groups and deliberately shot; some were shot while in the river, while others on the bank were shot and their bodies kicked into the water, many of them still living but unable to make any exertions to save themselves from drowning. Some of the rebels stood on the top of a hill or a short distance down its side, and called to our soldiers to come up to them, and as they approached, shot them down in cold blood; if their guns or pistols missed fire, forcing them to stand there until they were again prepared to fire. All around were heard cries of "No quarter! No quarter! Kill the damned niggers; shoot them down!" All who asked for mercy were answered by the most cruel taunts and sneers. Some were spared for a time, only to be murdered under circumstances of greater cruelty.[114]

As some Southern historians have pointed out, this report may exaggerate the extent of the "massacre," but three-fourths of the black garrison were killed whereas only one-third of the white Union soldiers died.[115] Moreover, in his report on the capture of Fort Pillow, General Forrest, who witnessed the killing and some believe ordered it, wrote with obvious approval that the Mississippi River "was dyed with the blood of the slaughtered for 200 yards. . . . These facts will demonstrate to the Northern people that negro soldiers cannot cope with Southerners."[116] Strikingly handsome, the powerful, six-foot-two-inch Forrest was an uneducated frontiersman from West Tennessee whose acute sense of "Southern" honor combined with his explosively ungovernable temper to involve him in numerous altercations, several of which left his adversaries dead. Before the war began, he moved from his Tennessee homeland to the cotton states, where, despite his near illiteracy, he became one of the best-known and wealthiest slave traders in the South. He also became the plantation owner of many slaves and a respected citizen. Although he did not believe that slaves were human beings, and he once killed a black Union prisoner in cold blood for no apparent reason, he may not have ordered the slaughter at Fort Pillow. In fact, about half of the men in the fort, including some blacks, were not killed at all but instead taken prisoner and treated reasonably well.[117] Still, Forrest's comments make it clear enough that he did not disapprove of the slaughter either.

Six days later, Confederate troops slaughtered all black soldiers taken prisoner at a battle in Arkansas including badly wounded men, whom they killed by driving heavily loaded wagons back and forth over them.[118] A few weeks later, the same atrocities were repeated.[119] For the remainder of the Civil War, black union soldiers shouted, "Remember Fort Pillow," often killing Confederates who attempted to surrender. President Lincoln also announced that the Union would execute one Confederate officer held as a prisoner of war for each Union officer put to death for leading black troops, and for each black soldier killed after surrendering, he would order one Confederate prisoner killed. For each captured black Union soldier forcibly returned to slavery, Lincoln threatened to place a "rebel soldier" at hard labor.[120] Despite these threats, the murder of Union black prisoners continued, and so did retaliation by black Union troops.

Despite the growing hatred between Confederate soldiers and black Union troops, their combat could sometimes take on an almost playful aspect, as a former black Union sergeant recalled of the fighting around Mobile near the end of the war:

> We were only ten days on the siege, and had nothing to eat but Parched Corn. But as luck would have it, I crept out of my hole at night and scared one of the Jonnys so bad that he left his rifle pit, gun and accouterments, also one corn dodger and about one pint of buttermilk, all of which I devoured with a will, and returned to my hole safe and sound. . . . We had to keep our heads down all the time or else run the risk of getting shot. So me and my friend of whom I was speaking had [done] it all that day, shooting at each other. Finally, he got hungry and cried out to me, "Say, Blacky, let's stop and eat some Dinner." I told him, "All right." By the time I thought he was done eating, I cried, "Hello, Reb." He answered, "What do you want?" I said, "Are you ready?" "No, not yet," he said. Then I waited for a while. I finally got tired and cried for a chew of tobacco. He then shot at me and said, "Chew that!" I thanked him kindly and commenced exchanging shots with him.[121]

At the very start of the war, substantial numbers of free blacks in the South displayed their intense patriotism by volunteering for military service in the Confederacy. An educated light-skinned African American, who along with many other educated black men attempted to enlist in the Confederate Army, was rejected for active service by a white officer who repeated the Southern insistence that blacks were not suitable to be soldiers because they were "natural cowards." The retort was an angry one: "Our fathers were brought here as slaves because they were captured in war, and in hand to hand fights, too. Pardon me, General, but the only cowardly blood we have got in our veins is the white blood."[122] Other free blacks in the South made clear their demand that if they were to provide gallant military service they should be treated as equals.

Slaves would provide invaluable labor to the Confederate cause, but if blacks, free or slaves, fought in combat, they did so rarely, and then in their roles as servants to their masters, not as members of combat units. Still, as the war wore on, some influential Southerners felt that the time had come to arm slaves. General Patrick R. Cleburne wrote this proposal to Jefferson Davis on January 2, 1864, at a time when the war might still have been won if the South's manpower shortage could have been overcome:

> The time has come when it would be madness not to look at our danger from every point of view, and to probe it to the bottom. Apart from the assistance that home and foreign prejudice against slavery has given to the North, slavery is a source of great strength to the enemy in a purely military point of view . . . but it is our most vulnerable point, a continued embarrassment, and in some respects an insidious weakness. . . . We propose . . . that we retain in service for the war all troops now in service, and that we immediately commence training a large reserve of the most courageous of our slaves, and further that we guarantee freedom within a reasonable time to every slave in the South who shall remain true to the Confederacy in this war. As between the loss of independence and the loss of slavery, we assume that every patriot will freely give up the latter. . . .
>
> . . . For many years, ever since the agitation of the subject of slavery commenced, the Negro has been dreaming of freedom, and his vivid imagination has surrounded that condition with so many gratifications that it has become the paradise of his hopes. To attain it he will tempt dangers and difficulties not exceeded by the bravest soldier in the field. The hope of freedom is perhaps the only moral incentive that can be applied to him in his present condition. It would be preposterous then to

expect him to fight against it with any degree of enthusiasm, therefore we must bind him to our cause by no doubtful bonds; we must leave no possible loophole for treachery to creep in. The slaves are dangerous now, but armed, trained, and collected in an army they would be a thousand fold more dangerous; therefore when we make soldiers of them we must make free men of them beyond all question, and thus enlist their sympathies also. We can do this more effectually than the North can now do, for we can give the Negro not only his own freedom, but that of his wife and child, and can secure it to him in his old home. To do this we must immediately make his marriage and parental relations sacred in the eyes of the law and forbid their sale. . . . Give him as an earnest of our intentions such immediate immunities as will impress him with our sincerity and be in keeping with his new condition, enroll a portion of his class as soldiers of the Confederacy, and we change the race from a dreaded weakness to a position of strength.[123]

Robert E. Lee eventually endorsed General Cleburne's proposal and urged haste in implementing it. Jefferson Davis reluctantly agreed, and on March 13, 1865, the Confederate Congress authorized the enlistment of 300,000 additional troops "irrespective of color," but the war ended before any of the new black recruits could see action. Before he could see what happened to his proposal, General Cleburne was killed in battle.

Women were not enlisted in combat units by either the Union or the Confederacy, but many black women as well as whites served heroically as nurses, braving the horror of tending to mangled men screaming in pain as well as the dangers of contagious diseases that ravaged hospitals both North and South. And Harriet Tubman, a small, gnarled former slave, with an enormous $40,000 reward on her head, had helped so many other slaves escape on the famous Underground Railroad that she became known as "Moses." She also frequently scouted behind Confederate lines for the Union, a dangerous role that some other former slave women willingly risked as well. In June 1863, Tubman served as a guide for Union Colonel James Montgomery, riding next to him as he led 300 black cavalrymen on a raid in South Carolina that destroyed millions of dollars worth of cotton and food supplies, then carried 800 slaves to freedom without the loss of a single man.[124]

In the period just preceding the war, about 50,000 slaves each year fled from their plantations. Many did so in search of their wives and children after they had been sold to a new owner, but others simply sought freedom. Most of the runaways were young men, and they were often helped by older women like Tubman.[125] Despite these courageous, dangerous flights for freedom through heavily armed mounted patrols and pursued by teams of savage dogs, many Southern whites interpreted the slaves' failure to rise in rebellion against their masters as further evidence of their inherent submissiveness and docility.[126] Others seriously asserted that the defeat of their white soldiers came about because they had inherited cowardice through the breast milk of their black wet nurses.[127]

Black Union troops played a vital role in the attacks that routed the Confederate Army of Tennessee, marking the beginning of the end for the South. In these battles, as in so many others, black troops had been ordered to lead the charge. As a Virginia-born Union commander rode over the battlefield looking at dead black soldiers in the front ranks, he turned to his staff to say, "Gentlemen, Negroes will fight."[128] An Irish-born Wisconsin cavalry officer agreed: "I never believed in niggers before, but by Jasus, they are hell in fighting."[129] Not all Union officers and men agreed. USCT men were sometimes ridiculed, and in at least one battle, white artillerymen who were ordered to fire on Confederate positions to support advancing black troops intentionally fired on the blacks instead. On a few occasions, drunken white troops attacked black Union troops with as much brutality as their former masters had done.[130]

The experience of Charles Wills, a white private in the 8th Illinois Regiment, was more typical. Before he met any black soldiers, he declared them "a brute species" that did not "average the ability of an eight year old child in taking care of themselves." After a month of sharing an encampment with black troops, he completely changed his mind, not only volunteering to fight to free the slaves but hoping that he might join a black regiment himself.[131]

Union General Benjamin F. Butler, who like Wills was initially skeptical about black soldiers, wrote this commendation of them after the bloody battle of New Market in October 1864:

In the charge on the enemy's works by the colored division of the 18th Corps at New Market, better men were never better led, better officers never led better men. A few more such gallant charges and to command colored troops will be the post of honor in the American armies. The colored soldiers, by coolness, steadiness, determined courage and dash, have silenced every cavil of the doubters of their soldierly capacity, and drawn tokens of admiration from their enemies, have brought their late masters even to the consideration of the question whether they will not employ as soldiers the hitherto despised race.[132]

A decade later in a speech to Congress advocating the granting of civil rights to the Negro, Butler referred to this battle again:

There, in a space not wider than the clerk's desk, and three hundred yards long, lay the dead bodies of 543 of my colored comrades, slain in the defense of their country, who had laid down their lives to uphold its flag and its honor, as a willing sacrifice. And as I rode along, guiding my horse this way and that, lest he should profane with his hoofs what seemed to me the sacred dead, and as I looked at their bronzed faces upturned in the shining sun, as if in mute appeal against the wrongs of the country for which they had given their lives, and whose flag had been to them a flag of stripes, in which no star of glory had ever shone for them—feeling I had wronged them in the past and believing what was the future duty of my country to them—I swore to myself a solemn oath: 'May my right hand forget its cunning, and my tongue cleave to the roof of my mouth, if ever I fail to defend the rights of the men who have given their blood for me and my country this day and for their race forever.' And, God helping me, I will keep that oath.[133]

The brutality of some of their former owners left deep scars, and occasionally black soldiers would have the opportunity to take revenge against their former masters. For example, in May 1864, the 1st Regiment USCT moved into Virginia very near Jamestown, where the first African slaves arrived in America. Several members of the regiment had been slaves on plantations in that region before their escape to the North. What they had suffered during their slavery was vividly relived when several slave women came to their camp bearing the wounds of a recent and brutal whipping. The following day, the former slave soldiers captured the man who had whipped the women, one "Mr. Clayton." He was stripped and tied to a tree before one of his former slaves, Private William Harris, was given the honor of laying on twenty hard lashes, bringing blood with each one while he reminded Clayton what it had been like receiving lashes from him during Harris' slave days.

Next, each of the slave women Clayton had whipped gave him twenty more lashes, leaving him blood-soaked and pleading for mercy.[134] Slave women could retaliate, too. Some were known to poison their owners and burn their houses.[135] When the war ended, a newly freed slave woman in Mississippi walked up to her mistress, bent over, and lifted up her dress, saying, "Mean and ugly, . . . kiss my ass."[136]

When Richmond finally fell to Union forces, over 12 percent of whom were black, the black 5th Massachusetts Cavalry was given the honor of being one of the first three regiments to enter the city:

> Richmond Negroes were beside themselves with joy. Here on horseback and afoot were men of color, in neat blue uniforms, their shoulders erect, their heads high, their eyes confident. The black admirers ran along the sidewalks to keep up with the moving column, not wishing to let this incredible spectacle move out of sight. In acknowledgment of their reception the Negro cavalrymen rose high in their stirrups and waved their swords. The cheers were deafening.[137]

TWO

"The War to Save Humanity"

Not everyone cheered. Most whites continued to ignore black contributions to the Union cause, including the sixteen black men who won the Congressional Medal of Honor.[1] Well after the war, for example, a biographer of General Ulysses S. Grant, who could hardly have been unfamiliar with blacks' Civil War record, nevertheless concluded, "The American Negroes are the only people in the history of the world, so far as I know, that ever became free without any effort of their own."[2] During the Civil War, many Northern soldiers wrote letters home agreeing with this conclusion.

The surprising fact revealed in a review of Union soldiers' diaries and letters is not that so many held anti-Negro beliefs; rather it is that these ideas persisted for so long, that anti-Negro sentiments proved so resilient to a fair measurement of the capacities of blacks, despite abundant evidence of their fortitude and loyalty. This was a sorry legacy to pass along to the next generation—and the next.[3]

At the war's end, except for the troops sent to the South to enforce "Reconstruction," 80,000 of whom were black, most of the large Union Army was quickly demobilized. Soon after the Civil War guns fell silent, the U.S. Army was reduced to about 55,000 men consisting of sixty-seven regiments, of which six would be "colored," as they were officially designated.[4] These six were soon reduced to four: two infantry regiments, the 24th and 25th, and two cavalry regiments, the 9th and 10th. White regiments had difficulty enlisting enough men to fill their rosters, but black recruits, almost all of them illiterate and desperately poor, tried to enlist in greater numbers than could be taken. From the outset, they were treated shabbily. Most white officers were unwilling to serve in "colored" regiments, although a few outstanding white officers eventually did so, later praising their black soldiers without reservation. One of these was Colonel Benjamin Grierson, who had led the most famous Union cavalry raid through the South during the Civil War and would now command the 10th Cavalry. Grierson was appalled to discover that almost all of his men's horses were so aged that they were virtually useless as cavalry mounts. His men, like those in the "colored" 9th Cavalry, also had shoddy equipment, old uniforms, useless artillery, very little ammunition, and broken saddles.

Nevertheless they were sent to the West, where they, along with the 24th and 25th Infantry Regiments would remain for more than two decades, far from the South, where racial tensions seemed to rise with each passing year of Reconstruction, a time when even southern moderates felt themselves threatened by the federal troops, some of whom were black, political reforms by "carpetbaggers," and "uppity" former slaves. Some of the rage of white southerners was directed at wealthy whites by poor ones, often called "rednecks," "crackers," "clay eaters," and worse, who had long lived on marginal agricultural land, rarely owned any slaves, lived in such rank poverty that it shocked northerners who saw it, and focused much of their anger on the indolent white planter class, or "Bourbons," as they were derisively called. These elite southerners preferred to be known as "chivalry."[5] Poor white southerners had no doubt that the Civil War had less to do with chivalry than "a rich man's war and a poor man's fight."[6]

In return, many freed blacks hated the "crackers" even more than their former owners. Still, few "Bourbons" and fewer "crackers" had any desire for black equality, and these feelings were intensified as the blatant corruption and incompetence of Republican Reconstructionists became more and more obvious, even to blacks themselves.[7] The favoritism shown blacks was especially galling to white southerners. For example, onlookers were shocked by the first postwar South Carolina legislature: "The Speaker is black, the Clerk is black, the doorkeepers are black, the little pages are black, the chairman of Ways and Means is black, and the Chaplain is coal black."[8] In most instances, these black legislators and officers were both illiterate and untrained.

To no one's surprise, southern vengeance against blacks erupted even before Reconstruction ended. Many "freed" slaves were held on their owners' plantations by force, while many thousands more took to open roads in search of freedom only to suffer terribly from hunger, lack of shelter, and white violence. Carl Schurz called it "a veritable reign of terror."[9] Blacks were murdered all over the South. In Texas, for example, from 1868 to 1870, 1,000 blacks were killed each year. In Louisiana, 1,884 were murdered in 1868 alone.[10] There were thirty race riots in the South during Reconstruction in which more than one life was lost, almost all of them black, and there were others in the North.[11] In addition to heightened white hatred of blacks, there was a widespread indifference to their well-being. Mark Twain captured the tenor of black-white relationships of the time in this exchange from *Huckleberry Finn*, published in 1884. After a steamboat engine exploded, Sally cries out:

> "Good gracious! Anybody hurt?"
> "No'm. Killed a nigger," Huck replied.
> "Well, it's lucky because sometimes people do get hurt."

Soon after the war, while federal troops were rapidly demobilized, conservative white southerners created white militias, and these men killed blacks in large numbers before being disbanded by federal law in 1867. Radical Republican state governments then countered by spending tax monies to mobilize black militiamen. As these black militias grew in size and strength, white southerners armed themselves to the teeth, with even fourteen-year-old boys carrying pistols wherever they went.[12] Black militiamen enraged white southerners by their prideful drilling, their expensive tax-funded weapons and uniforms, and their penchant for shooting white farmers' livestock and pet dogs.[13] Whites repeatedly clashed with these black militiamen, sometimes leaving many dead and wounded behind them. To cope with what they saw as this Radical Reconstructionist abuse of power, the conservative South created political-military organizations known as the White Brotherhood, White Line, White League, White Man's Party, Regulators, Jayhawkers, Pale Faces, and the like. Not related to the Ku Klux Klan, these quasi-military units would succeed in restoring white rule, and by 1877, the black militias either had been disbanded or were impotent.[14] Reconstruction had ended. What followed was called Redemption in the South.[15]

While the dramatic conflicts of Reconstruction were being played out in the South, African American soldiers did their best to protect the country's western frontiers against mounted Indians, who quickly named the black cavalrymen against whom they fought from the Dakotas to Texas and throughout the southwest "buffalo soldiers." The designation may have come from a perceived similarity in the hair of blacks and buffaloes, and Plains Indians complained about being unable to scalp these men properly, but they also regarded buffalo with great respect, often believing them sacred, and they were impressed by the fighting abilities of the black soldiers. The "buffalo soldiers" of the 10th Cavalry quickly added a buffalo to the regimental crest that would adorn their unit flag, something they had to invent for themselves because the army, perhaps as a calculated insult, had failed to give any of the "colored" regiments the unit flags, or "colors," that all white regiments possessed and that were such emotional rallying symbols for soldiers of that time.

Most of the posts where these black soldiers initially served not only were overcrowded but lacked even the simplest of amenities such as mattresses and blankets. Roofs leaked, there was no firewood, and kitchen facilities were primitive. The 25th Infantry lived in tents during freezing winters and broiling summers for two years. Their rations were dreadful and, despite their officers' best efforts, typically remained so throughout the years that these units served in the West. Outside these rudimentary posts—"forts," as they were called—the black soldiers faced racist hatred. Even settlers who had been saved from Indian raiders by black soldiers often expressed little appreciation and openly called for the "niggers" to be replaced by white soldiers. No matter how impoverished and uneducated the white settlers might be, they reserved the right to discriminate against black soldiers, and on several occasions black soldiers were shot and killed by white men who were never brought to justice. On two occasions, both near Fort Concho in Texas, when white men shot and killed unarmed black soldiers and were actually brought to trial, all-white juries found them not guilty so rapidly that it seemed to onlookers that the jurors had barely been seated before they handed down their acquittals.[16]

However, in 1867, after black cavalrymen routed a large band of marauding Indians, a leading magazine of the time carried this comment about the fighting ability of black troops:

A few months since, you could not have convinced a ranchman that there was "any fight in the colored troops." It is different now. I have not met a single frontiersman who has seen the dusky patriots "go for Indians" but is loud in their praise. "Why," quoth one of them the other day, "plague gone my cats if they don't like it!"[17]

There could soon be no question about the loyalty, discipline, and military accomplishments of these black soldiers. Some who enlisted were running away from criminal pasts, and not a few had histories of drinking heavily. But after a few years, the buffalo soldiers had lower rates of desertion and drunkenness than white regiments, and they rapidly won many battle honors. The 9th Cavalry shocked the army by reporting not a single desertion for a twelve-month period, an undreamed-of record in these hard times, and one the *New York Times* actually took note of.[18] As early as 1870, a sergeant from the 9th Cavalry won the Congressional Medal of Honor, an award that was later given to almost a score of other black soldiers during their years of service in the West. They fought in hundreds of battles against the Cheyenne in the North, against the Apaches in the South, and with Mexicans and rustlers in between.

After the eventual defeat and forcible relocation of the Seminoles, hundreds of their black allies went with them to Indian Territory, and scores of these men became uniformed scouts for the 9th and 10th Cavalry. Their white officers regularly described them with such superlatives as "extraordinary," "uncanny," "superhuman," and "excellent hunters and trailers and splendid fighters."[19] In 1875, one of these scouts, John Ward, received the Congressional Medal of Honor for riding back through heavy Indian rifle fire to rescue his unhorsed commanding officer. Soon after, scout Adam Paine received the same "highest" honor, being described by his commander as displaying "habitual courage and more cool daring than any scout I have ever known."[20] So impressed with these black soldiers was General William Tecumseh Sherman, who was Commanding General of the Army in 1877, that he recommended that the army integrate its units just as the navy had done. Changing his earlier attitude of mistrust toward blacks, he said that although he still preferred white soldiers to black ones, he was "willing to take black and white alike on equal terms, certainly a fairer rule than the present one of separating them into distinct organizations."[21]

There were few enough "fair rules" for African Americans in these post-Reconstruction years. Poll taxes and literacy tests greatly restricted voting rights, Jim Crow laws grew firmer in the racially explosive post-Reconstruction South, and similar, unwritten rules continued to hold sway in much of the North. A black newspaperman who had lived in Boston for ten years visited his home state of South Carolina, where to his surprise he encountered less discrimination than he had in the North.[22] Despite this man's positive experiences, the numbers of blacks who were lynched in the South after the end of Reconstruction rose dramatically. No longer of monetary value to their former masters, blacks could now be killed without concern for financial loss. In fact, during the last two decades of the nineteenth century, the number of lynchings far exceeded the number of lawful executions for capital crimes.[23]

Under pressure by Republicans and others who supported equal rights, twenty-five African Americans were appointed to West Point during the 1870s and 1880s. Only a dozen of these young men passed the entrance exams, and of these only three graduated. The first to do so was Henry O. Flipper in 1877. Although mercilessly hazed and completely ostracized, at his graduation Flipper was rewarded by a totally unexpected standing ovation from the white cadets, and West Point's superintendent praised him for his courage, quiet fortitude, and academic success under "severe mental strain."[24] Upon receiving his commission as a 2nd Lieutenant, he was assigned to the 10th Cavalry at Fort Concho. After five years of service, he was accused of embezzlement and conduct unbecoming an officer because, many have speculated, of his platonic but close relationship with a young, unmarried white woman, something that was deeply resented by white officers, at least one of whom coveted her for himself.[25] He was discharged dishonorably, and it was not until 1976, thirty-six years after his death, that the army cleared him of all charges. The following year, West Point dedicated a monument to Flipper on the 100th anniversary of his graduation.[26]

The African American cadets who did not graduate and receive commissions were driven out of West Point by ostracism, hazing, reportedly bad grades, and, in at least one instance, physical brutality. Cadet Johnson Chestnut Whittaker, son of a prominent white slave owner and a black slave mother, was found unconscious and bleeding from wounds to his face, so tightly tied to his bunk that it took some time to cut him free. Both an official inquiry and a subsequent court-martial concluded, with perfectly straight faces, that Whittaker had staged the entire event, including tying himself to his bunk. Only at the insistence of the War Department was this astonishing verdict later changed, but on that same day, Whittaker was expelled for academic failure.[27] Three

African Americans were admitted to the Naval Academy, one in 1872, another in 1873, and the third the following year. None of the three men lasted at the academy a full year, all suffering both ostracism and cruel hazing.

While the military academies were rejecting blacks, the South was rejecting black voters. In Missouri, the editor of the *Lexington Tribune* was quoted as saying, "No simian-souled, sooty-skinned, kink-curled, blubber-lipped, prehensile-heeled, Ethiopian gorilla shall pollute the ballot box with his leprous vote."[28] Senator Benjamin "Pitchfork Ben" Tillman of South Carolina used less florid language but made the same point: "We have scratched our heads to find out how to eliminate the last of them. We stuffed the ballot boxes. We shot them. We are not ashamed of it."[29]

And as the century drew to a close, public expressions of racial hate became ever more open. In April 1898, a politician in Missouri declared that blacks were "almost too ignorant to eat, scarcely wise enough to breathe, mere existing human machines."[30] In December of that same year, Senator John Sharp Williams of Mississippi offered this more genteel denunciation:

> You could ship-wreck 10,000 illiterate white Americans on a desert island, and in three weeks they would have a fairly good government, conceived and administered upon fairly democratic lines. You could shipwreck 10,000 negroes, every one of whom was a graduate of Harvard University, and in less than three years, they would have retrograded governmentally; half the men would have been killed, and the other half would have two wives apiece.[31]

Even America's leading literary magazines, such as *Harper's*, *Scribner's* (*Century* after 1881), and the *Atlantic Monthly*, regularly published articles containing racial slurs such as "pickaninny," "buck," "mammy," "coon," "darkey," "niggah," and, of course, "nigger." Blacks in these magazines were also given ludicrous names such as "Orang Outan," "Solomon Crow," "Piddlekins," "Napolean Bonefidey Waterloo," "Abraham Lincum," and many others, often including derisive titles such as "Colonel," "Senator," or "Sheriff." The stories these elite magazines carried regularly portrayed blacks as stupid, lazy, superstitious, immoral, and criminal, especially as petty thieves likely to target chickens.[32]

To some extent, the four "colored" army regiments were spared the rising tide of white hatred toward blacks by virtue of their western isolation. But in 1891, the 9th Cavalry was ordered to Fort Myer, on the outskirts of Washington, D.C., where they endured three grim years of racial segregation in all their post facilities, as well as unending hostility from the white residents of the capital city. In what may have been a blessing for these tormented men, whose stay in the nation's capital was never free from threats of violence, they were ordered back to the West in 1894. Two years earlier, over 150 blacks in the South had been lynched, many of them burned alive, their bodies cut to pieces as the mob fought for souvenirs; this death toll was duplicated in 1893.[33] Many of these attacks were in retaliation for alleged criminal acts, but others were carefully orchestrated to intimidate entire black communities that had begun to entertain hopes of voting or achieving some measure of social equality. Such a well-planned attack in Wilmington, North Carolina, in November 1898 killed twenty-five blacks outright while others who fled to the woods to escape later died of exposure to the cold.[34]

As oppressive as life had become for blacks in the South, as well as some parts of the North, educational opportunities were slowly improving with the opening of Howard, Atlanta, and Morehouse Universities in the 1860s as well as Spelman College for women in the 1880s. Oberlin College in Ohio had accepted some black students as early as 1860. At this same time, some elite black families, typically light-skinned and well educated, were achieving social prominence and considerable wealth in professions such as medicine, dentistry, and law as well as businesses such as banking, newspapers, insurance companies, and even funeral homes. By the late 1880s, Madam C. J. Walker had become the first black millionaire, thanks to her hair care and cosmetics businesses, which catered to white women as well as blacks, and her chain of beauty schools. Among several other houses, she built a magnificent 20,000-square-foot stone mansion in New York's Westchester County that still stands. She also contributed large sums to the NAACP (National Association for the Advancement of Colored People) in support of their antilynching campaign.[35] From this time on, a light-skinned black elite in America would grow and prosper, and although many supported civil rights issues, their exclusive, almost hidden lives would be spent far apart from the great majority of blacks, who would remain largely uneducated and poor.[36]

For well-to-do whites, on the other hand, the Gilded Age, as the late 1890s were known, saw young women playing lawn tennis, men learning to play golf, and both sexes bicycling and roller skating. Americans delighted in singing "There'll be a Hot Time in the Old Town Tonight," and Arthur Conan Doyle's *The Adventures of Sherlock Holmes* and Oscar Wilde's *The Picture of Dorian Gray* were read on both sides of the Atlantic. Commercial electricity was spreading widely, x-rays were invented, open-heart surgery was successfully carried out for the first time—by a black physician!—the game of basketball came into being, and gold was discovered in the Yukon Territory. But in 1893, 500 banks closed, and millions of Americans were out of work, and in 1894 Coxey's Army of unemployed men marched on Washington, D.C., only to be dispersed by force. A year later, 4,000 railroad workers living in the company town of Pullman, just south of Chicago, went on strike. When Mr. Pullman refused to negotiate, the strike spread to twenty-seven states and territories before it became violent and National Guard troops opened fire.

It was also a time when it was legal in almost all states to send seven- or eight-year-old children to work in textile mills for unlimited hours, while black adults were shut out of these new industries altogether. Except for the small black elite and some black townspeople who had never been enslaved, black poverty was often worse than it had been under slavery, and so was lynching. President McKinley pointedly ignored black pleas that he speak out against lynching. Instead, when he toured the South, he spoke of other matters while the United States flexed its muscles as a fledgling imperial power, with Spain's territories in the Caribbean and the Pacific its prime targets.[37] That Cuban and Filipino rebels were offering armed resistance to Spanish rule fed newspaper-generated American indignation and fueled ideas of territorial expansion. In 1895, when the Cuban rebellion broke out, Cuba's sugar harvest was worth $62 million; one year later, it was worth only $13 million.[38]

When the battleship U.S.S. *Maine*, sent to Cuba on January 25, 1898, to protect U.S. civilians and to intimidate the Spaniards, blew up and sank in Havana harbor on February 15—at the time thought by the Americans to be the work of a Spanish mine but later found to have been an accidental explosion caused by a boiler room fire—the United States erupted in a frenzy of jingoism, helped mightily by yellow journalism. The words "Remember the *Maine* and to hell with Spain," adorned not only William Randolph Hearst's newspaper headlines in the *New York Journal*, and those of Joseph Pulitzer in the *New York World*, but were actually on many people's lips. The United States had been quarreling with Spain about its treatment of the Cuban people for the past decade, so when the *Maine* sank, killing 252 Americans, 22 of them black, the nation demanded revenge.

That revenge would be known popularly as "The War to Save Humanity." White troops from Mississippi marched off singing:

> *Hurrah for the blue! Hurrah for the gray!*
> *Hurrah for the sons of them all.*
> *Together we come and united we stand*
> *To answer humanity's call.*[39]

Few war-hungry Americans realized that the U.S. Army at that time totaled a mere 28,000 men, whereas Spain had 400,000 regular army troops, 196,000 of them in Cuba, backed by another 40,000 Cuban militia.[40] State militias were called up around the United States and over 200,000 untrained volunteers stepped forward, but most would find virtually no uniforms, equipment, weapons, or ammunition available to them. Army regulars were armed with modern, smokeless Krag-Jorgenson rifles and carbines, but the volunteers would eventually be given old .45-caliber Springfields that belched black smoke with each shot. While a feverish but largely futile search for military equipment was under way, army planners made resistance to tropical diseases such as malaria and yellow fever a prime factor in selecting volunteers.

As a result, priority was given to men from the Deep South, especially blacks who were mistakenly thought to be doubly immune due to their African heritage and their years of exposure to tropical diseases since birth. Five so-called immune regiments were organized from black volunteers, but these men were not only untrained; there was not enough equipment available to send them into combat before the war ended, as it did only 113 days later. Their discipline was roundly questioned, even in the North. The *New York Times* carried an editorial saying that these men were "not 'immune' from anything but the obligations of law and discipline and decency. Wherever one of them has been it has left a trail of disrepute behind it." Noting that the officers of these units were appointed by "pull," the editorial concluded all these officers were "prima facie" incompetent and worthless . . . the men under their commands are not troops at all but mobs."[41]

While this new recruitment of "immunes" was under way, the army turned to its four regular "colored" regiments, which were therefore also thought to be immune. The 9th Cavalry hurriedly entrained from Nebraska, the 10th Cavalry and the 25th Infantry from Montana, and the 24th Infantry from Utah. As these African American soldiers left northern winter weather behind on their way to a tropical war, white crowds actually cheered them on their way with bands playing and flags waving.

But all that changed when these regiments reached the South, most of them detraining in Tampa, Florida, known as the devil's sandbox because except for the elegant, officers-only Tampa Bay Hotel, it was a ramshackle town ankle-deep in sand. A reporter for the *New York Times* wrote a highly favorable article about the discipline and demeanor of the 24th Infantry encamped near Tampa, but the South had not forgotten, much less forgiven, the use of black troops during the Civil War and Reconstruction, and they greeted the four "colored" regiments with jeers and curses.[42] Lakeland, Florida, where many troops were camped, followed a policy of "plenty of bourbon for the white man, but no gin for the nigger," as a sympathetic white soldier ruefully reported.[43] When confronted by Jim Crow laws like these, some of the soldiers openly objected, and when one barkeeper pulled a gun on them, he was shot dead. In other encounters, several black soldiers were killed as well.[44] Black and white soldiers sometimes fought, but at other times, blacks taught white troops to shoot "craps," one of their favorite gambling games not yet popular with whites.[45]

Potentially the most dangerous incident took place when men from the 24th and 25th Infantry learned that drunken whites from an Ohio volunteer regiment had amused themselves by firing their rifles at a two-year-old black child to see how close they could come to him without actually hitting him. One bullet cut through the terrified child's clothing. Outraged black infantrymen responded by smashing segregated businesses, including barbershops, bars, and brothels, beating any white soldiers they came upon. When neither local nor military police could end the riot, a regiment of white volunteers from Georgia was called in. They ended the fighting by beating the badly outnumbered blacks severely enough to send thirty of them to the hospital, some in serious condition.[46] The southern press reviled the rioting African

American soldiers but made no mention of the incident that had pre-cipitated the violence.

Even though each of the four "colored" regiments was so under-strength that it had to absorb hundreds of untrained, poorly equipped recruits, after this incident all four were rapidly shipped to Cuba, crowded into the holds of ships, the cavalry regiments' horses left be-hind for lack of space. Despite the crowding and inedible food, most regiments went to war singing "The Girl I Left Behind Me," the same sad song that British troops had sung half a century earlier when they sailed off to the Crimean War. Film of their landing in Cuba shows heavily laden troops slipping down steep gangplanks.[47] Two of these men slipped into the water, and despite the valiant efforts of a white captain, an ex-mayor of Prescott, Arizona, who dived in to save them, both men drowned.[48]

Although the U.S. Navy was far superior to the outdated, poorly trained, outnumbered, and dilapidated Spanish Navy, winning deci-sively in every battle they fought including the battle of Manila Bay, where Admiral Dewey's orders, "You may fire when you are ready, Gridley," have become legendary, most of the American army troops were not well prepared for battle. Neither were many of their senior of-ficers. General "Fighting Joe" Wheeler, a tiny, elderly, gray-bearded for-mer Confederate officer, continually referred to the Spanish as "Yan-kees" and at the height of a major battle implored his men to attack because "we've got the damn Yankees on the run."[49] The army was commanded by another Civil War veteran, Major-General William R. Shafter, a gouty sixty-three-year-old man who was so obese he could barely walk. His organizational skills were so very nearly nonexistent that few armies have gone to war so ill prepared.

Whether they were prepared or not, the fighting would soon begin. The American soldiers were badly fed, received wretched medical care, and had so little of their cherished tobacco that they resorted to smok-ing dried weeds, roots, and even dung. A plug of real tobacco that had previously sold for eight cents now cost two dollars.[50] They had little artillery, only a handful of machine guns and a few Gatling guns, and the volunteers were armed with obsolete, single-shot Springfield rifles that gave off a cloud of black smoke, clearly revealing the location of the men who fired. The veteran Spaniards were better armed with mod-ern, smokeless, multishot Mauser rifles, some Maxim machine guns, and light artillery. Their men were rugged Spanish peasants who were well trained and, contrary to American propaganda, unquestionably brave. They were not always well led, however, and their understanding of entrenchment was remarkably wrong-headed. Instead of digging their trenches as most armies did, at the so-called military crest of a hill—a point some distance from the hilltop that would allow them to fire at a downward angle toward attacking troops—they dug themselves in at the very top, making it nearly impossible for them to depress their weapons enough while under enemy fire to hit advancing troops below them without fully exposing themselves.

Even more serious for Spain, their disease-ravaged troops were scattered all over Cuba as they attempted to defend cities and towns against growing numbers of Cuban rebels. Armed with captured and stolen Mausers, and using Mauser ammunition Cuban prostitutes insisted that Spanish soldiers give them in lieu of money, then passed along to rebels, the Cuban rebels made it impossible for Spanish commanders to consolidate their forces against the American invaders. Attempts to move troop convoys along Cuba's almost impassable roads could be met with fearful losses as Cuban riflemen could fire into their columns while hidden in the dense jungle. Diseases were so virulent that perhaps half the garrison was too sick for combat when the Americans landed.[51]

Sweating profusely in their blue flannel winter uniforms and wearing red flannel "belly bands" under them to ward off disease, the dust-shrouded Americans first saw action on June 24 at El Caney when black troops of the 24th Infantry charged up a steep hill. White soldiers reported that these men "knew no such word as fear, but swept up the hill like a legion of demons."[52] Later, Teddy Roosevelt's 1st U.S. Volunteer Cavalry, or "Rough Riders," as they were known—the only U.S. troops in light-weight khaki uniforms—along with other white troops, attacked a Spanish blockhouse protected by barbed wire that dominated a ridge above the village of Las Guasimas. Outnumbered and outgunned by the powder-blue-and-white-uniformed Spanish soldiers, who wore white straw sombreros but fired modern Mauser rifles, the white American troops were taking heavy casualties when the 10th Cavalry attacked on their flank, drawing off Spanish fire, then driving the Spaniards away in retreat. As one white officer later said, if it had not been for the 10th, "the Rough Riders would have been exterminated; this is the opinion freely and openly expressed by the men of that regiment [Rough Riders] themselves."[53] The *Washington Post* carried this story about the same battle: "If it had not been for the Negro Cavalry, the Rough Riders would have been exterminated. I am not a Negro lover. My father fought with Mosby's raiders and I was born in the South, but the Negroes saved that fight and the day will come when General Shafter will give them credit for their bravery."[54]

In a later battle, General J. Ford Kent did everything short of begging to encourage the white 71st New York Infantry Volunteers to advance against a well-entrenched Spanish position. "But all in vain," he later said, "they fled like sheep from the presence of wolves."[55] Just then, the 24th Infantry, led by Colonel Emerson A. Liscum, came up, and General Kent ordered them to attack. Liscum answered, "General, my boys will not disgrace the flag."[56] The black men of the 24th charged over and through the prostrate men of the 71st, and although Liscum was hit, the Spanish were driven out of their position in a wild retreat. Another white southern officer, West Point Colonel James A. Moss, wrote:

> The first fight I was ever in, the battle of El Caney, Cuba, July 1, 1898, I had Negroes killed and wounded all around me, 20 percent of my company having been killed and wounded in about ten minutes' time, and the behavior of the men was splendid. At no time during that, and in subsequent fights, did my men hesitate at the command to advance or falter at the order to charge. . . . I do not hesitate to make the assertion that if properly trained and instructed, the Negro will make as good a soldier as the world has ever seen. . . . Anyone who says the Negro will not fight, does not of course, know what he is talking about.[57]

Various observers reported that the black soldiers were as cheerful as they were brave. This is from a white Lieutenant:

> The negro troops were in a high good humor. They had made the charge of the day; they had fought with a dash and vigor which forever established their reputation as fighters, and which would carry them down in the pages of history. To have heard them that night no one would ever have thought that they had lived for twelve mortal hours under a galling fire. They were laughing and joking over the events of the day, in the same manner they would have done had they been returning from a picnic.[58]

In subsequent battles, all four of the regular army black regiments fought gallantly against entrenched Spanish regular army troops, taking substantial casualties. The 10th Cavalry suffered a 20 percent casualty rate, and 50 percent of its officers were killed or wounded. Frank Knox, then a Rough Rider, who became Secretary of the Navy in World War II, said that the African Americans of the 10th Cavalry were the "bravest men he had ever seen."[59] And shortly after the battle of San Juan Hill, Theodore Roosevelt complimented the men of the 9th and 10th Cavalry for their bravery, saying that no Rough Rider would ever forget what they had done. Newspapers around the country carried a poem praising these men called "The Charge of the Nigger Ninth."[60]

"Black Jack" Pershing, then a captain in the 10th Cavalry, said, "We officers of the Tenth Cavalry could have taken our black heroes into our arms. They had again fought their way into our affections, as they here had fought their way into the hearts of the American people."[61] A white captain from the 10th Cavalry added this: "I am perfectly satisfied that if they were called upon to march through the gates of Hades they would do so in the same jaunty manner in which they went up San Juan Hill. I am perfectly willing to stake my all on their dashing gallantry."[62] During this battle, Spanish troops attacked the black 24th Regiment believing, as they had been told, that the black American soldiers were cowardly. The blacks held firm. It was the Spaniards who retreated.[63]

Major-General "Fighting Joe" Wheeler, who commanded the Cavalry Division during the campaign around Santiago, concluded, "The reports of all their commanders unite in commending the Negro soldier ... all speak of their brave and good conduct, their obedience, efficiency and coolness under a galling fire."[64] The last word on the heroism of black soldiers in Cuba can be left to George Kennan, a well-respected journalist who went to Cuba with Clara Barton as part of the Red Cross' extensive humanitarian efforts, which included 1,400 tons of food and medical supplies as well as doctors and nurses on board the hospital ship *City of Texas*. He wrote, "The fighting of all our soldiers, both at Caney and at San Juan, was daring and gallant in the extreme; but I cannot refrain from calling particular attention to the splendid behavior of the colored troops. It is the testimony of all who saw them under fire that they fought with the utmost courage, coolness and determination."[65] Five of these men were awarded the Medal of Honor. Kennan also reported that Roosevelt praised the squad of black soldiers, saying to them "that he never expected to have, and could not ask to have, better men beside him in a hard fight."[66]

Surprisingly, the cost of defeating Spain in Cuba was less than 400 men killed in battle, but another 5,000 soldiers would die soon after, most of them from tropical diseases exacerbated by dreadfully inadequate food and contaminated water, and some others from poorly tended wounds. All this was a sad commentary on army preparedness. In contrast, the far better prepared U.S. Marines wore cool uniforms, ate nutritious meals, and drank only boiled water, not scummy stream water as soldiers did. The Marines did not lose a single man to disease.[67] The United States annexed Puerto Rico, the Philippines, and Guam from Spain and also took sovereignty over Hawaii and Wake Island. President McKinley had to look on a map to find the Philippines, later admitting that they were not within 2,000 miles of where he thought they were located. He confessed that he did not know what to do with the islands but brought them under United States rule, "to educate the Filipinos, and uplift and civilize and Christianize them."[68]

Despite their heroism, when the black regiments returned home they faced even more violent racism. A black sergeant jotted down this question:

> I noticed that both white and colored soldiers had a brotherly affection for each other while on the way to Cuba, in Cuba and on the way back to the United States. They got along nicely together. During the whole campaign I never heard a cross word passed between them. Why can't it be so at home?[69]

After returning to the South, some veteran white soldiers who fought in Cuba protected black soldiers against white insults and violence, but many other white soldiers who had not fought in Cuba joined local whites in hurling insults at the "heroic" black veterans who had "saved" Teddy Roosevelt and others. Others actually attacked them, killing some without facing arrest. Blacks in the South welcomed the returning black soldiers with great pride, but one black Georgian correctly concluded that "the Negro's valor has *intensified* prejudice against him."[70] The more that newspapers praised these men, the more white southerners were determined to assert their everlasting supremacy. The South's cherished myth of black cowardice was not to be questioned, much less dramatically demolished.

As the black regiments headed north and west, away from the South, several of the troop trains carrying them were fired on by whites, and

numerous members of the Atlanta police force boarded the train carrying the 3rd North Carolina Volunteers home, going car to car viciously
clubbing the unarmed men. The same thing happened to the black 8th
U.S. Volunteers as their train was met in Nashville by 75 policemen and
200 white citizens who beat them with clubs and pistols.[71] Between the
end of Reconstruction and the Spanish-American War, the South was
searching for a solution to its "race problem," and there were southern
liberals as well as a few oases of tolerance such as New Orleans, but by
1900, blatant white supremacy was the rule everywhere, and poor
whites in particular were determined to enforce it.[72] The valor displayed
by black soldiers in Cuba was widely seen as a direct threat to the dom-
inance of these white people.

In December 1898, Mason Mitchell, a white actor who had served
with the Rough Riders, gave a dramatic presentation on the war in
Cuba in a Richmond, Virginia, theater. When he praised the gallantry
and bravery of the 10th Cavalry, "From all parts of the building came
cries of 'put him out' and 'stop him,' and hisses drowned the voice of
the speaker. Mr. Mitchell rebuked his audience, but to no purpose . . .
The hisses were continued until Mitchell had to ring down the curtain
and retire from the stage."[73]

Even Teddy Roosevelt, who had praised the courage of black soldiers
to the skies shortly after the fighting ended, now turned against them.
His political ambitions required the support of white voters who were
increasingly hostile to black soldiers in the North as well as the South.
Perhaps for that reason, when he published "The Rough Riders" in
Scribner's Magazine, early in 1899, he described the outrage he felt
when he saw black soldiers of the 10th Cavalry Regiment heading toward the rear during a crucial battle, saying that he had to threaten to
shoot them with his pistol to turn them back. A black eyewitness,
Sergeant Preston Holliday of the 10th, angrily denounced Roosevelt in
print, pointing out that these men were under an officer's order to go
to the rear to bring up essential supplies, something Roosevelt later acknowledged, but he refused to repudiate his published accusation of
cowardice.[74]

According to Frederick Remington, a former star football player at
Yale who accompanied Roosevelt to Cuba, and whose paintings made
him and the Rough Riders famous across America, Roosevelt was
"merely a hindrance" and "useless" as a soldier.[75] This judgment may be
unduly harsh, but there is no doubt that Roosevelt made "mistakes" as

a near-sighted soldier, just as he did later as a politician. In 1901, when he invited the elegant scholar Booker T. Washington to dine with him at the White House, the southern press, including many of its most influential newspapers, exploded in outrage. The *Atlanta Constitution* ran a cartoon of Roosevelt "cuddled up with a pop-eyed Negro wearing the traditional minstrel show costume of huge collar, gaudy shirt, speckled spats."[76] Not to be outdone by others who exploded with indignation, South Carolina Senator "Pitchfork Ben" Tillman was quoted as saying, "The action of President Roosevelt in entertaining that nigger will necessitate our killing a thousand niggers in the South before they will learn their place again."[77]

The four regular army black regiments had been returned to duty guarding the American Southwest against possible Mexican incursions, but in the spring of 1899, they sailed for the Philippines, followed soon after by two African American volunteer regiments, where they would become part of a 70,000-man force that would fight Filipino rebels who wanted independence, not an exchange of Spanish rule for "civilizing" American rule. The 50,000-man Spanish garrison in the Philippines had surrendered to American forces after only brief and desultory resistance, but the Filipino rebels, led by Emilio Aguinaldo—a man of mixed Chinese and Tagalog ancestry from a well-to-do landowning family—would prove to be much more determined fighters. Aguinaldo's small, untrained army quickly collapsed when it attempted to fight conventional battles against the American forces, but he then turned to guerrilla warfare hoping to wear down American willingness to govern such a fiercely resisting population.[78]

Although the black American soldiers felt bonds of kinship with the Filipino rebels as "people of color"—white American troops called them "niggers"—they fought valiantly against them even though white troops complained that they got along with Filipinos, especially Filipino women, altogether too well. Even so, the African Americans called Filipinos "gugus," not a complimentary term. From the perspective of the African American soldiers, they might as well have been back in the South. Strict Jim Crow segregation was practiced in all public places, especially bars and brothels, and both were numerous. White soldiers, who apparently knew or cared nothing about black heroism in Cuba, often refused to salute black officers and openly sang derisive songs about "coons" and "niggers."[79] One favorite song was "I Don't Like a Nigger Nohow."[80]

Faced by evidence of this open racial antagonism, along with a flood of Filipino insurgent propaganda leaflets urging the black troops to join them in their fight against white tyranny, many white officers expected black soldiers to desert in large numbers. To their surprise, throughout the three-year campaign, only five black soldiers deserted to the Filipino insurgents, many fewer than the numbers of white soldiers who deserted. The most notorious of these by far was Corporal David Fagen who did not desert for political reasons but because he felt harassed by his sergeant. Fagen fought with the rebels for two years, rising to the rank of captain before a bounty hunter brought his head to the Americans to claim the reward that had been offered. Although President Theodore Roosevelt, who had succeeded the assassinated William McKinley to that office in 1901, commuted the death sentences of fifteen white soldiers who had deserted to the rebels, two blacks who also deserted were inexplicably executed by firing squad.[81] Roosevelt was not the only politician who was now acutely aware that white attitudes toward blacks had become even more negative than they had been earlier.

The Spanish-American War, which was said by the Americans to have been fought "for the cause of humanity," became a war of conquest in 1899 when Aguinaldo's guerrillas refused to accept rule by the United States. Unlike the relatively bloodless war in Cuba, this one was deadly, with 4,000 Americans and 250,000 Filipinos killed. Many of these deaths came about because the Filipino rebels often resorted to extremes of brutality to control and intimidate peaceable Filipino villagers. Fifty-six Filipinos were reported to have been buried alive. Others were burned alive, beaten to death, or tortured and mutilated until they died. Women and children were killed along with adults, and many women were raped.

But many of the Americans were brutal, too. An American correspondent for *Outlook* wrote, "It is easy to understand how an ordinarily humane officer or soldier might regard himself as justified in dealing summarily, and even cruelly, with Filipinos who make war by burning other Filipinos at the stake, cutting out their tongues, tasting their blood, or burying them alive."[82] He was referring to the fact that at least ten officers and numerous soldiers and Marines were court-martialed for "cruelty and barbarity in the conduct of the war." One of these officers, Marine Corps Major Littleton W. T. Waller, testified that his commander, General Jacob H. Smith, ordered him to turn the large island of Samar into a "howling wilderness" and kill all Filipinos over the age of ten.[83] Two other Marine officers corroborated Waller's testimony, but Smith denied giving any such order. Whatever the truth of this case, innocent Filipino men, women, and children were shot down on many occasions. Richard O'Brien, a former corporal of the white 26th Volunteer Regiment, described numerous callous murders that he witnessed being carried out against helpless villagers.

> As we approached the town the word was passed along the line that there would be no prisoners taken. It meant that we were to shoot every living thing in sight—man, woman, and child. . . . Two old men, bearing between them a white flag and clasping hands like two brothers, approached the lines. Their hair was white. They fairly tottered, they were so feeble under the weight of years. To my horror and that of the other men in the command, the order was given to fire, and the two old men were shot down in their tracks . . . A man who had been on a sick-bed appeared at the doorway of his home. He received a bullet in the abdomen and fell dead in the doorway . . . a mother with a babe at her breast and two young children at her side pleaded for mercy. She feared to leave her home, which had just been fired. . . . She faced the flames with her children and not a hand was raised to save her or the little ones. They perished miserably. It was sure death if she left the house—it was sure death if she remained. She feared the American soldiers, however, worse than the devouring flames.[84]

What he saw were not isolated incidents. Throughout the war, white American troops often destroyed and stole private property, raped Filipino women, and killed rebel prisoners. One officer wrote, "I have six horses and three carriages in my yard, and enough small plunder for a family of six."[85] A soldier of the white 50th Iowa Regiment wrote:

> The soldiers made short work of the whole thing. They looted every house and found almost everything from a pair of wooden shoes up to a piano, and they carried everything off or destroyed it. Talk of the natives plundering the towns—I don't think they are in it with Fiftieth Iowa.[86]

A white Kansan wrote:

> Company 1 had taken a few prisoners and stopped. . . . Then occurred the hardest sight I ever saw. They had four prisoners and didn't know

what to do with them. They asked Captain Bishop what to do and he said, "You know the orders," and four natives fell dead.[87]

Another white soldier described the hundreds of Filipino bodies—"dead niggers"—he saw:

I don't know how many men, women, and children the Tennessee boys did kill. They would not take any prisoners. One Company of Tennessee boys was sent into headquarters with thirty prisoners, and got there with about a hundred chickens and no prisoners.[88]

There is also eye-witness evidence that white American officers and soldiers used water torture to extract information from Filipinos.[89] Two army officers admitted torturing Filipinos for information by hanging them by the neck for ten seconds at a time, and another testified that he put prisoners in the stocks, fed them on salt fish, and withheld all water until their thirst forced them to provide information.[90] It is possible that some black American troops committed similar atrocities, but there is no available evidence that they did so, and no black soldier was court-martialed for such an offense. Black troops fought many battles, killing rebels and losing men in return, but they were remarkably honorable in avoiding brutality or theft, and they brought back many prisoners alive.[91]

The U.S. Navy had long sailed racially integrated ships on which blacks and whites shared the same mess and sleeping quarters, and in which blacks sometimes served in combat roles. When Gridley obeyed Admiral Dewey by ordering American guns to open fire on the Spaniards at Manila Bay, that famous first shot was fired by Chief Gunner's Mate John Jordan, an African American. But the growth of Jim Crowism led to growing racial tension in the Navy, with brawls increasingly commonplace and shipboard integration less and less comfortable. With the rapid expansion of the Navy after 1900, huge, new, much more comfortable ships began to attract white recruits, who had previously refused to consider naval service. In response to the availability of these white sailors, the Navy rapidly eliminated black sailors and segregated its ships. Those few blacks who remained either stoked boilers or waited on white officers in their mess, and even this latter role was rapidly being taken over by Filipinos.[92] For example, in 1912, 6,000 U.S. Navy sailors paraded in the National Naval Review in New York. There was not a single African American among them.

By 1906, blacks constituted less than 5 percent of the Navy, and all black petty officers were transferred from combat ships to routine, unimportant shore duty. In that same year, the War College recommended that blacks not serve in artillery units because they were too unintelligent to manage such complex duties. The accomplishments of Gridley's Chief Gunner's Mate Jordan and others like him were not mentioned. In 1907, President Roosevelt sent his "Great White Fleet" of sixteen modern battleships—all in fresh white paint—to intimidate the Japanese, who had been emboldened by their defeat of Russia in 1905. However, they were infuriated by a Roosevelt-brokered peace conference that denied them any rewards for their victory, as well as by growing discrimination against Japanese immigrants on America's west coast. When these white ships arrived in Japan, the few black sailors who were still members of the ships' crews were kept discreetly below decks. So many black men left the Navy or were denied enlistment that black leaders appealed to Secretary of the Navy Josephus Daniels, complaining about discrimination against blacks. Daniels referred their complaint to Rear Admiral Charles J. Badger, Commander of the Atlantic Fleet. Less than six weeks later, on May 26, 1913, the *New York Times* reported:

> Secretary of the Navy Daniels and Rear Admiral Charles J. Badger have completed an investigation of the charge of discrimination in the navy against colored enlisted men and find that the charge is unwarranted as there is no evidence of discrimination.

In September 1904, maneuvers involving both black and white veteran soldiers of Cuba and the Philippines were held in Manassas, Georgia. Georgia's governor wrote the following comment to the *New York Times:* "The Georgia boy who refused to salute the negro officer at the Manassas manoeuvres showed true Georgia grit and we are all proud of him. He is a true Southerner, and I don't believe that any of our boys will depart from his example." An ex-governor of Georgia joined in, writing to the *Times,* "Any Yankee who thinks a Georgia soldier will salute a negro is a damned fool. Damn Yankees and negroes anyway."[93]

Racial hostility grew even worse in 1906, when a battalion from the 25th Infantry, recently returned from the Philippines, was ordered to Fort Brown in Brownsville, Texas, for training. The people of

Brownsville were so vehemently opposed to the presence of these men that the 25th's black chaplain predicted violent conflict. It was not long in coming. With Jim Crow law signs everywhere in evidence, including ones declaring that neither dogs nor blacks could enter a city park, black soldiers were on their best behavior but were nevertheless beaten or kicked for what white police saw as infractions. At midnight, after one such incident, as many as 150 shots rang out in an area near the fort. One white man was killed and at least two others were wounded. At dawn, cartridge casings from the army's new Springfield rifles were found lying in the streets, clear "proof" that the shooters had been soldiers. However, despite police pressure no soldier confessed, and there was no evidence linking any individual to the incident. Southern newspapers raged at the "black killers," and even though there was insufficient evidence to court-martial any individual soldier, President Roosevelt relied on an inquiry led by General E. A. Garlington, a South Carolinian, that declared the black soldiers guilty. Despite the absence of evidence sufficient to bring anyone to trial, Roosevelt took it upon himself to dishonorably discharge from the army every man in the battalion except a few who had been on leave. Those charged would never again be allowed to serve in the military or work for the federal government.[94]

Booker T. Washington joined other prominent black voices in expressing his dismay over Roosevelt's action, and a political opponent of Roosevelt's, Senator Joseph B. Foraker of Ohio, seized the opportunity to embarrass the president. An attorney, a Civil War veteran, and an aspiring presidential candidate, Foraker was able to show, among other things, that most of the bullets found at the scene did not come from Springfields and that those that did come from these weapons had been traced to individual rifles that either had not been fired that particular night or had been locked in a gun chest at the time. To make matters even more suspicious, the first five or six shots fired were from revolvers, and the black troops had no revolvers.[95] Only about 50 of the 150 cartridges found were from Springfields, and all these were in a ten-inch diameter circle. Most of the other bullets were found to have come from non-Springfields, a fact convincing Foraker that some citizens of Brownsville had staged the shoot-out, planting the cache of cartridges to frame the soldiers.

Infuriated by Foraker's challenge, Roosevelt called the men of the 25th "bloody butchers" who "ought to be hung" and soon after triumphantly announced the receipt of evidence that a former black soldier in the battalion had confessed to the shooting.[96] Foraker was quickly able to demonstrate that Roosevelt's claim was false. According to a Georgia sheriff who had subjected the man to a "most severe cross-examination," the accused had denied any wrongdoing. The sheriff went on to describe Roosevelt's report as a "willful misrepresentation of the truth."[97] After leaving office, Roosevelt wrote his autobiography, in which he failed to make a single mention of the Brownsville episode.[98] It was not until 1972 that the U.S. government corrected the record to show that all those black soldiers who had been dishonorably discharged deserved honorable discharges. By that time, only one of those men was still alive, Dorsie Willis, aged eighty-six. He was granted $25,000 in damages and medical care.[99] Willis pointed out that because of his dishonorable army discharge, he had never been able to obtain work beyond shining shoes or being a porter.[100]

In the same year, a less well-known but more destructive, and in many respects more ominous, riot took place in Atlanta, once again in a neighborhood called Brownsville. In 1906, Atlanta was a city of about 150,000 people, one-third of them African Americans. The inner city of Atlanta had attracted a good many people, white as well as black, who earned their living by less than altogether honest means. Many were armed and many were dangerous. As was the case in much of the South, whites lived in fear that their women would be raped by blacks. Many accusations of rape were well publicized by newspapers in Atlanta that year, and some of these rapes actually took place. For reasons that are still not completely clear, this pervasive dread exploded into mob violence, with whites attacking any blacks they came upon. Before it ended, twelve people were dead and seventy badly injured. None were said to have been actual rapists, nor did the violence put an end to rape. But the city of Atlanta was paralyzed for a week or more. Factories were closed down, railroad cars were left unloaded in the yards, the streetcar system was crippled, and there was no cab service (the cab drivers were African American); hundreds of servants left their employers, banks lost hundreds of thousands of dollars, and the state fair, which had been ready to open, failed.[101] An investigating committee concluded with this doleful report:

> As a result of four days of lawlessness there are in this glad Christmas time widows of both races mourning their husbands, and husbands of

both races mourning their wives; there are orphan children of both races who cry out in vain for faces they will see no more; there are grown men of both races disabled for life, and all this sorrow has come to people who are absolutely innocent of any wrong-doing.[102]

In the wake of this violence, the growing numbers of sexual relationships between white men and black women in Atlanta and throughout the South once again became the target for concern. In 1907, J. H. Currie, a district attorney in Meridian, Mississippi, addressed a jury as follows:

The accursed shadow of miscegenation hangs over the South today like a pall of hell. We talk much of the Negro question and all of its possible ramifications and consequences, but, gentlemen, the trouble is not far afield. Our own people, our white men with their black concubines, are destroying the integrity of the Negro race, raising up a menace to the white race, lowering the standard of both races and preparing the way for riot, mob [sic], criminal assaults, and, finally, struggle for racial supremacy. . . . We have tolerated this crime long enough . . . it is time to rise up and denounce this sin of the earth.[103]

After these riots in Texas and Georgia, relations between the races were frighteningly tense. A white women in Atlanta told a visitor from the North she did not feel like she "knew" African Americans any more: "Since the riot they have grown so glum and serious that I'm free to say I'm scared of them!" [104] Similar feelings could be found throughout the white South, and the Ku Klux Klan responded by becoming ever more visible and violent. Southern blacks were no less tense and many emigrated to the North. Racial tensions were not eased by repeated lynchings. For example, in early 1911, a black man accused of killing a white man was taken from his jail cell in Livermore, Kentucky, to the town's opera house, where an admission fee was charged to all those who wanted to watch his murder. Anyone who paid for orchestra seats was allowed to empty his revolver at the victim; those in the gallery were limited to a single shot. The NAACP was outraged, as were many other African Americans who learned about the killing.[105] There were no apologies given.

Not only did whites offer no apologies for the ways in which lynchings were carried out, but many pointedly insisted that once they believed that a crime had been committed by a black man, it did not matter which black was lynched for it. A southern military man, Captain McBane, explained this position as follows:

> Burn the nigger. . . . We seem to have the right nigger, but whether we have or not, burn *a* nigger. It is an assault upon the white race. . . . It would justify the white people in burning *any* nigger. The example would be all the more powerful if we got the wrong one. It would serve notice on the niggers that we shall hold the whole race responsible for the misdeeds of each individual.[106]

Sometimes, blacks fought back. For example, Robert Charles and a young black friend were sitting on Charles' doorstep in New Orleans when three police officers suddenly attempted to arrest Charles. When no reason for the arrest was given, Charles refused to cooperate and was clubbed. Charles then drew a revolver, wounding an officer before being wounded in return, then escaping. Soon after, several police came to Charles' home to arrest him but once again he resisted, killing two of the officers, a patrolman and a captain. New Orleans then offered a large reward for Charles, dead or alive, and a massive manhunt began with civilians called upon to join the police in their search.

They did so with vengeance, beating many wholly innocent blacks whom they happened to come across. They also looted pawnshops and began shooting blacks to death, including a seventy-five-year-old man on a streetcar and a woman in her own home.

After fours days the police learned of Charles' whereabouts and laid siege to his place of hiding. But Robert Charles made a notable last stand, fought a mob of 20,000, and before dying killed 7 of his would-be captors, seriously wounded 8, and left 12 slightly wounded. Charles was killed when the building in which he hid was set afire and he was forced to flee. The *Times-Democrat* announced that after Charles was pronounced dead his body was "shot, kicked, and beaten almost out of semblance to humanity." Even while the battle with Charles was in progress another black, apparently for no other reason than that he was black, was chased by a mob in the French Quarter and shot and stabbed to death.[107]

Charles, an earnest young employee of a "back to Africa" newspaper, became a hero to much of the black community.

It was in this atmosphere of escalating racial hatred that the unthinkable happened. A black man became the heavyweight boxing champion of the world. Boxing had become increasingly popular in America, and much of the country's adulation was focused on its white heavyweight champion, the immensely popular Jim Jeffries. By 1905, Jeffries had run out of challengers and retired. Soon, however, a challenger emerged in the person of Jack Johnson, a splendid boxer, an outspoken man on all subjects, and a very public patron of white prostitutes who often accompanied him arm-in-arm in public. The problem for Jeffries was twofold: Johnson was far too skillful for him and, to make matters worse, he was black. Johnson was a man white Americans loved to hate, and they implored Jeffries to fight—and knock out—this hateful man who openly consorted with white women, then boasted of his sexual prowess. In return, Johnson reveled in the role of "bad nigger," an idea made famous by the music of Leadbelly (Huddie Ledbetter) and Jelly Roll Morton.

Despite great pressure from outraged white boxing fans, Jeffries refused to fight Johnson, insisting that he was retired. However, the new heavyweight champion, Tommy Burns of Australia, was willing to fight Johnson for the title if the price was right. Publicly declaring that "all coons are yellow" (the cowardice myth had spread to Australia), and that Johnson was particularly "yellow," Burns expressed his hope that the fight could be arranged. It took place in 1908, and Johnson toyed with Burns, beating his face to a bloody pulp while taunting him mercilessly until police stopped the fight to save Burns from serious physical injury in addition to his now shattered pride. Whites in Australia, England, and America were aghast, and all the more so when Johnson flaunted his prowess in one public pronouncement after another. He also continued to appear in public with white women on his arm. Jeffries still avoided a fight with Johnson, but on July 4, 1910, with fireworks in the skies, he finally climbed into the ring with Johnson and suffered the same humiliatingly one-sided defeat as Burns. Johnson's embarrassingly easy victory set off gleeful celebrations by blacks in several cities, igniting deadly white violence against them. When the rioting ended, ten blacks were dead with hundreds badly injured.[108]

Despite intense hatred by white fans, Johnson proved unbeatable until 1913, when, after marrying a white woman, he was forced to flee to France to escape trumped-up charges that he had violated the Mann Act—transporting a female across state lines for immoral purposes. Desperate for money, but leery of returning to America, the then thirty-seven-year-old and paunchy Johnson agreed to fight a white Kansas cowboy named Jess Willard in Cuba, on April 5, 1915. Six-foot-six, weighing 238 pounds, Willard was the "Great White Hope" whom promoters across the United States had been searching for to defeat the hated Jack Johnson. Johnson was counted out in the twenty-sixth round, later claiming that it was a bribe, not Willard's punch, that had sent him to the canvas. Perhaps so, but it appeared to many that the out-of-shape Johnson had collapsed from heat exhaustion.[109] Willard went on to earn $650,000 in vaudeville appearances, and white Americans became still more triumphant because the next heavyweight champion would be the white Jack Dempsey, who, despite openly avoiding military service in World War I, went on to become America's favorite, the greatest fighter of his time. He was twice indicted for "draft dodging" but not convicted. Dempsey apparently saw no need to prove that he could fight outside the ring alongside so many Americans, including blacks, who were dying for their country.

In 1916, long-standing conflicts along the border with Mexico became more violent when Pancho Villa's men executed sixteen American miners they had taken off a train headed for Chihuahua City from El Paso. When this atrocity still did not bring about Villa's goal of a declaration of war by the United States against Mexico, he crossed the border to attack Columbus, New Mexico, killing five more Americans. With Europe in flames, the last thing the United States wanted was a military confrontation with Mexico, but President Woodrow Wilson finally ordered now-General Pershing to lead 15,000 men into Mexico to capture Villa, while avoiding any threat to the Mexican government. The black 10th Cavalry, Pershing's old regiment, led the attempt to locate Villa. On one occasion, the 10th, led by then Major Charles Young, relieved the embattled white 13th Cavalry. Major Thompkins, who commanded the 13th, greeted his rescuers saying, "By God, Young, I could kiss every black face out there."[110] Young replied that Thompkins could start with him. Later, a unit from the 10th ran into heavy machine gun fire from regular troops of the Mexican Army, taking many casualties and retreating in disorder after most of its officers had been killed. Before the black troopers could claim revenge, the war ended, and they were once again assigned to guard the border.

If more insight into a black man's "place" late in the nineteenth and early twentieth centuries should be needed, the life of Matthew A. Henson is an object lesson. Of light-skinned African American ancestry, Henson was born in utter poverty to a broken family, running away from home as a wholly unschooled eleven-year-old to escape a cruel stepmother. He became a cabin boy to a kindly ship's captain who taught him to read, and after some years at sea, followed by other jobs, he was recommended to then Lieutenant Robert Peary, who hired him as a "manservant" in 1887. Impressed by Henson's intelligence, loyalty, and indomitable spirit, Peary soon made him his "assistant," and Henson accompanied the explorer on his many attempts to reach the North Pole from 1891 to 1909. By the time the North Pole was finally reached in 1909, Henson, by then forty-three years old, had long been seen by Peary and other members of this and earlier expeditions as utterly indispensable. A carpenter, mechanic, great hunter, and expert dog-sled driver, Henson spoke Eskimo well and, according to Commander Donald B. MacMillan, a colleague of Peary, "He was easily the most popular man on board ship."[111]

Henson was devoted to Peary, saving his life on several of his expeditions, and Peary was the first to admit that he could not have reached the North Pole without his "assistant," who not only got Peary there but had to carry him to bring him back. When Peary's discovery was finally acknowledged after a challenge by a fraudulent competitor, he was made a rear admiral and retired with the thanks of Congress and the adulation of the public. After some delay—and no credit for his own achievements—Henson was given a civil service job at a customs house as a "messenger boy."[112] Despite his great courage and intelligence, history books routinely dismissed Henson as Peary's "colored manservant" until 1945, when the U.S. Navy belatedly awarded him a silver medal. A Navy captain read the inscription, but there was no one present to witness the award ceremony except Henson, who heard that he "had contributed materially to the success of the expedition." To no one's surprise, the Eskimos who also accompanied Peary to the Pole were still completely ignored. Henson's equal part in the discovery of the Pole was not publicly recognized until 1988, when his remains were disinterred and buried with full military honors next to Peary's in the Arlington National Cemetery, where a bronze plaque was displayed honoring him as "Co-discoverer of the North Pole, 1909."[113]

THREE

World War I

"Our Country, Our War"

Most Americans had leaned toward the Allied cause from the start of World War I in August 1914, when flag-waving French troops wearing blue jackets and bright red trousers–*pantalons*–marched north to war as laughing gray-clad German soldiers with flowers in the muzzles of their rifles swung south to meet them. French soldiers soon charged to their deaths against seemingly invincible field-gray-clad Germans, who were known vividly in the West for their military efficiency and their brutality against Belgian civilians. Among the French dead in these first battles were black soldiers from West Africa. Soon, British, Italian, Austrian, and Russian troops, among others, would join in the slaughter. With mounting horror, the American public read about the appalling casualties that followed.

Even though all the belligerent countries of World War I had sent military observers to witness the murderous war between Russia and Japan in 1904–1905, which should have proven even to the dullest of military minds that thanks to the advent of machine guns and barbed wire, frontal attacks were suicidal, all armies in the "Great War" attacked entrenched positions nonetheless, again and again, dying in enormous numbers. Nearly 1 million Frenchmen and Germans fell during the siege of Verdun in 1916. On July 1, 1916, 100,000 British troops surged out of their trenches to begin the Battle of the Somme. In less than half a day, 60,000 of them fell. Before 1917 ended, 700,000 men of Britain's "new army" recruited by Field Marshal Lord Kitchener had fallen on the blood-soaked fields of Flanders. Unwilling to face their own slaughter any longer, brave but too long suffering French troops actually mutinied in 1917 and had to be brought under control by artillery barrages and firing squads. When the war ended, 8 million soldiers and 7 million civilians lay dead.[1] In 1918, the war's aftermath contributed to an influenza epidemic that began in Spain and then spread across the world, leaving somewhere between 40 and 100 million dead.[2]

Few American homes had radios in 1912 when the *Titanic* sank, but only two years later, at the start of World War I, radios carried news of the war into millions of American living rooms.[3] What most Americans learned convinced them that their young men should not be sent to die in this seemingly senseless carnage. Even if the United States were somehow forced into the war, America's armed forces were too few in number to make an immediate impact, as Germany was well aware. Even so, America protested against the German Navy's unrestricted use of submarines against any shipping in the Atlantic that they believed might be aiding the Allied cause. All but the most isolationist members of the U.S. government were alarmed by this practice, as any ship might be sunk with no warnings and no apologies, and many were. Americans were repeatedly warned that they traveled at their own risk.

Slowly, tentatively, America strengthened its military forces. During the increasingly tense year of 1916, while the "Western Front" was stalemated in trench warfare and the Russian Army was near collapse in the east, the U.S. Army recruited 650,000 volunteers, only 4,000 of whom were African Americans. These "colored" soldiers, as they were still known, were assigned to one of the four regular army "colored" regiments still serving in the American Southwest—the 9th and 10th Cavalry and the 24th and 25th Infantry. In all, there were 10,000 troops in these four regiments, three of which would remain in the United States throughout the war while one would go to the Philippines. Another 10,000 African Americans served in various National Guard units in the North.[4]

Despite this unprecedented peacetime military buildup, most Americans still had no appetite for joining the war in Europe. Even the sinking of the British Cunard Line passenger ship *Lusitania* in May 1916, with the loss of 1,154 lives, 114 of them American, did not lead the United States to declare war against Germany and its allies. That did not take place until almost a year later, on April 6, 1917, after several other sinkings, and even then the vote was not unanimous—six senators and fifty representatives voted no. When President Wilson asked for a declaration of war against Germany, telling Congress, "The world must be made safe for democracy," most African American intellectuals, led by Dr. W. E. B. Du Bois, quickly pledged their full devotion to Wilson's cause, urging young black men to take up arms. Du Bois wrote, "Our country is at war. . . . if this is OUR country, then this is OUR war." He urged blacks to fight "shoulder to shoulder with our white fellow citizens," saying that the result of such loyal sacrifice would be "the right to vote and the right to work and the right to live without insult."[5]

Several African American intellectuals supported Du Bois, some saying that blacks would be considered cowards "for all time" if they did not join the war effort, but a few wondered aloud whether the world that was to be made safe for democracy included the South, noting, as one wrote, that President Wilson "believed in democracy for humanity but not for Mississippi."[6] Columbia University law student Chandler Owen reflected the views of some blacks when he wrote, "Did not the Negro take part in the Spanish-American War? . . . And have not prejudice and race hate grown in this country since 1898?"[7] But most black men, including many field hands who were so uneducated that they had never before heard of the war, or even of Germany for that matter, registered for the national draft that had quickly been put into place. Almost 5,000 draft boards staffed by local citizens were established throughout the country. With a very few exceptions in some northern states, these boards were all white, and many were not at all reluctant to defer large numbers of white men from service while refusing to defer African Americans, including those with several children, unless their labor was required by white plantation owners. One black man with a wife and five children aged seven years to six months was classified 1-A, whereas many single white men who worked for large planters were deferred.[8] For example, the local draft board in Fulton County, Georgia, exempted 526 of 815 white registrants but only 6 of over 200 African Americans. White farmers were well served by friends on many local draft boards.

Nationwide, by the end of the war, 34 percent of the black registrants had been conscripted compared to only 24 percent of whites.[9] Thirteen percent of all draftees were black, even though blacks constituted slightly less than ten percent of the American population. This pattern of conscription did not serve the needs of some southern whites who relied on black labor. In fact, in several parts of the Deep South, blacks' conscription in 1917 was delayed until after the cotton harvest in October.[10] Some southerners had other reasons for not being at all pleased by the large number of African Americans who appeared to be headed for military service. Senator James K. Vardaman from Mississippi, one of the South's most vocal racists, worried that "universal military service means that millions of negroes who come under this measure (the draft) will be armed. I know of no greater menace to the South than this."[11] One might wonder why "natural cowards" should be so threatening, but other southerners were not concerned, assuming, correctly as it happened, that almost all of the black soldiers would serve as unarmed laborers. Of the 400,000 African Americans who served during World War I, only about 42,000 would serve as combat soldiers. Vardaman need have had no worries about the U.S. Marine Corps, which refused all black recruits, or the U.S. Navy, which enlisted only 1 percent of its manpower from African Americans. During the Civil War, the Union Navy had been 25 percent black.

The average white recruit was twenty-two years old and stood five feet seven and a half inches tall, weighing 141-1/2 pounds. In general, black conscripts were larger men, many standing over six feet. An example was a six-foot, six-inch, 260-pound boxer, "Kid" Cotton, whose compassion for the hungry women and children he met in France revealed a heart as large as his frame.[12] Many more blacks than whites were illiterate, including nearly 90 percent of draftees from the rural Deep South, and even those with some education often spoke in a dialect that made them nearly incomprehensible to most whites, and to many northern blacks as well. Two university professors, Walter D. Scott and Robert M. Yerkes, were given the task of assessing the intelligence of the new recruits. Taking a more-or-less random sample of 160,000 men accepted for service, they administered a newly developed "intelligence test" that yielded alarming results. Although draft boards and physical examinations had supposedly eliminated "feebleminded" men, Scott and Yerkes found that 47 percent of the whites and 89 percent of the African Americans were "morons," that is, below the "mental age" of thirteen.

Even at the time, however, it was obvious that this "IQ" test was measuring education far more than generic intelligence. For example, it asked where the Overland Railroad car was manufactured, the definition of "mauve," and whether Scrooge appeared in *Vanity Fair, A Christmas Carol, Romola,* or *Henry IV*.[13] Given that 31 percent of all men tested, and the majority of blacks, were illiterate, it is hardly surprising that their scores were low. The military's response to the test results was to ignore low white test scores, whereas the low scores of blacks were used to confirm their lack of intelligence and their unsuitability for any complex military assignment. This was insisted upon despite clear evidence that many northern blacks outscored rural southern whites, an inflammatory report that angered many politically powerful southerners, who did their best to explain it away, then ignored it.[14]

Across the country, draft boards inducted men much faster than the Army could equip or train them. Most military camps were in southern states, where warm weather permitted year-round training, and it was to these far too few, too small, and unprepared training bases that the new soldiers flocked, some aboard trains and buses, others on foot. As they arrived, they often sang songs such as "Old Black Joe," "We'll Hang Kaiser Bill from a Sour Apple Tree," "Over There," "Swanee River," and rousing—if strange to today's ears—choruses of a song improbably said to be of Hawaiian origin, "Yaaka Hula, Hickey Dula."

Many men, particularly poor black farmers from the rural South arrived in tattered overalls with bare feet. Some urban men, including college-educated ones of both races, arrived in suits and ties. The clothes they arrived in would often have to serve them for weeks, as neither uniforms nor footgear were available in anything like sufficient amounts. Housing was grossly inadequate as well, and many men slept on the ground in hastily erected tents. Supplies of all sorts were unavailable, especially weapons, and so were qualified instructors. Surprisingly, in most camps food was plentiful, and the army's prescribed ration of almost 5,000 calories per day was usually met with a varied diet of food that was often far more nutritious and better prepared than most men had been used to. But there were exceptions. In Camp Hill, Virginia, 6,000 black draftees had to wear the clothing they arrived in from October until January. Many slept outside around fires or under trees. Few even had blankets. There were no bathing facilities, and what food there was had to be eaten outside, without mess kits, no matter the weather conditions.[15]

Conditions in many camps were sometimes so bad that regiments, especially black ones destined to serve as laborers loading supplies onto ships along the east coast of the United States or unloading them in France, were shipped out of camp after only two weeks of hopelessly chaotic "training." But as time went on, training camps became far better supplied and organized so that Camp Jackson in Columbia, South Carolina, was well prepared to receive the African American draftees of what would become the racially segregated 371st Infantry Regiment. Delayed by orders to harvest cotton crops in the Deep South, these rookie soldiers arrived on October 10, 1917, to the amazement of white officers and soldiers who looked on. This description is from a sympathetic white captain who would later learn to like and respect his black soldiers:

> The first intimation we had that the men had really arrived was the sound of distant yelling, catcalling, and laughter as our mob of embryo warriors was led up through the divisional area and through the crowds of convulsed white troops. No one who saw that outfit could keep from laughing. It was a sight never to be forgotten. There were big ones and little ones: fat ones and skinny ones; black ones and tan ones; some in rags and in tatters; others in overalls and every sort of clothing imaginable. They came with suit cases and sacks; with bundles and bandanna handkerchiefs full of food, clothing and knick-knacks. Many were barefoot. Some came with guitars or banjos hanging from their backs by strings or ropes. The halt, the lame, and the blind were there actually. Every colored derelict in certain districts must have been picked up when the draft was received. Our section of the camp became as busy as a hive of bees and almost as dangerous.[16]

White officers were there to oversee the training, but the army had failed to provide any noncommissioned officers. Educated men among the draftees had to become instant company clerks, supply and mess sergeants, and even sergeant drill instructors. They did remarkably well, and as a white officer recalled, organizing these young recruits into something resembling soldiers was easier than he expected:

> The draft boards had advised the men that when they reached camp they would be given brand new uniforms, consequently they left home, even if they possessed good clothes, in things that they expected to throw away as soon as they arrived. It was many days before we got uniforms for them, and the setting-up exercises and the drills, humorous in themselves, as they always are with recruits, were doubly so when almost every man was a living scarecrow. Large audiences from every section of the divisional area came to gaze upon us. . . . The men were light-hearted and

practically always in good spirits and were accustomed to taking orders and doing what they were told. Discipline was easily attained and necessarily strict, but just.[17]

In addition to the endless marching, the ever-present discipline, labor details, and an occasional bayonet drill, the new recruits would experience such wonders as hot showers, but also an unwelcome introduction to dentists. I remember distinctly. . . One company commander said,

the night that I put my newly arrived warriors into the shower baths. Very few of the men had ever heard of, much less seen, a shower and when stark-naked and clutching in their hands a cake of yellow laundry soap, a batch of twenty-five or thirty were pushed into the shower room and the water rushed down on them from the heads above, there was pandemonium. When they found that they were not hurt and that the water was warm, they yelled and danced in delight, and had to be ordered out to make room for the shivering and astonished squads waiting their turn outside.

Nor will I forget the day that my company marched up to the regimental infirmary to have their teeth looked at by the dentists. A large room had been equipped with chairs, and as I remember it, there were two dentists and their assistants, dressed in white coats and surrounded by glittering instruments on trays. I don't suppose that three men in my whole company had ever been in a dentist's hands in their lives. The company was lined up in single file, extending from the door through the hall, down the stairs, and out onto the parade ground.

The two dentists had to look at the teeth of the whole regiment and they had evidently made up their minds that if they started to do any filling the job would not be completed until the end of the war, consequently no filling was done. The poor victims were led in two at a time, their eyes popping from their faces and beads of perspiration sticking out on their foreheads. Their mouths were pried open and the doctors, making quick examination, commenced to yank out almost every tooth in which there appeared a cavity. Of course after the first yanks, the men began to scream bloody murder. Terror spread through the ranks in the halls and out onto the parade ground and a regular prayer meeting ensued. The poor victims waiting their turn shivered and shook, moaned and sobbed, calling on the Lord to save them from the agony that was coming. . . . I did not blame the poor devils for being terrified, for above the shrieks and groans, could be heard a sound which was very similar to hail upon a tin roof—the extracted teeth being thrown into tin buckets at the sides of the chairs. It was a terrible morning, and many a man was confined to quarters, having had from two to five teeth yanked out in almost as many seconds.[18]

Although the men of the 371st would not sing while under fire in France, while in training camp in South Carolina and in rest areas in France, they sang magnificently.

> The singing of our men individually and as a regiment was the envy of the entire camp. We assembled twice a week to learn the new army songs taught by the divisional song leader, David Griffin, such as: "Smiles," "There's a Long, Long Trail," "Little Liza Jane," "Pack Up Your Troubles," and the like. The real treat for us officers, and for the crowds that always collected whenever we were assembled for singing, was when some ex-preacher, called out from the ranks and perched high on the barrack steps, led our hundreds of men in some of their old-time spirituals. I never expect to hear again such wonderful harmony. Some of the songs they loved to sing were, "We Will Understan' It Better Bye and Bye, "I'se Gwyn to Die on de Battle Field," "Lil' David, Play on Yo' Harp," "Swing Low, Sweet Chariot," "Let the Lighthouse Shine on Me," and "I'se got Shoes, You got Shoes." When Ex-President Taft visited the camp, we were ordered to Headquarters one evening to sing for him. The men sang wonderfully and Mr. Taft seemed to enjoy it immensely.[19]

Of course, white Americans knew how well blacks could sing; it was their courage in combat that remained in doubt.

The combat training for the African American troops of the 371st, like that for other black draftees, was poor at best, but it served to weed out the least competent of the recruits, who were reassigned to labor battalions, where almost 90 percent of all black troops would serve during the war. But for most black recruits the dismal quality of the training was of less concern than the racial segregation they faced within these training camps and in the surrounding communities. Perhaps because they were southern black troops with no expectation of equality with whites, the men of the 371st Regiment did not complain openly about being led by white southern officers, or about the racial segregation they experienced at Camp Jackson, where they were surrounded by 25,000 white troops with more privileges than they, nor were there any reports of ugly racial incidents when these men went on passes to the nearby city of Columbia. The local newspaper carried an editorial saying, "We wish the black boys of the 371st to know that they behaved beautifully while in the cantonment here, and we have yet to hear of the first unfavorable criticism of the conduct of Negro soldiers in Columbia."[20] It might be noted that they were called "boys," not men.

That the men of the 371st escaped racial insults and violence was truly remarkable because South Carolina was prepared for the worst. Because theirs had long been a state in which blacks outnumbered whites and where Jim Crow laws were particularly stringent, South Carolinians were on guard following the racial violence that exploded in Houston in August 1917. As soon as the 3rd Battalion of the veteran all-black 24th Regiment of the regular army was sent to Houston, that city tightened its already strict Jim Crow laws. Regarding themselves as soldiers of the U.S. Army, not blacks, the men of the 24th not only ignored these laws but ridiculed them in public. In response, Houston police harassed and beat black soldiers, sometimes severely. On one occasion, a black soldier tried to intervene when he came upon two policemen beating a black woman. He was kicked, beaten, and arrested. After another such beating, a rumor spread that a black soldier had been killed. Outraged comrades marched into town, where they were met by armed white men including police, and shots were fired before the soldiers returned to camp. The conflict was not an organized one by the men of the 24th, but the resulting casualties were serious. Four black soldiers and seventeen white men, including five police officers, were killed, and others were wounded.

White troops were rushed into Houston to disarm the 24th. Soon after, sixty-three soldiers were court-martialed, and following brief and inconclusive testimony, all but five were found guilty. A few days later, without appeal, thirteen of these men were summarily hanged. Soon after, six more were hanged. An angry black community saw these men as martyrs who had been lynched by federal authorities. Many in the federal government agreed. Even Secretary of War Newton D. Baker told President Wilson that Houston's Jim Crow laws, not the black soldiers, were the cause of the conflict. Many white army officers were not convinced, expressing grave doubts about the wisdom of arming blacks, and white southerners, to no one's surprise after Houston, were even more determined than before to make black soldiers observe the color line. And nowhere was that line drawn more dramatically than in South Carolina.

When the African American soldiers who were sent to that state for training were from the North, it became particularly important to teach them their "place." So it was when a black soldier, Noble Sissle, a Broadway music arranger who later launched the career of Lena Horne, walked into the lobby of a "white's only" hotel in Spartanburg, South Carolina, to buy a newspaper. As other black soldiers looked on, he was beaten by the hotel's proprietor, and only the firm intervention of a black officer prevented a riot. In another incident, a black officer in uniform, who was a lawyer trained at Harvard, was cursed and forcibly dragged off a "white's only" streetcar by outraged citizens of Spartanburg. And black soldiers in uniform were frequently beaten for not removing their hats or not stepping off the sidewalk when they encountered a white person.

Before a black National Guard regiment from New York, the 15th, had arrived in Spartanburg, the town's mayor protested to the War Department:

> I was sorry to learn that the Fifteenth Regiment has been ordered here, for, with their northern ideas about race equality, they will probably expect to be treated like white men. I can say right here that they will not be treated as anything except negroes. We shall treat them exactly as we treat our resident negroes. This thing is like waving a red flag in the face of a bull, something that can't be done without trouble. We have asked Congressman Nicholls to request the War Department not to send the soldiers here. You remember the trouble a couple of weeks ago at Houston.[21]

After only two tumultuous weeks in Spartanburg, the New Yorkers of the 15th, now designated the 369th Infantry Regiment, were abruptly shipped off to France.

South Carolina was not alone in its racist views. African American troops were discriminated against throughout the South. Black soldiers seldom received passes to leave camp, and when they did, white military police joined local police in routinely harassing them. As in South Carolina, even officers were targeted. One black lieutenant traveling in uniform under orders to report to Fort Sill, Oklahoma, was arrested and imprisoned for riding on a train with white passengers.[22] White police were known to be brutal on many occasions, beating and even disfiguring uniformed black soldiers for trivial offenses. White civilians responded to any perceived violation of the color line by verbal abuse, blows, and threats of even worse violence. Sometimes the threats were real, with soldiers being savagely beaten, often with the help of military police. Others were threatened with lynching, a real enough possibility as there were seventy lynchings in 1917 compared to fifty-four in 1916, almost all of the victims being black. One of those lynched was a black accused of writing an insolent letter to a white woman in Georgia. That the man was known to be illiterate did not save him.[23] Any black could be expected to suffer for the deeds of any other black.

Race riots erupted as well. In East St. Louis, Illinois, during the summer of 1917, after an African American was rumored to have killed a white man, 3,000 white men hunted down, shot, beat, and burned blacks for four days without any interference from police or National Guardsmen. White women joined in the killing, one of them slashing the throat of a black woman; gangs of white girls beat any black woman they could lay their hands on. A black paraplegic was burned alive and a two-year-old black boy was shot, then thrown into a burning building.[24] In response, some blacks fought back, and before partial peace was restored, 8 whites were killed, 4 by bullets apparently aimed at blacks, and 100 blacks "were shot or mangled and beaten to various degrees of helplessness," as a U.S. senator later told an investigating committee.

Race relations within many southern training camps were tense as well. Insults were exchanged, fights sometimes occurred, and African American soldiers were typically openly discriminated against. For instance, recreational facilities available to white soldiers were closed to blacks. In some camps, black soldiers lacked sanitary and bathing facilities and were housed in tents, whereas whites lived in comparative luxury in barracks. Medical attention was sometimes unavailable for black troops, and they were often forced to work—rather than train—for long periods of time in the rain or snow, sometimes including all day on Sundays.[25] Amazing as it seems from a contemporary perspective, some white southern officers hired out black soldiers to civilian contractors to do such things as cut wood and dig potatoes for the contractors' and the officers' profit. One of these officers is said to have told a contractor that "the only way to get work out of Negroes was to work them three days and whip them three days."[26] Any black defiance to practices like these led to charges of mutiny and long prison terms. Many of these laborers in army uniform described themselves as "just same as slave is."[27]

Promotion for black troops was slow, if it occurred at all, and long sentences in the guard house followed even slight infractions of the rules set by white officers, most of them southerners.

> During Winter of 1917–18, general complaint was made of insufficient clothing, shortage in supply of overcoats, inadequate bedding, and tents without flooring and ofttimes situated in wet places, where ice formed in winter and where mud and malaria flourished at other times. A statement came from Camp Alexander, Va., that during the winter of 1917–18 men died like sheep in their tents, it being a common occurrence to go around in the morning and drag men out frozen to death.[28]

Men pronounced unfit for overseas service, and often unfit for any kind of military duty, were kept at these camps and forced to work long hours in all kinds of weather. Conditions in the North were somewhat better, but camp facilities were still segregated, including officers' clubs that admitted no African American officers and recreational facilities that were for whites only. Jim Crow practices, if not actual laws, were well entrenched in the North, as blacks were often refused service in restaurants and bars; certain parts of many northern towns and cities were strictly "off-limits" to blacks. When a black sergeant of the newly formed African American 92nd Division attempted to enter a movie theater in Kansas, he was denied a ticket and he responded angrily. Although acknowledging that the ticket seller had broken the law, the division's commander, Major-General Charles C. Ballou, issued Bulletin No. 35, which accused the sergeant of placing his pleasure above the general interest of the division. Ballou wrote that

> the sergeant is guilty of the GREATER wrong in doing ANYTHING, NO MATTER HOW LEGALLY CORRECT, that will provoke racial animosity. The Division Commander repeats that the success of the Division, with all that success implies, is dependent upon the good will of the public. That public is nine-tenths white. White men made the Division, and they can break it just as easily if it becomes a trouble maker.[29]

Ballou ordered his men to "avoid every situation that can give rise to racial ill will. Attend quietly and faithfully to your duties, and don't go where your presence is not desired." The men of the 92nd Division were joined by the black community in expressing their outrage about this order.

In response to the obvious need for black officers to lead the growing numbers of African American draftees, the army set up an officers' training school at Fort Des Moines, Iowa, where it was intended to train and commission 12,500 black men, 40 percent of whom were college graduates and another 50 percent of whom had either business or professional training.[30] Commissions were delayed by southern opposition to the idea of black officers, but after assurances that black officers would not command white troops, 639 of the original 1,250 candidates received commissions, 106 of them as captains, the rest as lieutenants. On the recommendation of the Fort Des Moines commander, all would be assigned to infantry regiments because they were thought to lack the intelligence necessary for the artillery or engineers.[31] Later, black officers and men did serve in artillery units, performing so admirably that whites were astonished.[32]

Colonel Glendie B. Young, commander of the 372nd Regiment, soon after concluded that the problems his regiment faced were a direct result of too many black officers. "There is no doubt," he asserted, "that the mental development of the white man is superior to that of the negro. Therefore, there is no question but that a regiment of all white officers would, as a whole, be more efficient. . . than one with colored officers."[33] While this officers' training program in Iowa was getting under way, Lieutenant-Colonel Charles A. Young, a black West Pointer, was still serving with the 10 Cavalry in Arizona, with whom he had previously served during combat in Cuba and Mexico. He had an exemplary record and had never missed a day of service, but he was soon to be sacrificed to placate southern racists.

A white southern lieutenant with the 10th Cavalry, who found it impossible to take orders from a black superior, complained to Senator John Bell Williams of Mississippi, who promptly wrote to President Wilson. Ever concerned about mending southern political fences, Wilson wrote this to Secretary of War Baker:

Senator Williams of Mississippi called my attention to a case the other day which involves some serious possibilities, and I am venturing to write you a confidential letter about it.

Albert B. Dockery, a first lieutenant in the Tenth U.S. Cavalry, now stationed at Fort Huachuca, Arizona, is a Southerner and finds it not only distasteful but practically impossible to serve under a colored commander. . . . I am afraid from what I have learned that there may be some serious and perhaps even tragical in-subordination on Lieutenant Dockery's part if he is left under Colonel Young, who is a colored man. Is there not some way of relieving this situation by transferring Lieutenant Dockery and sending some man in his place who would not have equally intense prejudices?[34]

Baker agreed to the transfer of Dockery, and soon after, other members of the Senate called for Young's removal. Despite his seemingly perfect health, Young was retired on medical grounds after he was ordered to have a physical exam that found him suffering from nephritis and advanced heart disease.[35] He rode his horse, Charlie, all the way from his home in Ohio to Washington, D.C., to prove his fitness but to no avail. He was reinstated only five days before the end of the war.

The first black troops to be shipped to France—stevedores in surplus Union blue uniforms left over from the Civil War—sailed under dreadful conditions. These men were assigned bunk space in the airless, stiflingly hot hold of a ship in June 1917. No mess facilities were provided, although the ship's white crew had a separate mess where they were served by black stewards and busboys. The black stevedores were compelled to eat their meals on deck in all sorts of weather, and the hold was so unbearably hot that most of them chose to sleep on deck as well. The few black officers who accompanied these men were denied access to the officers' mess.[36] They, too, ate on deck.

Conditions were no better when the 368th Infantry Regiment was shipped to France.[37] Prior to the arrival of these men, and many thousands of others who soon followed them under similarly degrading conditions, supplies in France were handled by Southeast Asians, Chinese, Maoris, Senegalese, Arabs, and others whom the Allies could bring to France from their colonial possessions. When the black Americans came ashore—literally as soon as their ships docked—they were put to work handling 100-pound crates with such ease that French onlookers were amazed.[38] French officials had hoped that the black American laborers could move 6,000 tons of supplies a month. On a single day, these stevedores first unloaded 42,000 men with their portable gear, followed by 5,000 tons of cargo.[39] Singing as they worked in all kinds of weather, night and day, black American laborers quarried stone for roads, built and repaired railroads, cut and stacked firewood, and unloaded everything from 100-pound sacks of flour to 90-ton naval guns. At the port of Brest, they unloaded almost 800,000 tons of war material during the month of September 1918 alone. On several occasions these unarmed troops in labor battalions repaired roads and railroads while under fire.[40]

Unlike celebrated moments for white American soldiers such as the time a newly arrived white officer addressed an adoring crowd in Paris with "Lafayette, we are here," newly arrived black American troops were more likely to meet hostile white military policemen than cheering French citizens. Most were quickly marched off to bases where they were kept as far away from French people as possible even though white soldiers received passes to leave their bases and visit nearby towns, which invariably included taverns and houses of prostitution.[41]

Even the YMCA, which had promised to serve black soldiers as well as whites, often practiced racial discrimination by refusing to sell food or nonalcoholic drinks to blacks. On one occasion, the YMCA refused to sell food to a black soldier even after he pleaded that he hadn't eaten for two days.[42] Despite the army's attempts to isolate them, some black soldiers were able to speak to French civilians, including French women, as unthinkable as that was to their white southern officers, and mutual friendship and respect was a common outcome. A few black soldiers complained about being overcharged for things by French proprietors but others greatly enjoyed giving toys, candy, fruit, and nuts to French children while their grateful mothers and grandparents looked on.[43] Other black soldiers voluntarily carried heavy bundles for French women and, more remarkably, even helped them harvest their crops.[44] One combat infantryman wrote to his mother, "Mammy, these French people don't bother with no color line business. They treat us so good that the only time I ever know I'm colored is when I look in the glass."[45] What is more, French officers treated black American officers as their equals, something that many white American officers could not accept.[46]

To many American military officials, the integration of their black troops with white French civilians and troops was considered to have the most dangerous implications for the future, when "uppity" black soldiers would return to America. Colonel J. L. A. Linard of the American Expeditionary Force Headquarters was at pains to explain this to the French in a document entitled "Secret Information Concerning Black American Troops." It was distributed to French officers who were likely to come into contact with American blacks, and to civilian officials in towns where black troops were likely to go. It told the French how African Americans *must* be treated and why:

In his "Secret Information" Linard explained that the French people must understand the position of blacks in America, whether or not they agreed with it. No use arguing this matter which some call "prejudice," Linard said; it was the unanimous opinion of white Americans on the "Negro question." The document went on to explain that the approximately 15 million Negroes in the United States presented a threat of race mongrelization unless blacks and whites were kept strictly separated. Since the danger did not exist in France, the French people were accustomed to being friendly and tolerant toward blacks; but such behavior deeply offended Americans as an attack on their national beliefs and aroused fear that it might give American blacks intolerable pretensions to equality—and have an adverse effect on American public opinion. . . . White Americans considered blacks to be lacking in intelligence, judgment, and civic or professional morals. . . . Therefore, Linard said, it was necessary to avoid any intimacy, beyond civil politeness, between French officers and black officers; the French should not eat with them nor shake hands with them, nor visit or converse except as required by military matters. And while it was all right to recognize their services in moderate and realistic terms, they should not be lavishly praised, especially not in the presence of white Americans.[47]

When the 369th Infantry Regiment arrived in France as the first of four black regiments that were to make up the 93rd Division, General Pershing somehow had no idea what to do with these men. While he pondered their fate, they were put to work laying railroad tracks, an activity they continued without any further combat training until the other regiments of the division arrived—the 370th, a reasonably well-trained National Guard unit; the 372nd, another former National Guard unit; and the 371st, as we have already seen, made up of draftees from the cotton fields of the Deep South. The hard-pressed French, still reeling from their huge losses at Verdun and the mutiny that followed, had long been pleading with Pershing to send them American troops to buttress their thin front lines. Pershing had steadfastly refused such requests from the French, insisting that American troops would fight in an autonomous American army or not at all. Although Pershing was known as "Black Jack," a nickname earned for his service with black troops in Cuba and Mexico, he displayed no confidence in the newly arrived black regiments. Despite his insistence that American troops fight under his command, he first tried to send the 92nd to the British for training, but they refused to accept the division. So in April 1917, he lent them to the French, who were happy to receive them. As Colonel William Hayward, the white commander of the 369th, put it, "Our great American general simply put the black orphan in a basket, set it on the doorstep of the French, pulled the bell, and went away."[48]

The French army had long employed African troops in combat with notable success, so-called Senegalese units earning many honors for their courage and ferocity, especially with knife and bayonet. The French expected the same from the black men of the 93rd Division, and they were not disappointed, praising the Americans for their use of "cold steel" against the Germans. Because the French had no ammunition for the Americans' Springfield rifles and the U.S. Army had not issued steel helmets to them, the French wholly reequipped them with French weapons, helmets, gas masks, and other gear. They also gave them some training in the complexities of trench warfare, with its heavy reliance on artillery barrages and machine gun emplacements, as well as patrols to check German positions, inspect their barbed wire, and capture prisoners for information. They also fed the Americans, not at all to their satisfaction at first because the French relied primarily on soup for their soldiers, something the Americans found "too light." However, the daily French wine ration was two bottles of red wine per man, per day! Instead of nursing the wine all day, as French soldiers were accustomed to doing, the Americans gleefully drank it down, with predictably undesirable results. Their white American officers quickly halted the wine ration for the troops, asking for more sugar instead, but these officers happily continued to draw the wine ration for themselves.[49]

All four of the regiments "lent" to the French distinguished themselves in battle, suffering 35 percent casualties. In April 1918, the 369th represented only 1 percent of American troops in France, but they held 20 percent of the front lines occupied by U.S. soldiers. Known to the Germans as "hell-fighters," and to the French as "men of bronze," officers and men of this regiment received 550 decorations by the French and Americans, including 180 awards of the Croix de Guerre.[50] They occupied front-line trenches for 191 days without yielding a foot of ground or having a single soldier taken prisoner. They took prisoner many "bush" Germans, as they called them, misunderstanding *Boche*, the French term for Germans during this war. They never hesitated to attack when ordered, as a black captain named Fairfax demonstrated when a black sergeant warned him that he was about to charge into the fire of German machine guns: "Do you know there is a nest of German machine guns ahead?" Fairfax answered, "I only know we were ordered to go forward and we are going." Fairfax was killed, as was another black captain who advanced with him.[51]

The conspicuous courage of many black officers and men was recorded by both French and white American officers. Several were honored for fighting hand to hand with Germans, often killing them with bolo knife or bayonet. Perhaps the most celebrated of these men was Private Henry Johnson of Albany, New York, who fought with the 369th who said, with "characteristic modesty":

There isn't so much to tell," said Johnson with characteristic modesty. There wasn't anything so fine about it. Just fought for my life. A rabbit would have done that.

Well, anyway, me and Needham Roberts were on patrol on May 15. The corporal wanted to send out two new drafted men on the sentry post for the midnight-to-four job. I told him he was crazy to send untrained men out there and risk the rest of us. I said I'd tackle the job, though I needed sleep.

German snipers had been shooting our way that night and I told the corporal he wanted men on the job who knew their rifles. He said it was imagination, but anyway he took those green men off and left Needham and me on the posts. I went on at midnight. It was moonlight. Roberts was at the next post. At one o'clock a sniper took a crack at me from a bush fifty yards away. Pretty soon there was more firing and when Sergeant Roy Thompson came along I told him.

"What's the matter men," he asked, "You scared?"

"No I ain't scared," I said, "I came over here to do my bit and I'll do it. But I was jes' lettin' you know there's liable to be some tall scrappin' around this post tonight." He laughed and went on, and I began to get ready. They'd a box of hand grenades there and I took them out of the box and laid them all in a row where they would be handy. There was about thirty grenades, I guess. I was goin' to bust that Dutch army in pieces if it bothered me.

Somewhere around two o'clock I heard the Germans cutting our wire out in front and I called to Roberts. When he came I told him to pass the word to the lieutenant. He had just started off when the snippin' and the clippin' of the wires sounded near, so I let go with a hand grenade. There was a yell from a lot of surprised Dutchmen and then they started firing. I hollered to Needham to come back.

A German grenade got Needham in the arm and through the hip. He was too badly wounded to do any fighting, so I told him to lie in the trench and hand me up grenades.

"Keep your nerve," I told him. "All the Dutchmen in the woods are at us, but keep cool and we'll lick 'em." Roberts crawled into the dugout. Some of the shots got me, one clipped my head, another my lip, another my hand, some in my side and one smashed my left foot so bad that I have a silver plate holding it up now.

The Germans came from all sides. Roberts kept handing me the grenades and I kept throwing them and the Dutchmen kept squealing, but jes' the same they kept comin' on. When the grenades were all gone I started in with my rifle. That was all right until I shoved in an American cartridge clip—it was a French gun—and it jammed.

There was nothing to do but use my rifle as a club and jump into them. I banged them on the dome and the side and everywhere I could land until the butt of my rifle busted. One of the Germans hollered, "Rush him! Rush him!" I decided to do some rushing myself. I grabbed my French bolo knife and slashed in a million directions. Each slash meant something, believe me. I wasn't doing exercises, let me tell you.

I picked out an officer, a lieutenant I guess he was. I got him and I got some more of them. They knocked me around considerable and whanged me on the head, but I always managed to get back on my feet. There was one guy that bothered me. He climbed on my back and I had some job shaking him off and pitching him over my head. Then I stuck him in the ribs with the bolo. I stuck one guy in the stomach and he yelled in good New York talk: "That black_____ got me."

I was still banging them when my crowd came up and saved me and beat the Germans off. That fight lasted about an hour. That's about all. There wasn't so much to it.[52]

The next morning, the Americans found four German bodies and enough abandoned equipment to suggest that perhaps thirty Germans had been engaged in the fighting and several dead or wounded appeared to have been dragged away.

Another black sergeant won a Distinguished Service Cross for, among other things, rescuing an American officer and five other men after killing ten of their German captors and taking prisoner a German lieutenant.[53] Despite such heroics, no African American soldier or officer received the Medal of Honor, this country's highest military honor, during all of World War I. After many years of pressure, in 1991, President George Bush awarded this medal posthumously to Corporal Freddie Stowers of the 371st Regiment. In late September 1918, Stowers was leading his squad in an attack on German lines when the Germans climbed out of their trenches, raising their hands in surrender. When the black Americans approached, the Germans jumped back in their trenches opening such intense fire with machine guns and mortars that half of Stowers' men fell in a matter of seconds. With the other NCOs and officers dead, Stowers rallied the survivors and urged them forward even after he was riddled by machine gun bullets that soon led to his death.

Other men of the 371st fought so well on various occasions that the French often praised them, and their white commanding officer said, "I'd take my chance of going anywhere with these black soldiers at my back." Another white officer said, "We were a little dubious about them. We did not know whether they would stand fire or not. But they did . . . and they were splendid fighters."[54] Killed in action were 4 officers and 109 men of the 371st, and 13 others died of wounds; 41 officers and 873 men were wounded. They had captured 3 German officers and 90 men, as well as eight trench mortars, thirty-seven 77mm guns, and nearly fifty machine guns.[55]

There were the usual rumors that a number of black troops had deserted during combat, but a regimental report filed later produced evidence that the missing men had either been separated from their units and joined others, had been evacuated to hospitals, or were among those killed. Almost every one of the alleged deserters was accounted for.[56]

French General Vincendon issued a General Order as follows to the black Illinois men of the 370th after they left the front lines:

> As Lieut. Colonel Duncan said November 28, in offering to me your regimental colors as proof of your love for France and as an expression of your loyalty to the 59th Division and our Army, you have given us of your best and you have given it out of the fullness of your hearts.
>
> The blood of your comrades who fell on the soil of France mixed with the blood of our soldiers, renders indissoluble the bonds of affection that unite us. We have, besides, the pride of having worked together at a mag-

nificent task, and the pride of bearing on our foreheads the ray of a common grandeur.[57]

Of the 370th Regiment, known as "Red Hand" after the French Division to which they were attached, French commander General Goybet wrote this:

Your troops have been admirable in their attack. You must be proud of the courage of your officers and men, and I consider it an honor to have them under my command. The bravery and dash of your regiment won the admiration of the Moroccan Division, who are themselves versed in warfare. Thanks to you, during these hard days, the division was at all times in advance of all other divisions of the Army Corps. I am sending you all my thanks and beg you to transmit them to your subordinates. I call on your wounded. Their morale is higher than any praise.[58]

He went on to write,

It is with deep emotion that I bid farewell to our gallant comrades of combat. For seven months we have lived as brothers in arms, sharing the same burdens, the same hardships, the same dangers. We have participated in the great battle of the Champagne which was crowned by such a magnificent victory. The 157th (Division) will never forget the irresistible and heroic rush of the colored American regiments up the "Cote des Observatoires" and into the "Plaine de Monthois." The most formidable defenses, the strongest machine gun nests, the most crushing artillery barrages were unable to stop them. These superior troops have overcome everything with a supreme disdain of death, and thanks to their courageous sacrifice, the Red (Bloody) Hand Division, for nine days of hard fighting always maintained the front rank in the 4th Army's victorious advance. Officers, non-commissioned officers, and privates of the 371st and 372nd . . . I respectfully bow to your glorious dead and salute your flags. . . . Dear friends from America, when you will have recrossed the ocean, do not forget the Red Hand Division. Our pure brotherhood in arms has been consecrated in the blood of the brave. These bonds will never be severed. Always keep the memory of your general, who is proud of having been your commander, and remember that you have forever his affectionate gratitude.[59]

The French erected a granite memorial monument to these black soldiers atop a hill where some of their greatest gallantry was displayed. When the Germans invaded France in 1940, they destroyed the monument.

After visiting African American soldiers on the front lines in France, Irving S. Cobb, a white journalist, wrote the following in the popular *Saturday Evening Post*:

> I am of the opinion personally . . . and I make the assertion with all the better grace, I think, seeing that I am a Southerner with all the Southerner's inherited and acquired prejudices touching on the race question—that as a result of what our black soldiers are going to do in this war, a word that has been uttered billions of times in our country, sometimes in derision, sometimes in hate, sometimes in all kindliness—but which I am sure never fell on black ears but it left behind a sting for the heart—is going to have a new meaning for all of us, South and North too, and that hereafter n-i-g-g-e-r will merely be another way of spelling the word American.[60]

Cobb was certainly right about the skill and courage that black troops would soon after display in combat, but how most Americans would think about African Americans after the war would not change. In fact, thanks to the reports by some white officers, most of them southerners, white Americans would come to believe that black troops in France had been shameless cowards. The source of this belief was a series of reports about the 92nd Division.

Black draftees from various parts of the country made up the four regiments—the 365th, 366th, 367th, and 368th—that together formed the 92nd Division, but these regiments never trained as a division before going into combat, and training for individual regiments was rudimentary at best. Many of the recruits who sailed with these regiments to France only joined them days before their departure. They had little equipment, lacking such essentials as wire clippers to cut the heavy barbed wire entanglements they would face, flares for night fighting, or grenade launchers. Although they would be asked to serve as a division, unlike their white counterparts they had no divisional artillery. One regiment was over 90 percent illiterate, and all contained men whose dialects were often impenetrable to their northern officers, whether white or black. Initially, only some 20 percent of their officers were white, most of them southerners who, according to the division's commander, General Charles C. Ballou, were racists who deliberately created confusion and conflict:[61] "It was my misfortune to be handicapped by many white officers who were rabidly hostile to the idea of a colored officer, and who continually conveyed misinformation to the staff of the superior units, and generally created much trouble and discontent. Such men will never give the Negro the square deal that is his just due."[62] When one such officer kicked a black soldier who had collapsed from exhaustion, black officers were barely able to prevent a riot.[63] By the time the division was assembled in France, many black officers had asked for and received transfers. Their replacements were whites, who soon made up half of its officer corps.

Black intellectuals and the black press watched the creation of the 92nd with growing concern. When Colonel Charles Young was not promoted to the command of the 92nd, influential blacks expressed their indignation, insisting that the army would never permit a black man to become a general, something that many white officers had said in public addresses.[64] It soon became clear that General Ballou was anything but an inspirational leader of the 92nd, and that many of the black officers assigned to the division were wholly untrained and in some cases unqualified to be officers. However, requests that more qualified black officers from other regiments be transferred to the 92nd were uniformly rejected by the army. In May 1918, *The Crisis* informed its readers, "Unless this decision is reversed, the Ninety-second Division is bound to be a failure as a unit. . . . Is it possible that persons in the War Department wish this division to be a failure?"[65] It was, indeed.

General Ballou was not always sympathetic to his black troops but he was not a vocal racist. However, the commanding general of the 2nd Army, to which the 92nd was assigned, was a white supremacist to the core. General Robert Lee Bullard was one of sixty-three Alabamans to graduate from West Point between the end of the Civil War and 1898. He had commanded a black volunteer regiment from that state during the Spanish-American War, but it did not see action. Perhaps because he had not seen black troops in combat in Cuba, he shared the southern conviction that blacks were inferior in all ways—in intellect, in moral stature, and in courage. One month after the 92nd joined his otherwise all-white Army, he wrote, "Poor Negroes! They are hopelessly inferior . . . with everyone feeling and saying that they are worthless as soldiers, they are going on quite unconcernedly."[66] Bullard's chief of staff, Colonel Allen C. Greer, may have had even greater contempt for African Americans than his commander. Ballou accused Greer of spreading false information about blacks in the 92nd to discredit the soldiers and their officers, but to no effect.[67]

Greer, who had won the Medal of Honor in the Philippines, had graduated from the University of Tennessee and earned a law degree at the University of Minnesota. Despite his education, Greer not only believed that blacks were cowards but was obsessed by his belief that blacks were insatiable rapists, often reporting that many rapes had taken place when, in fact, none had occurred. For instance, he wrote to Senator McKellar in his home state of Tennessee that there had been thirty rapes since the 92nd came to France. In fact, during the 92nd Division's six months of service in France, only one member of the division was convicted of rape.[68] Nevertheless, Greer wrote to Senator McKellar, "The undoubted truth is that the colored officers neither control nor care to control the men. They themselves have been engaged largely in the pursuit of French women, it being their first opportunity to meet white women who did not treat them as servants."[69] Bullard shared Greer's fixation on rape. He wrote this in his diary in late 1918: "They are brutes."[70]

In an attempt to capitalize on the growing racial tension in the 92nd Division, German aircraft dropped thousands of provocative, if sometimes stilted, leaflets urging the black soldiers to desert:

Hello, boys, what are you doing over here? Fighting the Germans? Why? Have they ever done you any harm? Of course some white folks and the lying English-American papers told you that the Germans ought to be wiped out for the sake of humanity and Democracy. What is Democracy? Personal freedom; all citizens enjoying the same rights socially and before the law. Do you enjoy the same rights as the white people do in America, the land of freedom and Democracy, or are you not rather treated over there as second class citizens?

Can you get into a restaurant where white people dine? Can you get a seat in a theatre where white people sit? Can you get a seat or berth in a railroad car, or can you even ride in the South in the same street car with the white people?

And how about the law? Is lynching and the most horrible crimes committed therewith, a lawful proceeding in a Democratic country? Now all this is entirely different in Germany, where they do like colored people; where they treat them as gentlemen and as white men, and quite a number of colored people have fine posi-

tions in business in Berlin and other German cities. Why, then, fight the Germans only for the benefit of the Wall Street robbers, and to protect the millions that they have loaned to the English, French, and Italians.

You have been made the tool of the egoistic and rapacious rich in America, and there is nothing in the whole game for you but broken bones, horrible wounds, spoiled health, or death. No satisfaction whatever will you get out of this unjust war. You have never seen Germany, so you are fools if you allow people to make you hate us. Come over and see for yourself. Let those do the fighting who make the profit out of this war. Don't allow them to use you as cannon fodder.

To carry a gun in this service is not an honor, but a shame. Throw it away and come over to the German lines. You will find friends who will help you. (German propaganda leaflet, dropped on the 367th Infantry, September 3, 1918)

The fact that so many men in the division were illiterate probably limited the impact of the leaflets, but so did loyalty. Virtually no one deserted.

In mid-September, the 92nd Division was ordered forward to take part in a major American attack on well-defended German positions in the Argonne. Major Ross of the 365th regiment of the 92nd described the difficulties of their night advance through deep mud and clogged traffic. He later provided evidence that contrary to widespread reports and Bullard's accusation, his men had not straggled.[71] Why the inexperienced 92nd was given a critical role in this attack as a liaison unit with the French is a puzzle, as they were still ill equipped, untrained, and inexperienced. The first units of the 368th Regiment, the one soon to be accused of cowardice, arrived in the Argonne only two days before the assault. No one was familiar with the terrain. The men were exhausted after traveling 100 miles in pouring rain and had received no food for two days. They had no hand grenades, no shears to cut barbed wire, no signal flares, no maps, and no clear objectives. Also, they had no artillery support during the five-day attack.[72] Their officers also did not speak French, and the regiment's commanding officer, Colonel Fred R. Brown, was an outspoken white supremacist. In the densely forested and deeply gullied terrain of the Argonne, with its units scattered, exhausted, and hungry, the 92nd was not ready for the complex assignment of advancing through enemy barbed wire and heavy artillery fire while maintaining contact with French units on its flanks. The result was a five-day battle marked by enormous confusion and only modest advances, although the 1st Battalion of the 368th advanced well. But there was a disorganized withdrawal by troops of the 2nd and 3rd Battalions, 368th Regiment. After a second attempted attack, both officers and men of the 3rd Battalion ran back to their trenches. However, their commander, Major Max Elsner, later stated that he ordered them to do so.[73]

General Bullard promptly blamed the entire 92nd division for the failure of these two battalions of one of its four regiments. Colonel Greer, with his usual contempt for blacks, if not impeccable English, said of the 92nd, "They failed in all their missions, laid [sic] down and sneaked to the rear, until they were withdrawn."[74] Word of the alleged flight of black troops under fire spread so quickly that in less than a week, a white surgeon, working well behind the lines, recorded this in his diary: "The 92nd (midnight) Division has been tried in the line and they didn't stick—labor for them hereafter."[75]

In this same battle, elements of the all-white 35th Division broke under fire at least as badly as the 2nd Battalion of the 368th Regiment. But the retreat of these white troops was officially and unofficially attributed to command failures, never to the inherent cowardice of the men. The accusations of cowardice by the black soldiers sometimes proved embarrassing to the officer who made them. One white officer of the 92nd who described his African American troops as cowards was later shown to have hidden in a ditch during the night of the battle. Max Elsner, the white major who initially reported that his black troops had fled in panic, later admitted that he had ordered their withdrawal before he became so hysterical he "placed his hands to his face and cried out to his personal runners to take him out of there, that he could not stand it."[76] He abandoned his command post and subsequently had to be hospitalized. More than one historian has concluded that the army made black officers and men into scapegoats to protect the reputations of white officers like these.[77] Neither of these white officers was punished—Elsner not only was not court-martialed but was later promoted—but thirty black officers were relieved of duty and five were convicted by courts-martial, with four sentenced to death and one to life imprisonment at hard labor. All five were later freed.[78]

Colonel Greer wrote nothing about these two derelict white majors nor about the successful attacks by other regiments of the 92nd at the same time, but in April 1920, he told the War College that "it is an undoubted fact, shown by our experience in the war, and well known to all people familiar with negroes, that the average negro is naturally cowardly."[79] Soon after, Greer illegally attempted to influence pending legislation by trying to convince Senator McKellar that blacks were unfit to serve in the postwar army: "They have in fact been dangerous to no one except themselves and women."[80] Among many other officers, General Bullard repeated his charges against black soldiers, saying, "Two days ago and again yesterday the 92nd Division would not fight; couldn't be made to attack in any effective sense."[81] He made no distinction among the three regiments that did advance and the two battalions among three of the one regiment that did not do so.

Greer and Bullard developed their opinions about African American soldiers from secondhand reports that came to 2nd Army headquarters, miles away from any combat. A white National Guard officer who led the 3rd Battalion of the 92nd Division's 365th Regiment into the Argonne battle told a dramatically different story. Major Warner A. Ross reported:

> In the battle line and out of the battle line, before the armistice and after the armistice, there was not a phase of military art or of the awful game of war at which this battalion did not excel. At going over the top, attacking enemy positions, resisting raids and assaults, holding under heavy shell fire, enduring gas of all kinds, at patrolling no-man's land, at drill, on hard marches, in discipline and military courtesy, at conducting itself properly in camp or in French villages, and in general all around snappiness, it excelled in all.[82]

Ross recommended some forty officers and men for medals for their bravery, but none, including Ross himself, ever received any decoration from any source. He reported that his recommendations reached headquarters but believed that "certain regular army officers saw fit to head them off."[83] Ross believed that no one in the entire 365th Regiment ever received a medal, yet he reported in vivid detail how these men took and held an important German position under heavy fire during the last days of the war. He recorded his pride in leading his 1,250 men toward that battle, listening to

> the muffled tread of their hob-nailed shoes. For I loved that Battalion. It was the pride of my life. And there was not one among all those hundreds

of big, black heroes of mine that would not have gone through *hell* for his Major. And no one knew it better than I.[84]

He wrote about the intensity of the battle at Metz that followed:

All day, all night and up to eleven o'clock next morning it lasted. By midnight the entire wood fairly reeked with gas. No one dared eat or drink because of it. Despite all our precautions and efforts, we were rapidly being wiped out. I have heard of officers and of men and of units—large ones and small ones, white and also colored, that became panic stricken and useless under fire that was feeble and light both in intensity and duration compared to this, but I am ready at any time to testify that twelve hundred and fifty officers and men (colored) *did* advance and that the command did hold *without showing the faintest symptoms of panic or retreat.*[85]

Ross described some scenes of the battle that he could not erase from his memory. One involved his search for a runner he had sent off with a message two hours earlier. After inadvertently stepping on a human hand, Ross followed a trail of blood until he found the man:

Not only was his right arm off at the elbow, but his right side and leg were badly mangled. I thought he was dead, but bent over and put my hand on his forehead. His eyes opened. In them was a wistful, faraway look. I spoke, and with an apparent effort he got them focused, they brightened with recognition, and immediately, almost to my undoing, his body straightened! His right shoulder and the stub of an arm jerked! Utterly helpless, trembling on the very brink of eternity, he had come to "Attention" and had *saluted* his Major!

Then I noticed he was making a pitiful effort to talk, and in some way, I can't explain just how, I got the impression that there was something in his pocket he wished to see. I took out a wallet and found what I knew he wanted. It was a post-card photo of a pretty colored girl holding in her arms a dark, smiling baby. Shells were screeching over. Just then one tore the earth nearby and sprinkled us with dirt. I propped his head against my knee and held the picture close to his eyes. A proud, satisfied look came into them, then a calm, tired smile. He seemed looking farther and farther away. Another terrific, bouncing jar and the bloody, mud smeared form relaxed. Another brave comrade had "gone west."

A little farther on I saw a private leaning against the splintered trunk of a tree, his bowels all hanging out. No one else was near. He seemed to be in delirium and was crying pitifully like a little child for "Mamma." When he saw me he stared for an instant, then jumped up and yelled, "Major Ross is with us! Go to it, boys!" and fell over–dead. Then I thought about all I had heard to the effect that you have to treat soldiers like dogs–especially colored ones–to gain discipline and inspire respect. I thanked God I didn't have to.[86]

After the battle, the unwounded survivors of the battalion were brought to attention by their black senior captain, Sanders:

Sanders saw me and knew what to do. . . . Those heels clicked. Their rifles, like one piece, in three clear-cut movements, snapped down to the "order." Again he yelled, or tried to yell "Present, arms!" Again two distinct and snappy movements. Sanders faced about standing at salute and there before me at "present arms"–not much larger than one company should be, stood all that was left of my wonderful Second Battalion!

I brought them to the "order" and stood spell bound. It was by far the most touching, the most thrilling, the most awe-inspiring ceremony I ever experienced or witnessed. There they stood–covered with mud, stained and spattered with blood, their clothes, what was left of them, torn and ripped to shreds. They looked emaciated–haggard, but about those erect, motionless figures, those big steady eyes, about their whole proud, manly bearing was something of that true nobility of unselfishness and sacrifice that is beyond description.

These men had suffered the tortures of the damned. They had faced all the engines of terror and destruction that fiendish man could invent. They had endured the shriek, the smash, the roar and pandemonium of hell. They had seen their comrades blown to bits or torn and mangled, and choked by gas. They had listened, powerless to help, through long, ghastly hours, to the pitiful, heart-breaking moans of the wounded and dying.[87]

After the war, Ross won an admission from General Pershing that his battalion had indeed taken and held their objective, but the reputation of the 92nd Division as a whole was tarnished forever, despite contrary evidence such as this final report by the Secretary of War concerning the "cowardly" 368th:

The circumstances disclosed by a detailed study of the situation do not justify many of the highly colored accounts which have been given of the behavior of the troops in this action, and they afford no basis at all for any of the general assumptions with regard to the action of colored troops in this battle or elsewhere in France. On the contrary, it is to be noted that many colored officers, and particularly three in the very battalion here under discussion, were decorated with Distinguished Service Crosses for extraordinary heroism under fire.[88]

This report, too, was ignored.

Even though the 92nd division suffered 1,700 casualties and had 21 of its men earn the Distinguished Service Cross—more than were awarded to the 6th, 35th, 81st, or 88th white divisions that fought nearby in the same 2nd Army—it would always be thought of by the Army as a cowardly, incompetent failure. Determined to embarrass Ballou, and perhaps everyone in the division, Bullard had General Ballou removed from command, returned to the United States, and reduced to his permanent rank of colonel. He also transferred Greer, who, despite his own open contempt for blacks, ironically and inexplicably had blamed Bullard's racism for the demoralization of the 92nd.[89] Bullard then asked the French to arrange for the 92nd's immediate return to the United States. When the French commander, Marshal Foch, declined, Bullard had Foch informed that "no man could be responsible for the acts of these Negroes toward French women, and that he had better send this division home at once."[90] Despite Bullard's warning, the much honored 93rd Division returned home before the 92nd did. Remarkably, before the 92nd left France, it passed in review before General Pershing, who told them, "Officers and men of the 92nd Division, I wish to express to you my appreciation for your co-operation during your stay in the A.E.F. This division is one of the best in the A.E.F., and the conduct of the officers and men has not been surpassed in any other."[91] General Bullard did not choose to write about this address in his war memoirs.

After the armistice was signed, the Allies staged a grand victory parade in Paris. Black African and West Indian soldiers who fought for France and Britain marched proudly to the loud applause of Parisians. No black American troops were permitted to participate. And the huge French war mural, *Le Panthéon de Guerre*, pictured those troops that had contributed to the Allied victory. Again, although French and British black troops were pictured, African Americans were not.[92] Instead, many black labor battalions were kept in France to search for and bury partially hidden, badly decomposed bodies. Despite miserable living conditions and the horrors of this task, they managed to locate and bury over 23,000 bodies.[93] Even when black troops were designated for shipment to America, their ordeal was not ended. Many were held in miserable conditions while white troops sailed home ahead of them.[94] The 369th, which had spent 191 days in combat, was forced to listen to hours of lectures on the science of rifle use by a young white lieutenant who had never been under fire.[95] Conditions were so tense that the heavily decorated 369th did not even dare to allow its band to play as it marched through the port of Brest, and after men of the 370th had coaled the U.S.S. *Virginia,* its captain refused to allow them to sail on the ship as their orders called for, because, he said, no blacks had ever sailed on that ship before.[96] African American soldiers had won the gratitude and respect of the French Army and the French people, but America's armed forces—like most ordinary Americans—were still a long way from opening their arms to them.

A white officer described the experience of a black captain, the only black among a complement of 400 officers who had been sent home on the *Siboney.* The dining room of the ship could seat only 200 at a time, but instead of two sittings of 200 officers each, three sittings were arranged for each meal—200 at the first, 199 at the second, and a third sitting for the black officer alone. The white officer recalled:

> Each night before retiring it was my habit to take a number of turns around the deck and the Negro captain did the same, walking in the opposite direction. The first time we passed, I always said "Good evening, Captain," and he would reply "Good evening, Lieutenant." To the best of my belief these were the only words spoken to him during the nearly 10 days we were at sea.[97]

FOUR

From Triumph to Despair

In the spring of 1917, Colonel William Hayward, a distinguished lawyer and former public service commissioner from New York, was doing his best to train the black porters, chauffeurs, elevator operators, and waiters who made up the 15th New York National Guard, recently renamed the 369th Infantry Regiment. In the absence of rifles, his men drilled with broomsticks, and their drilling was so uncoordinated that when Colonel Hayward led them on a parade through Harlem in the hope of attracting new recruits, an onlooker derisively referred to their formation as a "column of bunches." In August 1917, after the 369th had grown in numbers and greatly improved its drilling, Colonel Hayward asked permission for his men to march through New York City on their way to report for duty at a training camp in South Carolina. His request was denied. Badly hurt by what he saw as a gratuitous slight, Hayward swore that after the war the 369th would march through New York City in triumph.

In February 1919, the 369th did exactly that, fifty-five years after black Union soldiers had received a warm New York City welcome. *The World*, a major Pulitzer New York newspaper of that time, reported the parade with extraordinary, front-page enthusiasm on February 18, 1919:

In official records, and in the histories that youngsters will study in generations to come, this regiment will probably always be known as the 369th Infantry, U.S.A.

But in the hearts of a quarter million or more who lined the streets yesterday to greet it, it was no such thing. It was the old 15th New York. And so it will be in this city's memory, archives and in the folk lore of the descendants of the men who made up its straight, smartly stepping ranks.

New York is not race-proud nor race-prejudiced. That this 369th Regiment, with the exception of its eight or nine white officers, was composed entirely of Negroes, made no difference in the shouts and flagwaving and handshakes that were bestowed upon it. New York gave its old 15th the fullest welcome of its heart.

Through scores of thousands of cheering white citizens, and then through a greater multitude of its own color, the regiment, the first actual fighting unit to parade as a unit here, marched in midday up Fifth Avenue and through Harlem, there to be almost assailed by the colored folks left behind when it went away to glory.

Later it was feasted and entertained, and this time very nearly smothered with hugs and kisses by kin and friends, at the 71st Regiment Armory. Still later, perfectly behaved and perfectly ecstatic over its reception, the regiment returned to Camp Upton to await its mustering out. . . .

When a regiment has the medal honors of France upon its flags and it has put the fear of God into Germany time after time, and its members wear two gold stripes, signifying a year's fighting service, on one arm, and other stripes, signifying wounds, on the other, it's a whole lot different outfit from what it was when it went away. . . .

At the official reviewing stand at 60th Street, the kinsfolk and admirers of the regimental lads began to arrive as beforehandedly as 9 o'clock. They had tickets, and their seats were reserved for them. The official committee had seen to that—and nine-tenths of the yellow wooden benches were properly held for those good Americans of New York whom birth by chance had been made dark-skinned instead of fair. BUT this was their Day of Days, and they had determined (using their own accentuation) to BE there and to be there EARLY.

The first-comers plodded across 59th Street from the San Juan Hill district, and it was fine to see them. There seemed to be a little military swank even to the youngsters, as platoons of them stepped along with faces that had been scrubbed until they shone. Had a woman a bit of fur, she wore it. Had a man a top hat—origin or vintage-date immaterial—he displayed that. All heads were up, high; eyes alight. Beaming smiles everywhere. No, not quite everywhere. Occasionally, there was to be seen on a left sleeve a black band with a gold star, which told the world that one of the Old 15th would never see the region west of Columbus Circle, because he had closed his eyes in France. And the faces of the wearers of these were unlaughing, but they held themselves just as proudly as the rest.

Few of the welcomers went flagless. No matter whether a man or woman wore jewels or a pair of patent leather boots as a sign of "class," or tramped afoot to the stand or arrived in a limousine, nearly every dark hand held the nation's emblem.

Nearly every one wore white badges bearing the letters: "Welcome, Fighting 15th," or had pennants upon which stood out the regimental insignia—a coiled rattlesnake of white on a black field. . . .

Just why it was that when Governor Smith and former Governor Whitman and Acting Mayor Moran and the other reviewers appeared behind a cavalcade of mounted policemen, the youngsters struck up that army classic, "Oh, How I Hate to Get Up in the Morning," no one could tell, but it gave the reviewers and the crowd a laugh.

With the state and city officials were the members of the Board of Alderman, the Board of Estimate, Major Gen. Thomas J. Barry, Vice Admiral Albert Gleaves, Secretary of State, Francis Hugo; Rodman Wannamaker and—in a green hat and big fur coat—William Randolph Hearst. Secretary Baker of the War Department was unable to attend, but he did the next best thing and sent his colored assistant, Emmett J. Scott.

It was 11:26 when the old 15th stepped away from 23rd Street and Fifth Avenue. They looked the part of the fighting men they were. At an exact angle over their right shoulders were their long-bayonetted rifles. Around their waists were belts of cartridges. On their heads were their "tin hats," the steel helmets that saved many a life, as was attested by the dents and scars in some of them. Their eyes were straight forward and their chins, held high naturally, seemed higher than ever because of the leather straps that circled them. The fighters wore spiral puttees and their heavy hobbed hiking shoes, which caused a metallic clash as they scraped over the asphalt.

At the head of the line rode four platoons of mounted police, twelve abreast, and then, afoot and alone, Col. Hayward, who organized the 15th, drilled them when they had nothing but broomsticks to drill with, fathered them and loved them, and turned them into the fightingest military organization any man's army could want.

The Police Band was at the front of the line of march, but it was a more famous band that provided the music to which the Black Buddies stepped northward and under the Arch of Victory—the wonderful jazz organization of Lieut. Jimmie Europe, the one colored commissioned officer of the regiment.

When Colonel Hayward was organizing the 369th, he recruited James "Jimmie" Europe, the Broadway arranger for Irene and Vernon Castle. Although recently commissioned as a combat officer, Europe agreed to direct the regiment's much larger than regulation band, one that later toured twenty-five French cities to enthusiastic acclaim:

But it wasn't jazz that started them off. It was the historic Marche du Regiment de Sambre et Meuse, which has been France's most popular parade piece since Napoleon's day.

One hundred strong, and the proudest band of blowers and pounders that ever reeled off marching melody—Lieut. Jimmie's boys lived fully up to their reputation. Their music was as sparkling as the sun that tempered the chill day.

Four of their drums were instruments which they had captured from the enemy in Alsace, and ma-an, what a beating was imposed upon those sheepskins! "I'd very much admire to have them bush Germans a-watchin' me today!" said the drummer before the march started. The old 15th doesn't say "Boche" when it refers to the foe it beat. "Bush" is the word it uses, and it throws in "German" for good measure.

Twenty abreast the heroes march through a din that never ceased. They were as soldierly a lot as this town, now used to soldierly outfits, has ever seen. They had that peculiar sort of half careless, yet wholly perfect, step that the French display. Their lines were straight, their rifles at an even angle, and they moved along with the jaunty ease and lack of stiffness which comes only to men who have hiked far and frequently.

Colonel Hayward, with his hand at salute, turned and smiled happily as he saw his best friend, former Governor Whitman, standing with his other good friend, Governor Al Smith, with their silk ties raised high over their heads. It was the Governor's first review in New York and the first time he and Mr. Whitman had got together since Inauguration Day. They were of different parties, but they were united in greeting Colonel Bill and his Babies.

From the stand, from the Knickerbocker Club across the street, from the nearby residences and from the curbing sounded shouts of individual greetings for the commander and his staff. But these were quickly drowned as a roar went up for Lieutenant Europe's band, with its commander at the head—not swinging a baton like a common ordinary drum-major, but walking along with the uniform and side-arms of an officer.

Half way down the ranks of the 2,992 paraders appeared the colors, and all hats came off with double reverence, for the Stars and Stripes and the blue regimental standard that two husky ebony lads held proudly aloft had been carried from here to France, from France to Germany and back again, and each bore the bronze token with its green and red ribbon that is called the Croix de Guerre. Keen eyes could see these little medals swinging from the silk of the flags, high toward the top of the poles.

Then [came] one of the most famous of the whole war. Henry Johnson! That Henry, once a mild-mannered chauffeur, who to protect his comrade, Needham Roberts, waded into a whole patrol of "bush Germans" with a lot of hand grenades, his rifle and his trusty "steel" in the shape of a bolo knife, and waded into them so energetically that when the causalities were counted there were four dead foemen in front of him, thirty-four others done up so badly they couldn't even crawl away, and heaven knows how many more had been put to flight.

And now Henry, in commemoration of this exploit, was riding alone in an open machine. In his left hand he held his tin hat. In his right he held high over his head a bunch of red and white lilies which some admirer had pressed upon him. And from side to side Henry—about as black as any man in the outfit if not a trifle blacker—bowed from the waist down with all the grace of a French dancing master. Yes, he bowed, and he grinned from ear to ear and he waved his lilies, and he didn't overlook a bit in the way of taking (and liking) all the tributes that were offered to him.

A fleet of motor ambulances, back of Henry, carried the wounded men who were unable to walk, nearly 200 of them. But though they couldn't walk they could laugh and wave and shout thanks for the cheers, all of which they did.

From this point north the welcome heightened in intensity. Along the park wall the colored people were banked deeply, everyone giving them the first ranks nearest the curb. Wives, sweethearts and mothers began to dash into the ranks and press flowers upon their men and march alongside with them, arm-in-arm. But this couldn't be, and Colonel Hayward had to stop the procession for a time and order the police to put the relatives back on the sidewalks. But that couldn't stop their noise.

The residents of the avenue paid fine tribute to the dusky marchers. It seemed inspiring, at 65th Street, to see Mrs. Vincent Astor standing in a window of her home, a great flag about her shoulders and a smaller one in her left hand, waving salutes. And Henry Frick, at an open window of his home at 73rd Street, waving a flag and cheering at the top of his voice.

At the corner of 86th Street was a wounded colored solider wearing the Croix de Guerre and the Victoria Cross as well. Colonel Hayward pressed to his side with a hearty hand shake, exclaiming: "Why, I thought you were dead!" It was one of his boys long ago invalided home. "No, sir, Colonel, not me. I ain't dead by a long ways yet, Colonel, sir," said the lad.

The real height of the enthusiasm was reached when, after passing through 110th Street and northward along Lenox Avenue, the heroes arrived in the real Black Belt of Harlem. This was the Home, Sweet Home for hundreds of them, the neighborhood they'd been born in and had grown up in, and from 112th Street north the windows and roofs and fire escapes of the five and six story apartment houses were filled to overflowing with their nearest and dearest.

The noise drowned the melody of Lieut. Europe's band that was now playing "Won't You Come Home, Bill Bailey?" Flowers fell in showers from above. Men, women and children from the sidewalks overran the police and threw their arms about the paraders. There was a swirling maelstrom of dark humanity in the avenue. In the midst of all the racket there could be caught the personal salutations: "Oh, honey!" "Oh Jim!" "Oh, you Charlie!" "There's my boy!" "There's daddie!" "How soon you coming home, son?" It took all the ability of scores of reserve policemen between 129th Street and 135th Street, where the uptown reviewing stand was, to pry those colored enthusiasts away from their soldiermen.

There was one particular cry which was taken up for blocks along this district: "O-oh, you wick-ed Hen-nery Johnson! You wick-ed ma-an!" and Henry the Boche Killer still bowed and grinned more widely than ever, if possible.

"Looks like a funeral, Henry, them lilies!" called one admirer.

"Funeral for them bush Germans, boy! Sure a funeral for them bushes," shouted Henry.

As rapidly as possible the fighters were sent down into the subway station and loaded aboard trains which took them down to the 71st Regiment Armory at 34th Street and Fourth Avenue.

As each company came up from the subway the friends and relatives were allowed to go through the lines, and, while the boys stood still in ranks, but at ease, their kinsfolk were allowed to take them in their arms and tell them really and truly, in close-up fashion, what they thought about having them back.

When the entire regiment was in the Armory, the civilians in the gallery broke all bounds. They weren't going to stay up there while their heroes were down below on the drill-floor! Not they! They swarmed past the police and depot battalion and so jammed the floor that it was impossible for the tired [soldiers] even to sit down. Most of the boys had to take their chicken dinner—served by colored girls, and the chow, incidentally, from Delmonico's—standing up with arms about them and kisses punctuating assaults upon the plates.[1]

Major Arthur W. Little could not have been more proud to march with "his" regiment, the "15th New York" that day:

The multitude of fellow citizens who greeted us that day—the tens of thousands who cheered, the women who wept—the men who cried "God bless you, boys!"—all were united to drown the music of Jim Europe's Band. They did not give us their welcome because ours was a regiment of colored soldiers—they did not give us their welcome in spite of ours being a regiment of colored soldiers. They greeted us that day from hearts filled with gratitude and with pride and with love, *because ours was a regiment of men, who had done the work of men* [italics in original].

Upon the 17th of February, 1919, New York City knew no color line.[2]

Similar parades honoring returning black soldiers took place in Chicago, Washington, Cleveland, and other cities where onlookers' expressions of respect and affection seemed to promise better times ahead for race relations, a grateful white reward for the gallantry of black American soldiers. But in only a matter of months, that promise was shattered by deadly race riots in many of these same cities, including Chicago, Washington, and even New York City itself. At the same time, exceptionally brutal lynching spread throughout the South.

Even before the African American combat and labor troops left France, racial segregation and discrimination by white officers, troops, and military police had led to violent confrontations, including what appear to have been numerous summary executions of black soldiers. A U.S. senator presented a Senate investigating committee with a list of sixty names of black soldiers allegedly executed without court-martial.

One black soldier was photographed hanging from a tree limb, and members of the Graves Registration Service testified that some men whom they had reburied had rope burns on their necks, indicating that they, too, had been hanged.[3] When questioned, many officers denied these charges, but one officer testified that he had been in charge of the executions of two black soldiers and that one had been drugged to "keep him quiet" before he had been hanged.[4] Despite shockingly compelling testimony like this, the Senate quickly dismissed the charges, concluding that they were "without foundation."

No sooner had America entered the war "to make the world safe for Democracy," than lynchings in the South increased in number and in brutality. In 1918, there were sixty-two "lynchings," one of them of a pregnant woman who had threatened legal action after her husband was murdered. She was tied to a tree upside down, doused in motor oil, and set on fire. While she was still alive, screaming in agony, her abdomen was cut open, and her unborn child was intentionally crushed under the feet of the mob.[5] A few days later, a member of the mob that had killed her gleefully boasted to Walter White, a blond-haired, blue-eyed man who easily passed as white but identified black, "Mister, you ought to've heard the nigger wench howl."[6] In 1919, with the return of the troops, seventy-seven blacks were lynched, at least ten of them veterans still in uniform.[7] Two of these men were burned alive.[8] Surprisingly, white police occasionally managed to fight off white mobs bent on lynching a prisoner. During the summer of 1923 in Savannah, Georgia, police killed one white man and badly wounded several others while refusing to yield a black prisoner to a white lynch mob, but local authorities rarely intervened in lynchings.[9]

A Vietnamese visitor to the United States at this time named Nguyen Sinh Cung made himself an expert on lynching, a practice that appalled him even though he did not feel personally threatened by it. He collected clippings such as the following notices from newspapers in the South:

TODAY A NEGRO WILL BE BURNED BY 3,000 CITIZENS . . .
(NEW ORLEANS STATE).

NEGRO J.H. TO BE BURNT BY THE CROWD
AT ELLISTOWN THIS AFTERNOON AT 5 PM.
(JACKSON DAILY NEWS).[10]

Later, Cung wrote an article in French describing an actual lynching:

Imagine a furious horde. Fists clenched, eyes bloodshot, mouths foaming, yells, insults, curses. . . .

Imagine in this human sea a flotsam of black flesh pushed about, beaten, trampled underfoot, torn, slashed, insulted, tossed hither and thither, bloodstained. . . .

In a wave of hatred and bestiality, the lynchers drag the Black to a woods or public place. They tie him to a tree, pour kerosene over him, cover him with inflammable material. While waiting for the fire to be kindled, they smash his teeth, one by one. . . .

The Black is cooked, browned, burned. But he deserves to die twice instead of once. He is therefore hanged, or more exactly, what is left of his corpse is hanged. . . .

When everybody has had enough, the corpse is brought down. The rope is cut into small pieces which will be sold for three or five dollars each. Souvenirs and lucky charms are quarreled over by the ladies. . . .

While on the ground, stinking of fat and smoke, a black head, mutilated, roasted, deformed, grins horribly and seems to ask the setting sun, "Is this civilization?"[11]

When Cung returned to Vietnam, he changed his name to Ho Chi Minh.

As shocking as the hangings and burnings by gleeful mobs like these were to the returning veterans, what they encountered in northern as well as southern cities was in some respects even worse. Before the bloody summer of 1919 had ended–the "Red Summer" as it became known–thousands of people, both black and white, had been killed, injured, or left homeless in racial violence that swept through Chicago, New York, Washington, and Omaha, as well as southern cities such as Charleston, South Carolina; Norfolk, Virginia; Knoxville, Tennessee; Longview, Texas; and Elaine, Arkansas. Whites blamed these clashes on the newly emboldened postwar blacks, whom they described as "armed and defiant," whereas blacks saw the violence as desperate white attempts to reestablish their racial supremacy in all things.

It is true that many black veterans who knew all too well the horrors of war and the cost of their many contributions to the Allied cause returned home expecting to be treated as men, not the "coons," "darkies," or "niggers" they quickly learned they still were. Some black men who had earlier despaired of any hope of racial equality now demanded change, while many white men were just as determined to reassert their superiority. Members of the Ku Klux Klan proudly donned their robes, swearing to kill as many blacks as necessary to make the South safe once again for white women—and for white supremacy. In 1920, hundreds of white-robed Klansmen paraded through Richmond in open automobiles, a new means of asserting white power. Five years later, as many as 85,000 robed Klansmen, many of them from the North, marched through Washington, D.C. The police looked on, seemingly in favor of this show of force.

This reaction by the police was not surprising. The nation's capital had felt itself embattled since early July 1919, when the *Washington Post* reported a black "crime wave" in the city, openly suggesting that white troops stationed in the city take care of the problem. On July 19, 1919, they did so by invading an African American neighborhood, where they beat any blacks they found, sending many to the hospital. The police did nothing to protect the victims, so the next day black men, many of them army veterans, took up arms and fought back, causing the *New York Times* to headline that "Armed and Defiant Negroes Roam about Shooting Whites." In reality, although the fighting was intense, the conflict took place first in black neighborhoods. Only later did blacks drive through white neighborhoods firing. The death count remains uncertain, but it is possible that more whites than blacks were eventually killed. For the first time, government forces took action to end the killing. The black gunfire had made the cost of white supremacy very high.[12] Only after over 1,000 troops moved in was the rioting quelled. One black woman recorded this reaction:

> The Washington riots gave me the thrill that comes once in a lifetime. I was alone when I read between the lines of the morning paper that at last our men had stood like men, struck back, were no longer dumb, driven cattle. . . . The pent-up humiliation, grief and horror of a lifetime—half a century—was being stripped from me.[13]

Later that same month, Chicago exploded. Chicago's so-called Black Belt was home to 125,000 African Americans, many of them impoverished and illiterate new immigrants from the South who had arrived to find a prosperous black settlement on the South Side of Chicago, where middle-class blacks owned five banks, seven drug stores, and many other businesses and cooperatives, as well as large and prosperous churches. But there were also scores of bars and nightclubs where whites and blacks mingled to the growing disgust of Chicago's white population. Black voters helped to put some white politicians in power, and at the time of the riot, two blacks served on the city council. When black veterans returned to reclaim their jobs and demand even more civil rights, some saw reasons to hope for progress. Instead, racial tension grew and a deadly spark was struck.

The explosion began when outraged white bathers in Lake Michigan threw stones at black swimmers who had crossed an imaginary line into a "whites only" area. A seventeen-year-old black boy drowned. When blacks asked a police officer to arrest the stone thrower, he refused, arresting a black man instead. Blacks assaulted the officer, freeing his prisoner. Rioting followed, with the fighting again being confined to African American neighborhoods. A white mob seized a young black woman with a three-month-old baby. After beating and stabbing the woman, they beat the baby's brains out against a telephone pole. One young white rioter severed the mother's breasts and carried them aloft on a pole "triumphantly while a crowd hooted gleefully."[14] After six days of violence with both races exchanging gunfire, 38 people were dead, over 500 injured, and over 200 arrested, the majority in all three categories being black. Ironically, an autopsy of the seventeen-year-old whose drowning had set off the mayhem showed no evidence of a wound that could have been inflicted by a thrown stone.[15] When the rioting ended, large numbers of blacks fled Chicago for what they saw as the comparative safety of the South.[16]

Not all blacks fled. Some, like an anonymous black attorney, wrote in the *Messenger*, September 1919, that the riot proved that many blacks were well armed—he referred to 1,000 rifles and "enough ammunition to last for years"—and ready, willing, and eager to defend their rights. He even applauded the slow intervention of troops because it gave blacks an opportunity to prove their manhood:

> The riot will make the future relations between the races decidedly better. . . . The colored man must not be kicked about like a dumb brute. Our white friends, seeing the danger that besets the nation, will become more active in our cause, and the other whites will at least have a decent respect for us based on fear.

This optimism was premature. More riots soon followed in other cities in both the North and the South. After a bloody riot in Omaha that once again had to be controlled by white troops, the *New York Times* wrote that "Omaha is not ashamed but Omaha is frightened."[17] New Yorkers' spirit of racial tolerance created by the triumphal march of the 369th lasted less than six months. Race relations in this and other northern cities would worsen in the years to come. So would race relations in the South. Beginning with a bloody riot in Phillips County, Arkansas, that killed perhaps 200 blacks, racial violence would sweep through the South as savagely as it ever had even during the years soon after the Civil War and again following the end of Reconstruction.[18]

Perhaps the bloodiest riot of all took place in 1921 in Tulsa, already an oil-rich city that had attracted a large black population. Apparently in response to a complaint by a white woman elevator operator that a black man had attacked her, whites in Tulsa came together in a dangerous mood. When the *Tulsa Tribune* ran an awkward but ominous headline reading "To Lynch Negro Tonight," some 10,000 white men and boys, joined by police officers and a local National Guard unit, burned thirty-five blocks of Greenwood, a formerly thriving black business district, shooting any black people they could find, while several airplanes flew overhead actually dropping bombs. Perhaps as many as 300 people were killed, the great majority of them black, but perhaps 50 whites were killed as well. When the killing ended, the elevator operator declined to press charges.[19] The city government, Tulsa's schools, and most white residents of Tulsa did everything they could to cover up the mass murder. Along with other evidence, the *Tribune* headline disappeared. All but a few of the victims were buried in unmarked mass graves by Tulsa whites and have yet to be exhumed.[20]

As one historian has noted, blacks fought back, but they did not dynamite churches, murder pregnant women, organize lynch mobs, kill small children, or carve up and sell the flesh of their victims, pictured on best-selling postcards.[21] If there can be a high road in racial violence, it was taken by black Americans, not whites.

While race riots swept across America after the war, Europe was reeling under a barrage of German propaganda about the "Black Horror on the Rhine," the alleged presence of 50,000 "coal-black" African "savages" as Allied occupation troops. These black troops, French Tirailleurs Sénégalese, were said to be roaming out of control across the Rhineland, raping German women at will, infecting the population with venereal diseases, and "polluting" German blood.[22] In reality, there were never more than 5,000 African troops stationed in Germany,

TOP: Black soldier in the Union Army. (© Minnesota Historical Society/CORBIS)
MIDDLE: Black soldiers in the U.S. cavalry known as buffalo soldiers. (© Underwood & Underwood/CORBIS) *BOTTOM:* Black Soldiers in bayonet training. (©Bettmann/CORBIS)

TOP: Black troops in France with French equipment. (National Archives). *BOTTOM:* In 1918, Ike Sims of Atlanta, Georgia, 87 years old, had eleven sons in the service. (National Archives).

TOP: Parade of the famous 369th Infantry on Fifth Avenue, New York City, 1919. (National Archives). *BOTTOM:* Five black aviation cadets get a final look at a map before taking off on a training flight at Tuskegee, Alabama, 1943. (© Bettmann/CORBIS)

TOP: A gun crew of six African Americans who were given the Navy Cross for standing by their guns when their ship was damaged by enemy attack in the Philippine area, 1945. (National Archives) *BOTTOM:* Brig. Gen. Robert N. Young, commanding general of the Military District of Washington, assists Melba Rose, aged 2, daughter of Mrs. Rosie L. Madison, in viewing the Silver Star posthumously awarded her father, 1st Lt. John W. Madison of the 92nd Infantry Division, who was killed in action in Italy. (National Archives).

TOP LEFT: Pvt. Lloyd A. Taylor, who knows Latin, Greek, Spanish, French, German, and Japanese, studies a book on Chinese. A former medical student at Temple University, he nevertheless served as a transportation dispatcher with the rank of private. (National Archives). *TOP RIGHT:* Admiral C. W. Nimitz pins the Navy Cross on Doris Miller at a ceremony on board a warship in Pearl Harbor. (National Archives). *BOTTOM:* Coxswain William Green observes safety precautions in checking his pistol while Albert S. Herbert, quartermaster first class, stands by with a clip of ammunition and holster belt, ready to complete the formalities. (National Archives).

TOP: In 1944, fliers of a P-51 Mustang Group of the 15th Air Force in Italy in the shadow of one of the Mustangs they fly. (National Archives). *BOTTOM:* Capt. Andrew D. Turner signals to the chief of his ground crew before taking off from a base in Italy to escort heavy bombers en route to enemy targets. (National Archives).

TOP: Lt. General George S. Patton pins the Silver Star on Private Ernest A. Jenkins of New York City for his conspicuous gallantry in France. (National Archives). *MIDDLE:* A U.S. Army soldier and a Chinese soldier together just before the first truck convoy in almost three years crossed the China border over the Stilwell road in 1945. (National Archives). *BOTTOM:* Private Jackson Brown and Private Roy Williams sit at the air raid shelter of the Anzio-Nettuno beachhead. They are members of the Fifth Army forces holding the bulge against Nazi onslaughts. (© Bettmann/CORBIS)

TOP: Members of an African American mortar company of the ridiculed 92nd Division near Massa, Italy, 1944. (National Archives). *BOTTOM:* Seeking to rescue a Marine who was drowning in the surf at Iwo Jima, this sextet of African American soldiers narrowly missed death themselves when their amphibian truck was swamped by heavy seas. (National Archives).

and all of these were withdrawn by France by June 1, 1920. The Rhinelanders themselves made no protest about these men, whom they described as well behaved. The propaganda flowed out of Berlin, Munich, and other distant German cities. It became grist for Hitler's claims about Allied "de-Germanization" and "Negrification" of the German people.[23]

During World War I, the growing need for labor in the industrial cities of the American North had drawn some 500,000 blacks out of the South, many of them urged on by labor recruiters who traveled throughout the South offering to pay likely job prospects the cost of train travel to the North.[24] Most of these migrants were poorly educated, often with fragile family relationships, and never with any reserves of money. They tended to congregate in run-down urban slums, where they became easy targets for violence when white southerners also moved North in search of jobs, and when white soldiers returned from France wanting their former jobs back. Blacks were excluded from labor unions, squeezed out of federal jobs, and no longer wanted in numerous crafts such as barbering, where they had previously earned a living. After dominating Texas and Oklahoma, the Ku Klux Klan moved North as well, gaining a large following there, especially in Indiana, a state it controlled for years.

The "Roaring Twenties" are remembered for the antics of flappers doing the Charleston and gangsters defying Prohibition, but this was also a time of intense racial hatred. White politicians in the South openly espoused white supremacy at any cost, a principle widely, if less openly, shared in the North. In response, African Americans expressed their views through the increasingly confrontational NAACP and National Urban League, as well as popular black newspapers like the *Chicago Defender* and the *Pittsburgh Courier*.

Racial tensions smoldered throughout the 1920s, sometimes flashing into deadly violence, but much of white America paid little mind to these problems as its college-educated men and women threw themselves into new-found sensual freedom. It was the age of "college men" cradling ukuleles or banjos, not books, while "flappers"—a British slang term for young women who were worldly beyond their years—drenched themselves in perfume, bobbed their hair, and wore short dresses with silk stockings rolled down to their knees. Corsets were abandoned as men demanded a more "natural" feeling, especially as they more openly pursued passionate embraces with young women in what was newly called "petting," or if confined to above the shoulders, "necking." Some flappers openly carried condoms, but relatively few appear to have "gone all the way," as they put it. Instead, they sang a song, "Never Let a Fellow Go an Inch Above Your Knee."

But women as well as men did smoke heavily, drink often, and dance the latest "craze," such as the Charleston, during very loud all-night parties. Popular songs included Al Jolson singing, "How You Gonna Keep 'Em Down on the Farm After They've Seen Par'ee," while party-goers sang "Ain't We Got Fun," and "Yes, We Have No Bananas." Fads of all sorts sprang up, from mah-jongg and dominoes to implausible marathon dancing, and even more unlikely flagpole sitting. When Prohibition was enacted, making "bathtub gin" a household phrase, still more young women joined their male friends in the clubs, saloons, or "speakeasies," which sprang up in cities across the country. One of the most famous was Texas Guinan's speakeasy in New York City, where well-heeled young men and women drank heavily while listening to the latest blues or jazz pieces. Another club featured the melancholy voice of the beautiful "octoroon," as she was known, Helen Morgan. While sitting on a piano, she sang "Why Was I Born?" with such feeling that no one could doubt that she truly did not know. A very heavy drinker, she died in an alcoholic haze at the age of forty-one, one of many thousands to die of apparent alcoholic excess during an era when the sale of alcohol was prohibited by law.

The roar of the 1920s was enjoyed primarily by affluent white people in the cities of the North, where places such as 21 and the Stork Club prospered in New York City. In small towns across America, the "high life" of the flappers and their escorts might as well have been taking place on another planet. The lives of most Americans continued to revolve around family, work, and church. But even the most remote small towns and farm communities were influenced, and soon transformed, by the technological changes of that time. As mentioned earlier, when World War I began, the radio—or wireless as it was then known—was relatively unknown in American homes, including those of the wealthy.

But by 1925, America's radio audience was 50 million people who sat for long hours transfixed by a new world of music, soap operas, murder mysteries, comedies, Christian sermons, newscasts, and endless advertisements for almost everything that could legally be sold including patent medicines and rejuvenation potions.[25] There were evening serials, too, such as *The Lone Ranger* and *Jack Armstrong the All-American Boy*. But none was as popular as *Amos 'n' Andy*. From 1923 until 1951, when it was serialized on television, its deeply accented black humor—scripted by white writers—somehow made it the most popular program on radio. Perhaps audiences enjoyed the middle-class values the program promoted as much as its minstrel humor.[26]

In 1929, Erich Maria Remarque published *All Quiet on the Western Front*, and Ernest Hemingway produced *A Farewell to Arms*. It was a time when Robert Benchley and Dorothy Parker fascinated white Americans, while superb black poets went unnoticed. There were dozens of new magazines, too, with *Life*, *Vanity Fair*, the *New Yorker*, *Harper's Bazaar*, and the *National Geographic* joining the *Saturday Evening Post*, *Redbook*, *McCalls*, and many others like *Good Housekeeping* and the *Atlantic Monthly* in flooding American homes with advice, stories, and advertisements of all kinds. At the same time, automobiles spread across the American landscape. In 1924, a Model T Ford cost $290, and one rolled off the assembly line every ten seconds.[27] By 1926, Chevies were as popular as Fords. Despite appalling road conditions that even federal subsidies for road repair did little to alleviate, the 6,771 personally owned autos that existed in the United States at the end of the war in 1919 grew to over 23 million only ten years later, one for every four and one-half residents.[28]

Sports benefited enormously from radio, magazine, and newspaper information expansion, as well as fans' new automobile-borne mobility. Jack Johnson and Jim Jeffries fought in virtual obscurity compared to Jack Dempsey, who fought during the 1920s. Babe Ruth became a household hero in the same decade, and so did football player Red Grange, and Man O' War became perhaps the most famous horse of all time. Tennis player Bill Tilden, golfer Bobby Jones, and swimmer Johnny Weismuller became famous, too. Movies swept across the country as well, with Charlie Chaplin dominating silent movies along with Clara Bow, until "talkies" came in and her harsh Brooklyn accent, along with a few scandals, destroyed her career. When Rudolph Valentino died in 1926 at the age of thirty-one, over 100,000 people attended his funeral. Newspapers featured comic strips, or "funnies" as they were known, such as *Popeye*, *Joe Palooka*, *Mutt and Jeff*, *Moon Mullins*, *Dick Tracy*, *Gasoline Alley*, and *Little Orphan Annie*.

The new motion picture industry was hugely popular. In 1920, 35 million Americans went to a motion picture theater once a week, where admission was often only a nickel. Stars like W. C. Fields, Mae West, and the Marx Brothers became household names. With the introduction of sound in 1927, the numbers of moviegoers rose to 57 million, and by 1929, 80 million Americans—one out of every two people in the country—were reported to have seen a movie every week of the year.[29] What they saw can have done little to endorse racial tolerance much less racial equality. Instead, Al Jolson's 1927 talking movie, *The Jazz Singer*, which featured him singing "Mammy" in blackface, seemed to reaffirm the separation and inequality of the races. Earlier, films like *The Birth of a Nation* had portrayed every imaginable racial stereotype, including white supremacy and black rape. What movie audiences saw on their many trips to theaters were racial stereotypes acted out by performers like Bill Robinson, Louise Beavers, and, in especially crude caricature, the "shuffling, lazy, stupid" roles played by an actor named Lincoln T. M. A. Perry, who took the ultimate "Sambo" screen name of Stepin Fetchit.

A few small-budget, racially sensitive films produced for black audiences appeared during the 1930s, but no film sensitive to blacks attracted a large audience until 1939, when *Gone with the Wind* premiered in Atlanta. Hattie McDaniel won an Oscar for her portrayal of "Mammy," and some black viewers were said to have been pleased by the relative lack of black stereotypes in the film.[30] But many others detested the film, seeing during its nearly four hours on the screen the usual racial stereotypes, only more subtly portrayed. Some thought Hattie McDaniel should not have agreed to play Mammy, or to accept the Academy Award.[31] She replied with candor: "The only choice permitted us is either to be servants for $7.00 a week or portray them for $700.00 a week."[32]

Early in the 1930s, Paul Robeson, former All-American football player at Rutgers, Rhodes Scholar, Columbia Law School graduate, and much acclaimed baritone, starred in the movie made of Eugene O'Neill's play *The Emperor Jones*. Unfortunately, as one critic wrote in 1935:

"The Emperor Jones" maintained unbroken the chain of white chauvinism forged in the carbon-arc lights of the Hollywood studios. Paul Robeson is presented as a vainglorious braggart, a murderer, a tin-foil Napoleon who imposes upon and exploits heartlessly members of his own race. And when finally they rise against him his false front falls away.

He is revealed for what he is, and by extension, what all Negroes are supposed to be, creatures who stand trembling in a murky land of shadow, peopled with the ghosts that rise up out of the swamps and jungles of the primitive mind.[33]

In *The Green Pastures*, which was a great success on Broadway, the black cast played Jews, comparing their travail to that of blacks, and one of the characters was God, a blasphemy that caused the play to be banned in Britain.[34]

Dr. Lawrence Reddick, curator of the Schonenberg Collection at the New York Public Library, listed the following white American stereotypes about blacks, all of which were reinforced by Hollywood movies: the savage African, the "happy savage," the devoted servant, the corrupt politician, the irresponsible citizen, the petty thief, the social delinquent, the vicious criminal, the sexual superman, the superior athlete, the natural-born cook and musician, the perfect entertainer, the superstitious churchgoer, the chicken and watermelon eater, the razor and knife "toter," the uninhibited expressionist, and the mental inferior.[35]

Black Americans were attending college in some numbers for the first time during the 1920s, and a good many achieved local prominence in business or church work, while others became known nationally through their civil rights activities. There were many doctors and professors, too, including Daniel Hale Williams, the first open-heart surgeon,[36] but most remained out of sight and out of mind for white Americans. If white Americans knew anything about African Americans beyond their alleged childishness, stupidity, cowardice, and propensity for rape, it was their music. The blues and jazz—"black music"—spread from the bars, clubs, and brothels of New Orleans to Kansas City, Memphis, Chicago, New York, and many other cities throughout the country, especially after 1917, when the Secretary of the Navy forced the red-light district of Storyville in New Orleans, with its famed musicians but growing rates of venereal disease, to close down. Jelly Roll Morton claimed to have invented jazz, but it was King Oliver's Creole Jazz Band that took New York by storm, and thanks to the new medium of record players, or "victrolas," black jazz men like Louis Armstrong, "Fats" Waller, and "Kid" Ory, along with blues singers such as Bessie Smith and Ethel Waters became popular entertainers even in northern households that believed fervently in white supremacy. White musicians responded by forming their own "Dixieland" jazz bands, especially in Kansas City and Chicago. Chicago's Leon "Bix" Beiderbecke achieved great popularity as a white jazz cornetist. And of course, white bands such as those led by Paul Whiteman and Red Nichols and the Five Pennies were popular as well.

None of this should suggest that white Americans were welcoming black Americans into their restaurants, hotels, or homes. Even major hospitals in New York were strictly segregated. There was little to suggest popular sentiment for racial integration, but the musical *Show Boat*, with music by Jerome Kern (who had previously written "Smoke Gets in Your Eyes" and "They Didn't Believe Me" among other hit songs) and with a racially mixed cast, brought an antiracist message to the country in 1927. Its signature song, "Old Man River," seemed to affect white audiences with the pathos of black subjugation, but there is little to suggest that racist attitudes changed as a result.

Instead of reducing their racist intolerance toward blacks, white Americans extended their hostility to white immigrants. The Bolshevik Revolution had created fears of communist revolution led by the "hordes" of eastern European Jews. There were also fears of Catholics from southern Europe who were trying to eke out a living in American cities, whereas California felt itself endangered by the "yellow menace" of Chinese and Japanese immigrants. A popular saying was "Chink, Chink, Chinaman, eat dead rats."[37] Even parts of Western Canada welcomed the Klan in the mid-1920s to combat the influx of eastern European and Catholic immigrants. Now representing themselves as "old-stock, Nordic Americans," the Ku Klux Klan targeted Jews, Catholics, and alien foreigners for surveillance, insisting that they accept "Native, White, Protestant Supremacy."[38] Some Klansmen thronged to Texas to resist Mexican immigration, and others went to California to repel Asians, and to the Northeast to resist the Catholic "menace" in that part of the country. Billy Sunday joined other churchmen in denouncing the new white immigrants as "paupers and criminals dumped" on American shores.[39] At the same time, of course, neither Billy Sunday nor the Klan reduced their hatred of blacks, some of whom, like Marcus Garvey, responded to America's rejection of them by proposing a "Back to Africa" movement that, like earlier ones, failed to lead to any large exodus of blacks from America.

The 1920s were not a time of religious tolerance, either. In 1925, a high school teacher named John Scopes was tried for teaching "Darwinism," rather than biblical creation. Defended by Clarence Darrow and prosecuted by William Jennings Bryan, Scopes was eventually found guilty and fined $100, which he was never required to pay. Bryan died five days after the verdict, widely seen in the North and overseas as the loser to Darrow. More generally, the United States—especially Tennessee where the so-called "monkey trial" took place—was scorned as a primitive bastion of fundamentalism that had humiliated itself in the eyes of many in Britain and Europe.[40]

While this kaleidoscope of social events was changing the face of America, policymakers within the armed forces were evaluating the performance of black soldiers and officers in World War I. Ignoring all evidence of martial skill and gallantry, they concluded that black soldiers were inadequate for any service except labor. At the same time, black officers were "discriminated against, ridiculed and discredited in every conceivable way."[41] To the surprise of no one, Lieutenant-Colonel Greer agreed emphatically, adding that black officers were not only colossally ignorant but dishonest as well, and that African Americans should never again be used as combat troops. They should serve only as laborers.[42] In early 1920, a questionnaire was sent to white officers who had served in the 92nd Division asking them to evaluate the performance of black officers during the war and to comment on the role they should play in the future. The responses were derogatory at best. One colonel rejected black officers because of their inherent "inferior intelligence, carelessness, false pride, and easy discouragement." A white colonel, Fred R. Brown, who had commanded the 368th Infantry, declared, "History has repeatedly proven that normally the negro as a race, is and always has been lacking in bravery, grit and leadership."[43]

The army leadership readily accepted the racial stereotypes then current in this country about African Americans' lack of intelligence. Based on studies that had actually been faked, their brains were said to be smaller and less heavily convoluted than whites'; it was also said that they could memorize but not truly understand, and, of course, that they were "born cowards."[44] Reacting to ideas like these, as well as the frequently expressed opinions of many senior officers, in 1925 the Army War College issued a report written by Major-General H. E. Ely, Commandant, entitled "The Use of Negro Manpower in War." About black troops, it provided this by now foregone conclusion: "In physical courage, it must be admitted that the American Negro falls well back of the white man and possibly all other races."[45] The report went on to declare that black officers were not only cowardly but unintelligent, vain, and pleasure-seeking men who banded together for self-interest, and that all of these inherent faults were exaggerated by wearing an officer's uniform.[46] The report recommended that future black officer candidates be trained alongside whites to the same standard but concluded that only one in ten blacks could hope to meet it. It added that those who proved to have sufficient intelligence to succeed would do so because of their white blood, but even so, their lack of moral character—unlike intelligence, something that apparently could not be inherited from their white ancestors—would continue to limit their effectiveness. As ludicrous as this report seems in light of the historical record, it would dominate military thinking for many years to come.

In that same year of 1925, General Bullard published his reminiscences of the war, in which he declared that his memories of the 92nd Division were a "nightmare." He described blacks as cowards who were so sensual as to be "depraved," a reference to his fear that they would—and in his mind, did—repeatedly rape white women.[47] Walter White soon after wondered in print why for 200 years prior to 1830, Americans of African descent showed no greater propensity for sex crimes than white Americans. In fact, White found no evidence that any black had ever been charged with rape before 1830.[48] From 1830 to 1860, some blacks were lynched for varying reasons, but fewer blacks were lynched than whites during this period. The reason, White argued cogently, is that a black slave had substantial value to his master that should not be wasted. After Emancipation, all that changed, and valueless "freedmen" were lynched in growing numbers.

Led by the NAACP, several newspapers in the North criticized Bullard for his unfounded attack, pointedly noting his Alabama roots and his many earlier racist comments. The most forceful criticism came from Congressman Hamilton Fish, the former Harvard football player who had served in combat as a captain with the black 369th Infantry Regiment in France. He chided Bullard for his hostility to African American soldiers, pointing out that a senior officer like General Bullard should be well aware of "the deeds of heroism performed by Negro soldiers in all our wars." Fish was less ready to spring to the defense of black officers, about whom he had some reservations, but he characterized Bullard's comment about black cowardice as "a gross calumny against fearless soldiers."[49]

Although black newspapers and organizations continued to criticize Bullard and others while defending black officers and soldiers, there is little evidence to suggest that white Americans were listening, and ample evidence that the War Department was not. When a new War College report was issued more than a decade later, in 1936, it continued to describe blacks with racial stridency:

> As an individual, the negro is docile, tractable, lighthearted, care free and good natured. If unjustly treated he is likely to become surly and stubborn. . . . He is careless, shiftless, irresponsible and secretive. He is unmoral, untruthful and his sense of right doing is relatively inferior. Crimes and convictions involving moral turpitude are nearly five to one as compared to convictions of whites on similar charges.[50]

In fact, as we shall see, even after the onset of World War II, both the War Department and the Army were still citing the cowardice and incompetence of the 92nd Division as reasons not to employ blacks in combat. With so many white officers, some of them from the South, praising blacks for their heroism throughout American history, this verdict is difficult to understand. Unless, of course, the historical evidence was intentionally ignored.

On the civil front, there was continuing racial violence, but black activists won an occasional political victory. In August 1925, the *Chicago Defender* noted that since the conclusion of World War I, the U.S. government had pardoned numerous criminals including spies and other foreign agents, while twenty-nine men from the 24th Infantry who had been convicted of taking part in the Houston riot of 1917 were still in Leavenworth Penitentiary. By 1925, the NAACP had collected large numbers of signatures asking President Calvin Coolidge to commute the death sentences of the Houston prisoners and later to reduce their sentences. It was pressures like these that finally led Coolidge to appoint an investigatory board of the War Department to look into the sentencing of the twenty-nine remaining prisoners. On the board's recommendation, the sentences were reduced, and by 1929, all twenty-nine men had been freed.

In that same year, the stock market crashed and the Great Depression began. Just before the crash, famous psychologist John B. Watson, doyen of the school of belief that experience can mold people into virtually any shape or form, declared that during the Roaring Twenties sex had become "so free and abundant . . . that it no longer provides the thrill it once did. . . . Gambling in Wall Street is about all the thrill we have left."[51] Some Americans did pursue the stock market with something akin to sexual fervor, but in fact, no more than 1.5 million people, or about 1 in every 200 Americans were investors in the stock market, but most of these bought stocks on a 10 percent margin, and because few had any savings, they would not be able to pay the 90 percent they owed on short notice if they were required to do so. In 1929, the market fell precipitously, wealthy investors sold their stocks, and brokers demanded their 90 percent from the majority who had bought on margin. The result was market collapse, the Great Crash, and a downward spiral of the entire economy. Banks closed, locking out depositors, factories and businesses shut down, and millions of Americans who had bought goods on installment plans faced repossession and foreclosure.[52] In 1932, a New York revue opened called *Brother Can You Spare a Dime?* "Okies" streamed out of the Dust Bowl to California, and while the death rate per capita actually lowered slightly during 1930–1933, there were bread lines, soup kitchens, and widespread hunger. Some actual starvation occurred.[53]

The Great Depression brought suffering to many, and terrible suffering to blacks, particularly sharecroppers in the Deep South, who lived in far worse housing and had less to eat than slaves did during slavery. In 1934, British journalist Naomi Mitchison visited black sharecroppers working on Arkansas cotton plantations, describing their lives as a "nightmare":

> I have traveled over most of Europe and part of Africa but I have never seen such terrible sights as I saw yesterday among the share-croppers of Arkansas. Here are people . . . being treated worse than animals, worse than farming implements and stock. . . . They are dressed in rags, they have barely enough food to keep them alive; their children get no education; they are a prey to diseases which the scientific resources of modern civilization could easily eliminate. I saw houses, if one can call them that, in which whole families lived in conditions of indescribable misery. Here was a log cabin half sunk in flood water and in it eight people, one of them a mother yellow and boney with malaria with a newborn child in her arms. The only furniture in the house was a table, a bench and stove and two beds for everyone. In another home a bed this time out of old bits of rusty iron, patched with rags. The youngest child was two years old but his mother was still nursing him; she could at least be sure he got some milk that way. She herself was gray haired with a face of such misery that it seemed scarcely possible she could go on living.[54]

Conditions were also dreadful for blacks in urban areas, where many women had previously been employed. For example, in 1930, 57 percent of all black females over the age of ten in Atlanta were employed. Soon, most were without work, vulnerable to crime, and near desperation. Occasionally, unemployment brought some blacks and whites closer to one another in a camaraderie of shared misery. There were even a few racially integrated bread lines and soup kitchens in the North, where blacks were twice as hard hit as whites, but blacks were often taken out of line and beaten by police for no reason apparent to onlookers.[55] But Jim Crowism remained throughout the country, and although lynchings declined in number, they still took place. A black man lynched in Virginia in 1936 was burned to death, then hacked into hundreds of pieces by eager souvenir hunters. Even pieces of bone were taken. After several particularly ghastly lynchings like this one, picture postcards of the mutilated body were made and widely sold.[56]

Flagrantly rigged trials continued, too, such as the one in 1931 that sentenced nine "Scottsboro Boys" to prison for rape on perjured testimony.[57] Like many poor whites, destitute black men often "rode the rails" in freight trains looking for work. Accused of rape, these nine black youths were taken from a train, and eight of them were quickly sentenced to death. Thanks to legal assistance by communist and black organizations, they were eventually freed. Despite its obvious communist rhetoric, this appeal for help moved many Americans:

> We have been sentenced to die for something we ain't never done. Us poor boys have been sentenced to burn up on the electric chair for the reason that we is workers—and the color of our skin is black. We like any one of you workers is none of us older than 20. Two of us is 14 and one is 13 years old. What we guilty of? Nothing but being out of a job. Nothing but looking for work. Our kinfolk was starving for food. We wanted to help them out. So we hopped a freight—just like any one of your workers might a done—to go down to Mobile to hunt work. We was taken off the train by a mob and framed up on rape charges. . . . Working class boys, we asks you to save us from being burnt on the electric chair. We's only poor working class boys whose skin is black. We shouldn't die for that. . . . Help us boys. We ain't done nothing wrong.[58]

The fact that the alleged rape victim repudiated her allegations of rape four years later finally led to the dismissal of charges against the nine young men.

At the height of the depression years, Adam Clayton Powell, Sr., pastor of the large Abyssinian Baptist Church of Harlem, and a devoted proponent of the "meekness of Jesus" as he put it, wrote, "Each race has a contribution to make to the other. My race needs the white man's courage, initiative, punctuality, business acumen and aggressiveness. The white man needs the Negro's meekness, love, forgiving spirit and the emotional religion expressed in his folk songs."[59] Southern slave owners of a century earlier could hardly have endorsed this creed of "meekness" any more fervently, and neither could the War Department. Powell's son, Adam Clayton Powell, Jr., who would be elected to Congress in 1945, would take a radically different view of relations between blacks and whites.

As the Depression years wore on, most white Americans were oblivious of black suffering just as they were of black achievements. As early as the eighteenth century, former slave Benjamin Banneker became a respected mathematician and astronomer. A few black scientists received some acclaim, as Dr. Percey Julian did in 1935 for inventing the foam method of extinguishing flame and synthesizing a drug for the treatment of glaucoma, and even earlier, Dr. Louis T. Wright would make signal contributions to brain surgery, but their accomplishments, like those of other distinguished African Americans, such as Booker T. Washington, were unknown to all but a handful of white Americans.[60] Similarly, the poetry of Langston Hughes was virtually unknown to whites. Richard Wright's novels—*Uncle Tom's Children*, *Native Son*, and *Black Boy*—were somewhat better known but far from bestsellers with white Americans. Walter White's novel *The Fire in the Flint* was more successful. Describing the life of a black medical student in the North who returns to the South hoping to ease racial tension only to be lynched, the novel sold only fairly well in the United States but did better in Europe, the Soviet Union, and, surprisingly, in Japan.[61]

Black music did achieve popularity with many whites, but most of its live performances were still confined to night clubs where Cab Calloway, "Fats" Waller, and Count Basie held sway. One of the most famous was Harlem's Cotton Club, where Duke Ellington's orchestra was playing his complex compositions like "Mood Indigo," "Flamingo," "Perdido," and "Sophisticated Lady" and that of a colleague, "Take the 'A' Train." Nonetheless, Ellington was routinely introduced to white audiences by the club's white master of ceremonies as "the greatest living master of jungle music." Radio and phonograph records brought Ellington's new "swing" style into millions of white homes, but Ellington's orchestra never performed in a concert auditorium until two white undergraduate students who heard him perform in a noisy Los Angeles nightclub invited him to play at UCLA's new 2,000-seat Royce Hall in 1937. His orchestra played to a full house of white college students and faculty for four spectacular hours, but despite his growing esteem in white America, he would not be invited to another concert stage for six more years, when his orchestra finally performed at Carnegie Hall.[62] Taking a controversial "no color bar" position, Benny Goodman's very popular "white" orchestra and quartet both regularly employed black musicians, but when Goodman went to Hollywood to make the movie *Sweet and Low*, he was forced to use only white musicians. Despite Goodman's protests, his quartet was all white in the film.

One of the most popular female black vocalists in the 1930s was Billie Holiday. In addition to her many recordings, she was a regular performer at Café Society, a racially integrated Greenwich Village cabaret. In 1939, Abel Meeropol, a thirty-six-year-old English teacher from the Bronx took his song, "Strange Fruit," to Barney Josephson, the owner of Café Society, hoping that he would urge Holiday to sing it. Josephson not only gave the song to her but made certain that the audience would listen by ordering that all service be halted, that waiters, busboys, and cashiers all stand up and be still, and that the lights be turned off except for a tiny spotlight on Holiday's face.

Holiday's voice and her obvious pain mesmerized the audience:

> *Southern trees bear a strange fruit*
> *Blood on the leaves and blood at the root,*
> *Black body swinging in the Southern breeze,*
> *Strange fruit hanging from the poplar trees.*
> *Pastoral scene of the gallant South,*
> *The bulging eyes and the twisted mouth,*
> *Scent of magnolia sweet and fresh,*
> *And the sudden smell of burning flesh!*

When she finished, she walked off the stage without waiting for applause and taking a bow. Over the years, she sang it less often. According to one of the musicians who accompanied her, "She would cry every time she would do it."[63] Still, she did perform it often over the years. In 1946, she sang "Strange Fruit" at a club in Chicago for a group of naval officers. One man recalled the experience vividly: "When she finished there was no applause, but everyone in the club just stood up with their heads bowed. It was one of the most moving experiences of my life."[64] She also recorded "Strange Fruit" four times and performed it on television in London in 1959, the year of her death.

During the 1930s, many black musicians became popular with white Americans, especially in the North, but the two African Americans who received the greatest respect from whites at this time were athletes: "The World's Fastest Man," Jesse Owens, and "The Brown Bomber," Joe Louis. Modest, soft-spoken sprinter Jesse Owens—the son of Alabama sharecroppers—became an American hero when he embarrassed the Nazi regime and Hitler himself in the 1936 Olympic Games in Berlin by winning the 100- and 200-meter dashes and the long jump, as well as running the opening leg of America's victorious 400-meter relay, while athletes from the "Master Race" trailed far behind. What Owens achieved brought him great popularity in the United States, with his name in headlines and on Broadway marquees, while newsreels trumpeted his victories.[65] But except for the Olympic Games, track and field did not attract many fans, and the 1940 Olympics, where Owens might have starred again, were canceled because of World War II. Owens felt the pain of racial discrimination throughout his life, but even so, at his death, few Americans were honored as extensively as the Olympic hero.

Boxing was a much more popular sport than track, and still a racially tense one. Joe Louis Barrow, like Owens the son of nearly destitute Alabama sharecroppers, was taken to Detroit as a young boy, and despite going hungry many times, he grew to be a six-foot, one-and-one-half-inch-tall, 200-pound heavyweight boxer. Always a hero to the black community—Langston Hughes saw old black women sitting on a curb weeping after he lost one fight—Louis had to prove that he was not a second Jack Johnson before white fans would accept him. Joe did sometimes wear flashy clothes, and there were many women in his life, but he was reasonably discreet about them, modest about himself, and not one to challenge the color line. He first endeared himself to white fans when he knocked out Italian Primo Carnera in 1935 while Italy's brutal invasion of Ethiopia was taking place. But in 1936, he was knocked out by Germany's Max Schmeling. Blacks were crushed, but despite heavy radio, newsreel, and newspaper coverage of Louis's defeat, most whites did not yet picture Schmeling as a Nazi, and at that time Americans were just beginning to be aware of what Hitler's government was or would soon after become.

When Louis won the heavyweight title in 1937 by knocking out Max Baer in Chicago, 25,000 blacks ran joyously, proudly, and peacefully through the streets of the South Side.[66] In 1938, Louis fought a rematch with Schmeling in Yankee Stadium before some 80,000 fans, including several governors of states, the postmaster general, the German ambassador, and many movie stars, including Clark Gable, Douglas Fairbanks, and Gary Cooper. Where Hitler was leading Germany was now much clearer, and the prefight publicity left no doubt that this was a fight between the United States and Nazi militarism. Although many young white men dressed in Nazi uniforms heckled Louis at his training camp, and many of those people in attendance at the fight cheered more loudly at the introduction of Schmeling than they did for Louis, the fight had obvious patriotic meaning. Before the bout, President Roosevelt met with Louis, telling him that he must "prove that *we* can beat Germany."[67] As perhaps the largest radio audience in American history listened in, Louis knocked Schmeling out in the first round, thrilling white as well as black listeners all over the country. It was a triumph that newsreels and print media documented as no previous fight in history.

Louis went on to win many more fights, achieving celebrity status and many invitations to Hollywood as a result. When World War II broke out, and he was quickly drafted, he was probably the best-known and best-liked black man in America. He received some preferential treatment in the Army, but his accomplishments in the ring did nothing to ease the burden of Jim Crow for other black soldiers or sailors. Since the end of World War I, the Army had been devoted to cleansing itself of its "cowardly, depraved" blacks. By 1930, only one soldier in forty was of African descent. Only nine northern states maintained black National Guard units, and troops from the 9th and 10th Cavalry were being assigned to act as stable boys and groom white officers' polo ponies. Men of the two infantry regiments served as cooks, truck drivers, and grooms as well.[68] All four of the "colored" regiments were supposed to be combat-ready, but only one, the 25th Regiment, received even rudimentary combat training after World War I.

Charles H. Houston, a black army officer during World War I, and later a special counsel to the NAACP, was one who refused to accept the racial status quo of the 1930s. In 1934, he confronted Douglas MacArthur about the Army's neglect of blacks, pointing out that the military should not expect to be able to make them instant patriots by waving the flag in time of war after treating them wretchedly in times of peace.[69] Soon after this inconclusive meeting, Houston wrote to the *New York Times* to assure the Army's general staff that if it "thinks that Negroes in the next war are going to be content with peeling potatoes and washing dishes," they had badly misread the minds of African Americans.[70] Later, he insisted that blacks must demand the right to serve in combat under black officers, and not only in the Army but the Army Air Corps, Navy, and Marines as well.

Houston's words had little effect, but by 1938 Congressman Fish had introduced three House bills intended to widen opportunity for blacks in the military and lessen discrimination against them. One of these bills called for a segregated black division, but after opposition by the NAACP, Fish withdrew it. The remaining two bills died in committee in 1939. In 1940, with the threat of war growing with every passing day, still the military did nothing to alter its rejection of blacks while "public sensibilities remained profoundly segregationist and hostile toward any suggestion of racial equality."[71] Even the passage of this country's first-ever peacetime draft bill in September 1940 did nothing to change either the Army's or the Navy's opposition to racial equality in the military. Selective Service Director General Lewis B. Hershey said that he regretted the discriminatory segregation and racial quotas of the military, "but unfortunately the army gets the final say. What we are doing, of course, is simply transferring discrimination from everyday life into the army. Men who make up the army staff have the same ideas [about race] as they had before they went into the army."[72]

He did not say, as well he might have, that racial segregation of the military was enforced by powerful southern politicians who, among other positions of power, led the House Military Appropriations Committee and the Senate Armed Services Committee. One documented example among many undocumented ones was brought about by a plan by some individuals in the War Department to reduce racial discrimination by purchasing 55,000 copies of *Races of Mankind*, a pamphlet by anthropologists Ruth Benedict and Gene Weltfish exposing the myth of white supremacy and calling for racial equality. Congressman Andrew J. May of Kentucky, chairman of the House Military Appropriations Committee, threatened to cut off the War Department's funding if the pamphlets were distributed. All copies were burned.[73]

But black Americans were growing in political power, too. Knowing full well that African Americans now stood together as a voting bloc that he might need in 1940 for reelection against Wendell Willkie, who was campaigning as a foe of racism, President Franklin D. Roosevelt listened to the entreaties of powerful black lobbyists to end discrimination in the military. In October 1940, Roosevelt's press secretary, Stephen Early, responded with a seven-point plan for the "fair and equitable utilization of blacks" in the military:

1. Negroes will be drafted in proportion to their population ratio—about one to every eleven men.
2. They will be used in every branch of the service.
3. Negro reserve officers will serve with outfits which already have negro officers.
4. They will be given a chance to earn reserve commissions when officers' schools are set up. (But except for the established black National Guard units, black units would be officered by whites.)
5. They will be trained as pilots and aviation mechanics.
6. Negro civilians will have an equal chance with whites for jobs at arsenals and army posts.
7. Negro and white soldiers will not serve in the same regiments.[74]

Early's statement added that racial segregation had served the military well for many years and that change would be detrimental to the national defense.

In the face of black criticism about this policy of continued segregation, Early lied to the press that black leaders like Walter White and A. Philip Randolph had sanctioned it. FDR had to apologize in writing for Early's deceit. Soon after this lamentable affair, a black New York City police officer inadvertently blocked Early's entrance to the presidential train after FDR had given a speech at Madison Square Garden. Early kicked the officer in the groin. FDR again apologized for Early, who was made to apologize to the officer and the New York Police Commission.[75] It was not the best of times for the president.

Clearly, despite Willkie's election-year threat, there had been no changes in military policy relating to segregation. Black leaders continued to react angrily, denouncing Roosevelt's plan as racial segregation. In an attempt to calm the storm and deliver the black vote for Roosevelt, the administration made an important gesture by appointing Dean William H. Hastie of the Howard University Law School as a civilian aide to Secretary of War Henry Stimson. What is more, the War Department decided to create black aviation units and reaffirmed the formation of black combat units. A former federal judge, a magna cum laude valedictorian from Amherst, and a distinguished graduate of the Harvard Law School in 1932, Hastie declared, "We will be anything that any other American should be in the whole program of national defense. But we won't be black auxiliaries."[76]

Judge Hastie's words had no visible effect on military planning. At the end of 1940, the army had been so thoroughly cleansed of blacks that there were only 4,179 African American soldiers in the entire army and only 5 black officers, 3 of them chaplains. The 2 nonchaplains were Colonel Benjamin O. Davis, who commanded the 369th Regiment, still a part of the New York National Guard but no longer remembered for its World War I heroism, and his son, Lieutenant Benjamin O. Davis, Jr., a West Point graduate who would become famous in World War II as a fighter pilot. One week before the election, the White House announced that it had nominated Colonel Davis for promotion to brigadier general, and he soon after became the first African American ever to attain that rank. Despite more than eight years of honorable service, however, he was never promoted beyond this one-star rank. When Davis became a general, there were only 353 blacks in the Officers' Reserve Corps, less than 0.5 percent of the total.[77] Judge Hastie's memorandum was ignored throughout 1941 as draftees poured into the armed forces. Only six days before Pearl Harbor, General George C. Marshall, Chief of Staff, and a Virginian, responded to Hastie by announcing that "the settlement of vexing racial problems cannot be permitted to complicate the tremendous task of the War Department."[78]

When Japanese bombs fell on Pearl Harbor, a black mess attendant named Dorie Miller on the battleship U.S.S. *West Virginia* carried the ship's wounded captain away from the exposed bridge before manning a machine gun on deck. Although he had no training in the use of this weapon, he shot down at least two Japanese planes. One historian wrote, "As he did so, his usually impassive face bore the deadly smile of a berserk Viking."[79] His heroism earned him the Navy Cross but no change in duty assignment. Two years later, he was still serving meals to white officers when a Japanese torpedo sank the escort carrier U.S.S. *Liscome Bay*. Miller was lost at sea.

FIVE

"Made Perfect Fools of Themselves"

On September, 30, 1938, three months after Joe Louis knocked out Schmeling, British Prime Minister Neville Chamberlain flew back to England following his meeting with Hitler in Munich to announce a treaty that would guarantee "peace for our time." Six months later, German troops marched into Prague without a shot being fired. In September 1939, German tanks overran Poland with the assistance of Soviet troops, who also crushed Finland in that same year. When Poland was invaded, bringing declarations of war from France and Britain and igniting World War II, there were all of 3,640 black soldiers in the U.S. Army. By June 1940, Norway, Denmark, Holland, Belgium, and France had all fallen while Britain was under heavy siege from the air. On September 16, 1940, two years after Chamberlain's guarantee of "peace for our time," the war had become so threatening that President Roosevelt signed into law his country's first peacetime military draft. But by the end of 1940, the draft had added only 539 black soldiers to the Army.[1]

However, the War Department had stipulated that African Americans would be drafted in proportion to their numbers in the American population, and by the time of Pearl Harbor, one year later, almost 100,000 had been inducted into the Army. One year after Pearl Harbor, the number had risen to almost half a million. With the partial exception of the Coast Guard, wherever blacks served in the military during World War II, they encountered rigid racial segregation within their training facilities and camps. They also faced racial discrimination throughout

America, but especially in the South, where deadly violence continued unabated, with police brutality, lynching, and racist court decisions unaffected by the war effort.

The black men—and later women—who served in World War II were better educated than their predecessors in World War I, less accepting of "color lines," and more determined to serve as equals to whites, including every form of combat. As police beat and shot blacks without provocation, as lynching continued as savagely as ever, and as Jim Crow refused to yield, a worker for the NAACP said, "White people are sitting on a powder keg . . . blind to what is developing. I expect to see race riots flare up all over the country unless something is done to give the Negro a real opportunity in the war effort."[2] Black political protest would grow, too. The NAACP was founded in 1909 by two white men, one of them a southerner, and a white woman. In 1940, it had 50,000 members. By 1945, its membership had grown to 450,000, and these people had been increasingly vocal during the war.[3]

And the riots did come. Poet Langston Hughes, who vocally supported the war effort, nevertheless wrote this:

Looky here, America
What you done done—
Let things drift
Until the riots come

Now your policemen
Let the mobs run free.
I reckon you don't care
Nothing about me.

You tell me that hitler
Is a mighty bad man.
I guess he took lessons
From the ku klux klan.

You tell me mussolini's
Got an evil heart.
Well, it mus-a been in Beaumont
That he had his start—

Cause everything that hitler
And mussolini do

> *Negroes get the same*
> *Treatment from you*
>
> *You jim crowed me*
> *Before hitler rose to power—*
> *And you're still jim crowing me*
> *Right now, this very hour.*
>
> *Yet you say we're fighting*
> *For democracy.*
> *Then why don't democracy*
> *Include me?*
>
> *I ask you this question*
> *Cause I want to know*
> *How long I got to fight*
> *BOTH HITLER–AND JIM CROW.⁴*

Jim Crow would not yield, and race riots would continue to sweep the country.

White America would not readily change its racist ways, and the War Department was no exception. Referring to the post–World War I "authoritative" conclusions of the army policymakers that blacks were both unintelligent and cowardly, and their officers useless, Roosevelt's new Secretary of War, Henry L. Stimson, declared in 1940 that he could not support the provision of the Selective Service Act that "there shall be no discrimination against any person on account of race or color." He was even less willing to support racial integration in the military as proposed by African American leaders, saying:

I saw the same thing happen twenty-three years ago when Woodrow Wilson yielded to the same sort of demand and appointed colored officers to several of the Divisions that went over to France, and the poor fellows made perfect fools of themselves and one at least of the Divisions behaved very badly. The others were turned into labor battalions.⁵

In fact, Stimson "saw" no such thing. He served briefly in France with a field artillery unit attached to the all-white 77th Division. He had no experience serving with the 92nd Division or any other black unit.

His ignorance about the heroism and success of the 93rd Division—hardly composed of labor battalions—is astounding.

While professing a hatred for slavery, Stimson—a wealthy New Yorker who was educated at Andover, Yale, and Harvard Law School—would do as much as any member of his government to defend southern values of racial supremacy, as Judge Hastie was quick to point out.[6] Stimson did not hesitate to let it be known that much as it pained him to say so, blacks were too unintelligent to cope with modern weapons, especially tanks and airplanes, and they were wholly incapable of performing adequately as officers. His convictions, like those of many others who agreed with him, were founded on traditional racial stereotypes as well as now well-entrenched military doctrine about the 92nd Division in World War I. Furious, Judge Hastie accused the army of adopting "the traditional mores of the South."[7]

And with the draft of 1940 came a new source of evidence about black inferiority. When tested by the Army General Classification Test (AGCT), blacks on average scored significantly lower than whites, "proof" to the War Department that they were less intelligent than whites, and less able to perform military duties except labor. The self-evident fact that the AGCT tested knowledge, not intelligence, and that blacks with similar years, even if not equal quality, of schooling as whites scored as well as whites did was pointedly ignored. What the Army wanted was black laborers to free whites for combat duty, and the AGCT provided the proof of inferiority the Army was looking for.[8] Over 80 percent of the blacks tested fell into the lowest two grades—IV and V—reflecting grossly inadequate education. Almost all of these blacks, like equally low-scoring whites, came from the South. Yet the stereotype-driven conclusion reached by Secretary Stimson, and by most others in the military, was the same one reached during World War I: Blacks were innately stupid, whereas poor white southerners who scored badly on the AGCT suffered only from educational deprivation.[9] Stimson actually admitted that the Army "adopted rigid requirements for literacy mainly to keep down the number of colored troops."[10]

Even highly educated black draftees were often assigned to labor battalions, and whatever their AGCT score and wherever they were sent for training, black draftees encountered racial segregation and prejudice. White officers and soldiers routinely addressed them as "nigger." The one exception to such prejudice was Officer's Candidate School (OCS), which was racially integrated from the start. Despite the insistence of Stimson and others that blacks could not become effective officers, in OCS blacks trained with whites, ate at the same mess, and slept in the same quarters without any reports of racial confrontations.[11] But OCS was a lone exception to a climate of racial discrimination and conflict that plagued America's new military. At the war's outset, a two-star general, the commanding officer at Selfridge Field, Michigan, far from the Deep South, called all his white and black officers together to tell them that "as long as I am in command there will be no socializing between white and colored officers."[12] He added that he would deal personally with anyone who had a question about his order. There were no questions asked.

At that same time, at an Army base in Pennsylvania, white officers—most, but not all of them, from the South—issued an order that "any association between colored soldiers and white women, whether voluntary or not, would be considered rape. And the penalty would be death."[13] Elsewhere, other white officers banned the possession of black newspapers in training camps. And accepting the demands of the military services, the Red Cross maintained racially segregated blood banks, a policy that continued until the outbreak of the Korean War in 1950![14] Ironically, the pioneer who developed the blood plasma bank techniques used by the Red Cross was Dr. Charles R. Drew, a black man.[15]

Training camps in the North as well as the South were every bit as segregated during World War II as they had been during World War I. Not only were blacks housed, fed, and trained apart from whites, but their facilities were almost always inferior. There was growing tension between the races on these bases, with sublethal violence a common occurrence, and deadly conflict sometimes taking place in the North as well as the South. Some of the worst violence occurred in the North in places like Camp Shenango, Pennsylvania, in 1943, where large numbers of heavily armed white soldiers opened fire on unarmed black soldiers one night, killing several and wounding many others. As one of the black soldiers lay on the ground wounded in three places, he heard a man with a "southern" accent standing above him say, "Where I come from . . . we shoot niggers like we shoot rabbits."[16] Violence was even more common in southern camps, one of the worst incidents taking place at Camp Stewart, Georgia, after a rumor sparked rioting that left several soldiers and military policemen dead and many others hospitalized.[17] Similar violence was reported from several other camps, north and south, including March Field and Camp San Luis Obispo, in California.[18]

When black troops went on maneuvers in the Deep South, something that occurred often, violent confrontations with southern civilians and local policemen were commonplace. These frequently led to an armed stand-off when black troops threatened to open fire rather than allow one of their comrades to be arrested. At other times, unprotected black soldiers were arrested, beaten savagely, and sometimes shot to death by local police and white military police. In April 1941, a black soldier was found hanged, his hands tied behind his back, in a wooded portion of Fort Benning, Georgia.[19] No one was charged. In 1943 in Centerville, Mississippi, a white sheriff intervened in a fistfight between a white soldier and a black one. After the black man got the upper hand, the sheriff shot him to death, then asked the white soldier, "Any more niggers you want killed?"[20]

Black troops expected trouble when they left their training camps in the South, and they were seldom surprised. In the North, they were often ignored, insulted, or denied service, but in the South, their reception was far more hostile. One black officer remembered a white woman spitting in his face because he had the temerity to be uniformed as an officer.[21] Other soldiers were dragged off buses and beaten, or threatened by drivers wielding guns if they did not move to the rear. Many men were badly injured and some were killed. Black civilians were also targeted. During 1943, there were 242 race riots in forty-seven cities.[22] One of these riots, in Harlem, left 6 people dead, with 550 arrested and 1,450 stores destroyed or severely damaged.[23] Shortly before his election to Congress, Adam Clayton Powell, Jr., said that the cause of the Harlem riot was "the whole, sorrowful, disgraceful bloody record of America's treatment of one million blacks in uniform."[24] He did not share his father's respect for meekness.

But even this violence was less painful to many black soldiers than the repeated experience of seeing German or Italian prisoners of war eating and laughing with friendly white military police and civilians in restaurants that had just denied service to the blacks.[25] At Fort Lawton, Washington, black soldiers were so angry about the preferential treatment received by Italian war prisoners that they attacked and badly beat thirty of them.[26] Black officers encountered all sorts of prejudice, too, as Lieutenant Jackie Robinson—who in 1947 would become the first black to play Major League baseball—poignantly described. Many black officers suffered in silence, but Robinson was not one to turn the other cheek. After he refused to sit in the back of the bus while still on an Army post, he was charged with being drunk (he had never had a drink in his life), with disrespect to a commanding officer, and with conduct unbecoming an officer. Soon after the charges were dropped, he was honorably discharged.[27]

Even more than was apparent during World War I, these forms of racial oppression engendered profound hostility, even hatred, toward whites in the minds of many black troops. A former sergeant who had served in the Pacific Theater said after the war that black troops were routinely accused of cowardice, stealing, and rape by white officers who had no respect for them. In turn, he reported that he and his fellow soldiers had "utter contempt" for white officers and enlisted men alike.[28] Others recalled the insults and humiliation they had endured with great bitterness long after the war. A former black sergeant remembered hearing these shocking words from a black soldier after German planes bombed a neighboring camp of white American soldiers on Sicily:

Goddamn, Jerry [the Germans] bombed the hell out of our big-mouth Southern brethren. Well, I do believe Jerry damn near massacred the bastards, now ain't that just too bad! . . . Our camp was scarcely a mile away and not one bomb landed in our area. I felt it then and I feel the same now: they got exactly what they deserved.[29]

Such hatred can be better understood in light of events like ones in which southern white soldiers from what blacks called the "all-cracker" 29th Division forced black soldiers to "dance" in a bar by firing at their feet until armed black soldiers arrived, killing five or six of the white soldiers. A black sergeant who took part in this conflict commented, "I have an idea making Negro soldiers do the jig did not long remain a favorite form of entertainment among the men of the 29th."[30]

When another former black sergeant wrote that the "real" enemy was not the Germans or Japanese, but "whitey," he was hardly alone in his views, as an incident in Italy illustrates. Some white southern soldiers were beating a few badly outnumbered African American soldiers when a truckload of Japanese American soldiers that was passing by, stopped and joined in the brawl. All too familiar with white insults, not to mention internment camps, these Nisei soldiers used judo-like moves along with their fists, leaving the white soldiers dazed, battered, and sprawled on the ground. As one of the black soldiers later said, "It was beautiful. I must admit I felt a little sorry for the crackers who looked like a bulldozer had run over them." The Nisei then boarded their truck, waved to the astonished but grateful blacks, and said only one word: "Anytime."[31]

Black troops were surprised when they arrived in Britain to receive a warm welcome, even by British women. Although the American-staffed Red Cross in Britain refused to serve African American troops, British pubs extended warm hospitality.[32] In response, many white American officers placed British pubs, and even whole villages, off limits. The resulting tension led to several dangerous confrontations in which British bystanders stood alongside blacks, before General Dwight D. Eisenhower issued an order that no attempt to curtail association between black soldiers and British civilians would be tolerated. His order helped somewhat to reduce racial tensions in Britain, but troubles remained elsewhere. Black troops sent to Trinidad in the Caribbean had to be recalled, not simply because they were black, but because that country's British rulers feared that they would stir up rebellious thoughts among the island's large African-descended population.[33] Belgian officials in what was then the Belgian Congo also objected to African American soldiers being stationed there, again fearful that their relatively high incomes and ideas of racial equality would incite unrest.[34] And black American soldiers brawled with Australians in Brisbane.[35]

There were problems elsewhere, too, several of them nearly erupting into large-scale conflict, and rioting at home was not easily avoided. In June 1943, 25,000 white employees of a Detroit plant that made military engines went on strike because 3 blacks had been promoted. William White heard one white agitator with a "thick southern accent" screaming to a crowd in front of the plant, "I'd rather see Hitler and Hirohito win the war than work beside a nigger on the assembly line."[36] A few days later, rioting broke out, again fueled by rumors of rape by blacks and murder by whites that were only too readily believed by both races. After 30 hours of looting, burning, and shooting, much of it by outrageously out-of-control white police officers, 34 people were dead and 600 injured, and the destruction of property was enormous. There were glimmers of hope in the heroism of 3 white sailors, who at great risk saved a black from a frenzied white mob, as well as the fact that black and white workers at the plant itself did not fight.[37] But the racial hatred would not soon be forgotten, and other riots would soon follow.

Even before riots rocked Detroit, Harlem, and forty-five other cities, the racial hatred that had so dangerously divided black and white soldiers, threatening to weaken the war effort even more than it already had, brought several camps together to seek a remedy. Black leaders, including Walter White of the NAACP, joined Republican politicians such as Wendell Willkie in attempting to interest Hollywood in making films about racial tolerance, if not actual equality. At the same time, the War Department's Information and Education Division, now manned by prominent Hollywood filmmakers like Frank Capra, as well as distinguished university professors such as John Dollard of Yale University and Samuel Stouffer of the University of Chicago, were hoping to create a documentary film vehicle to reduce racial unrest. Hoping to improve race relations in the Army, General George C. Marshall encouraged Capra to pursue the project.[38] The task of creating the film script fell to a young black film writer from Columbia University named Carlton Moss in the summer of 1942.[39] Capra liked what Moss produced, calling it "an emotional glorification of the Negro war effort."[40] Others, like John Dollard, disagreed, finding the script "corny," and too likely to open past wounds.

Moss agreed to rewrite the script before it was filmed in black-and-white using the most advanced cinematographic techniques Hollywood had to offer. Finished in 1943, *The Negro Soldier* was delayed by numerous second and third thoughts within the War Department until it finally screened in early 1944. Featuring Carlton Moss as a young minister, it began with a choir singing in an all-black church congregation. With its men in Army uniforms or dressed in suits and ties, and its women wearing dark dresses and hats, the congregation listened intently as Moss read from Hitler's *Mein Kampf* about his plans for world domination and the inferiority of many peoples, including his observation that blacks were "born half-apes." After a clip of newsreel film showed Joe Louis knocking out "Nazi" Max Schmeling—a clear portent of Hitler's fate—the history of African Americans in America's wars from Crispus Attucks to San Juan Hill was shown. The Civil War, a still highly sensitive subject in the South, received only glancing mention with no black soldiers shown, but the courage of black soldiers in World War I was highlighted through film footage of the 369th in action in France, followed by its triumphant postwar march through New York. Its hero, Henry Johnson, was pictured as well. Viewers then saw a montage of black doctors, scientists, and leaders; the growth of black colleges; and the victories of Jesse Owens, followed by the graves of prominent military men such as Colonel Charles Young.

The film continued with footage of the terrible destruction brought about by German and Japanese forces in World War II, including moving shots of tragic human suffering. In response, black men—and some women—were shown volunteering for military service. Racial segregation was downplayed as the recruits were shown training to use all kinds of modern weapons from machine guns, antiaircraft cannon, heavy field artillery, and tanks to combat aircraft. Finally, fully equipped for battle, thousands of men were pictured in their steel helmets, marching precisely, as if they were off to battle. As viewers watched the parade passing by, first the church choir, then the entire congregation, sang "Onward, Christian Soldiers," followed by "Joshua Fi't the Battle of Jericho," and finally, "My Country, 'Tis of Thee."

The film received very high approval ratings by black soldiers who saw it, and nearly as favorable endorsements from white soldiers.[41] A shortened version of *The Negro Soldier* was shown in theaters in various parts of the country, but it was poorly attended. Still, it raised racial sensitivities. A censor banned it in Memphis, an outcome not indicative of the racial harmony that the filmmakers had hoped for, but by the end of 1944, *The Negro Soldier* had become a vehicle for both black and white opponents of racial intolerance. Near the end of the war, the same filmmakers produced a second movie, *Teamwork*, showing black fighter pilots in action as well as heroic black truck drivers in the "Red Ball Express," delivering essential supplies to General George Patton's embattled troops in the Ardennes. Inexplicably, it did not note that many of the bravest of Patton's embattled men were also black.

At the same time, MGM studios produced a very popular film called *Bataan*, starring the well-known Broadway actor and singer Kenneth Spencer as a black American soldier who fights the Japanese in a fully integrated Army unit. Completely accepted by his white comrades, Spencer's character is a paragon of kindness, intelligence, good humor, and courage. Critics applauded the film, and the NAACP gave it a special award.[42] Audiences at the time probably did not know that there were no racially integrated Army units in the Philippines during the Japanese invasion, perhaps because throughout the war, network radio broadcasts in America carefully made no mention of racial segregation in the armed forces.[43]

Despite films like these, both on the homefront and overseas, black servicemen and women continued to be either misunderstood, invisible, or the subjects of unchanging racism. For example, another movie, *The March of Time*, showed black men and women dancing the jitterbug, the dance craze of the war years. After the dance sequence was shown, an interview with prominent psychoanalyst Dr. A. A. Brill appeared in which he "authoritatively" identified jitterbugging as "a generic African-ism."[44] This conclusion must have baffled all those African scholars—something Brill decidedly was not—who had failed to discover this African trait in their own research. It would also have surprised the millions of young white Americans who jitterbugged throughout the war years.

The entertainment industry rushed into action in many other ways. United Service Organization (USO) troupes entertained white servicemen with comedians like Bob Hope and Joe E. Brown and glamorous movie stars such as Ginger Rogers, Lauren Bacall, Judy Garland, Marlene Dietrich, Dorothy Lamour, and Veronica Lake. "Pretty Girl" pinup drawings were augmented by pinup girl photos of Chili Williams of polka-dot bathing-suit fame, Jinx Falkenberg, Betty Grable, and most famous of all, lingerie-clad Rita Hayworth. For music, there were Bing Crosby, the Andrews Sisters, and Glen Miller. None of this was intended for black troops, although on some occasions, black servicemen were allowed to attend the shows. Few entertainers performed for blacks, and for all the talent of Bill "Bojangles" Robinson and singer Paul Robeson, there were no beautiful black actresses or pinup girls. Although Lena Horne sang for black troops at Fort Huachuca in 1942, the great black female vocalists did little to entertain troops, and neither did most famous black musicians. In the United States, the USO set up many clubs where music, dancing, and food were available, but most of these were racially segregated. Some all-black USO services were made available, but they were relatively few in number.[45]

Thanks to the remarkable persistence of Senator Harry Schwartz from Wyoming, a state that then had virtually no black constituency, Congress agreed to make black flight-training schools, such as the one at the Tuskegee Institute, eligible to receive government equipment for flight instruction. The instruction would be segregated, and although there was no guarantee that the Army Air Forces would ever accept black airmen, who had long been "officially" declared lacking in the intelligence necessary for such duty, it was a hopeful first step. Flight training began at Tuskegee while thousands of black draftees were assigned to so-called aviation squadrons at nine other bases around the South. But to the great and growing impatience of many blacks, including Judge Hastie, these thousands of men divided their time between trash collecting, tending lawns, and close-order drill.[46]

In the wake of Charles Lindbergh's wildly celebrated transatlantic flight to Paris in 1927, blacks joined white Americans in their enthusiasm for flying, and although few whites knew it, a black American had flown in combat with the French in World War I at a time when whites "knew" that blacks lacked the brain power to fly. Eugene J. Bullard left South Carolina as a young man to go to France, where he joined the French Foreign Legion at the war's outbreak in 1914, was wounded, and after convalescing, requested and received flight training. He was credited with shooting down two German planes, becoming known to the French as the "Black Swallow of Death." But when he volunteered to fly for America after her entry into the war, despite the severe shortage of American pilots, he was rejected.[47]

Soon after Lindbergh's flight, black pilots made long-distance flights across the United States and, in 1932, a round-trip transcontinental flight. A black woman aviator operated a flying school in Chicago, and another put on aerial circus shows throughout the West. Still, the idea that blacks could successfully fly in combat, or even on transport missions, was rejected by almost everyone in the newly formed Army Air Forces. Nonetheless, thanks in large part to the urgings of Eleanor Roosevelt—who was accused by southern conservatives of having promiscuous sexual relations with black men[48]—the White House pressed ahead with flight training at Tuskegee despite the vocal opposition of Secretary of War Stimson, who adamantly believed that black officers had already proven themselves to be failures and had dismissed the idea that blacks could contribute to the war effort as airmen.[49] Judge Hastie did everything he could to change Stimson's mind, but to no avail. In response, the War Department and senior Army officers "deliberately waged a campaign to dishearten" Hastie.[50]

Despite opposition at seemingly every turn, the 99th Pursuit Squadron began to take shape in late August 1942 at Tuskegee under the command of Benjamin O. Davis, Jr., a West Point graduate and the son of the Army's only black general. He would prove to be a splendid leader, although not the most gifted pilot in the squadron.[51] As young black officers and enlisted men learned to fly and to maintain aircraft, their segregation in Alabama was complete. Because they were not welcome off the base, not even at nearby air bases where they sometimes had to land, Tuskegee became their entire world, and it was a demanding one. The training was so intense that the attrition rate was approximately 50 percent, owing in part to an inadequate screening of the black aviation cadets.[52] The black pilots were acutely aware of the intensity of the scrutiny they were under, with the fear of failure seldom out of mind. When the P-40 fighter plane flown by one cadet burst into flames in mid-flight, its pilot, Lieutenant Mac Ross, parachuted to safety, all the while dreading the accusation that the fire was a result of pilot error, certain to be seized upon as further and very damaging evidence that blacks should not attempt to become aviators. An investigation showed that the fire was due to an engine problem, not Pilot Ross, but he still felt that all black flyers were on trial every time he took to the air.[53]

Soon after black pilots were beginning their training at Tuskegee, the Army took the advice of General Benjamin O. Davis to train a black parachute battalion "for purposes of enhancing the morale and esprit de corps of the negro people."[54] It began to take shape at the parachute-training facility at Fort Benning, Georgia, in 1943, when the Army agreed to commission several officers to lead the all-black 555th Parachute Infantry Battalion, soon to be proudly known as the "Triple Nickels." Joined by black noncommissioned officers and other men rigorously selected for their physical ability and high morale, the 555th grew from platoon strength to eventual battalion size under the always demanding eyes and voices of white southern instructors who, according to one black officer, betrayed no sign of racial discrimination.[55] Although the Triple Nickels reached battalion strength too late to see service in Europe, then Major-General James M. Gavin, commander of the highly decorated 82nd Airborne Division, was so impressed by their morale and their proficiency as airborne infantry that he invited them to march with the 82nd's white troops down New York's Fifth Avenue in a postwar victory parade. Soon after, he integrated these men into the 82nd Division. Widely respected for his courage in combat, General Gavin had learned to respect black soldiers when he served with the black 25th Infantry in 1930–1932. Now he extended that respect and encouragement to black officers as well.

When it became clear by late 1942 that the Air Force had ignored three reports by white inspectors that declared the 99th ready for combat and, moreover, that the only blacks who were receiving any flight training were those at Tuskegee while the others still languished doing odd jobs at the other southern air bases, Judge Hastie finally exploded in indignation, then resigned in disgust. In response, the Army Air Forces predictably enough defended all of their racial policies, but although they had not planned to use the 99th Pursuit Squadron in combat, Judge Hastie's very public resignation, combined with the unexpectedly acute need for tactical air support during the impending Allied invasion of North Africa, led them to relent.[56]

When the 99th arrived in North Africa, it was poorly trained for combat, as were many other squadrons that had been hurried through their training in the United States to join the Allied offensive. The 99th had flown many hours but had received none of the combat training needed for modern aerial combat. Fortunately, Colonel Philip G. Cochran, an experienced training officer, was available to ease them through their growing pains as they learned to navigate more effectively and combine accurate machine-gun fire with the aerobatics needed to contend with experienced German pilots. Within a month, a black flyer shot down a German fighter, and overall, the 99th's performance rapidly improved. However, Colonel William W. Momyer, commandant of the group of which the 99th was a part, became outraged when Captain Davis asked that his men be given a three-day rest period during the fighting on Sicily because they were exhausted. Momyer admitted that the men of the 99th had displayed the skills necessary to be effective fighter pilots but questioned their motivation and discipline, saying, "They have failed to display the aggressiveness and desire for combat that are necessary to a first-class fighting organization."[57]

Momyer's superiors agreed with this assessment, and it appeared that the 99th had seen the last of front-line air combat; however, before this step could be taken, the War Department referred this sensitive matter to its Advisory Committee on Negro Troop Policy, chaired by Assistant Secretary of War John J. McCloy. The committee learned that the 99th had not, in fact, received adequate combat training, and Captain Davis explained that his request for rest did not reflect a lack of motivation. Because the squadron had fewer pilots than white fighter squadrons, men of the 99th had to fly many more hours than comparable white units in order to keep their planes in action.[58] Fatigue was an unavoidable result. While these discussions were taking place, the combat effectiveness of the 99th was improving, and with the growing need for more tactical airpower to cover the fighting on Sicily and the forthcoming invasion of Italy, the 99th was not only retained in place but was joined by other black fighter squadrons. Before the end of the war, four black fighter squadrons would see extended combat as the 332nd Fighter Group.

During the fighting in Italy, men of the 332nd proved their skill and courage in aerial combat as well as in dangerous low-level attacks on enemy boats, trains, and trucks. By the end of the war, seventy-five different pilots were credited with shooting down 111 German aircraft, including one of Germany's new, jet-powered Messerschmitt Me 109s, and destroying 150 other planes on the ground. They also destroyed or damaged hundreds of locomotives, box cars, trucks, barges, and boats, as well as gun emplacements, radar installations, and fuel dumps. By attacking repeatedly, six fighter planes even sunk a German destroyer, an unheard-of achievement that was ignored by the press.[59] Black fighter pilots of the 332nd were awarded close to 1,000 medals, including 150 Distinguished Flying Crosses.[60] Seventy-six African American flyers were killed in action; others died in training accidents.

In addition to these achievements against German air and ground forces, the 332nd achieved a truly phenomenal record of success in escorting U.S. and British bombers in missions all over German-held Europe, including the notoriously deadly air over the heavily defended Ploesti oil fields in Rumania. Although the Germans regularly sent up their best fighters, including jets, to shoot down these bombers, the men of the 332nd had a remarkable record of success against them. Although many bombers were shot down by German antiaircraft fire, no German fighter ever succeeded in breaking though the 332nd's fighter escorts to shoot down an American bomber. It was no surprise, then, that the "Red Tails," as the 332nd was known after their unit insignia, were highly regarded by white bomber pilots. As a former Red Tail pilot, Lieutenant Herbert Barland, recalled:

Naturally, we were most esteemed by bomber crews. This was paradoxical because I never had a bomber guy stop me to shake my hand or buy me a drink who didn't have a Southern drawl. All of the pilots of the 332nd were aware of this. It was probably the one time in American history our white southern brethren appreciated black men.[61]

This appreciation did not lead to integration. Just as segregation continued to be the rule at training facilities in the United States, black airmen were segregated from whites oversees. The 332nd's base in Ramitelli, Italy, was all black—flyers, mechanics, and specialists in intelligence, weather, and communications, as well as ground crews and supply. A former black captain at Ramitelli recalled an occasion when bad weather forced a white bomber squadron to land at this "blacks-only" base and remain there for several days. The white air crews ate in the black mess and slept in the same rooms, with blacks often giving them their beds and sleeping on pallets on the floor. They played cards, had "bull sessions," drank together, and made friendships: "They found we lived the same, spoke the same language, didn't smell up the place, and were doing the same job and doing it well . . . some of the guys actually had tears in their eyes as they bid us good-bye."[62] Captain Samuel Fuller, a communications officer and a graduate of Howard University, observed that it took an act of God to integrate the Army Air Forces for a few days, adding that in his experience only "an emergency or something most unusual can bring about a healthy integrated situation."[63]

Another example came from an incident at Tuskegee when a white major from Mississippi crashed, sustaining serious injuries and losing so much blood that he needed a blood transfusion. Told that the only available blood of his type was "black," he steadfastly refused to receive it. When his wife was told that her husband would die before blood from a white blood bank could be obtained, she urged doctors to use the black blood. A black witness to this exchange later wondered if the major, who survived, ever knew what he was "carrying around with him."[64]

There would be no "emergency or unusual situation" to bring about the integration of ground troops. Most black soldiers had no illusions that racial segregation would end, but those who had been trained for combat saw that as a kind of equality with white troops and hoped to put their training to use as soon as possible. In late 1943, the black 2nd Cavalry Division, consisting of the 9th and 10th Cavalry, among others, was sent to North Africa, their hopes of taking part in the fighting there seemingly about to come true. But when they went ashore, they were disarmed and put to work unloading ships, an action enraging these soldiers and their officers alike. Walter White of the NAACP arrived soon after they did to find them the most depressed troops he had ever seen. Their sense of betrayal was all the greater when it was discovered that nearly 50,000 white "misfits" who had been relieved from combat duty were camped nearby doing nothing.[65] The men of the 2nd Cavalry were certain that they had been assigned to work as stevedores solely because they were black. That the white troops continued to do nothing while the black troops labored long hours confirmed their belief. When White complained to the War Department, he was assured that the assignment of the 2nd Cavalry had nothing to do with race. Cavalry, he was told, were obsolete, so they had no role in combat. The fact that they, like most cavalry in most armies, had also been trained to fight dismounted as infantry was ignored.

White's caustic and angry inquiries about the 2nd Cavalry seem to have had little effect, but those of Republican Congressman Hamilton Fish once again did. Fish spoke out in Congress in February 1944, noting that after twenty-six months of combat during World War II, black soldiers had yet to be assigned a role in ground combat. He went on to remind everyone of the bravery of the men of the black 93rd Division, with whom he served in World War I, and wondered why, after twenty-years of improved education for African Americans since then, black men could not "master modern weapons" today, an accusation still being made by Secretary of War Stimson. Because it was clear that Republicans would attack the administration's refusal to use blacks in combat during the forthcoming 1944 elections, which promised to be close, the White House listened to Fish and pressure was brought on the War Department. The 25th Infantry landed in Guadalcanal, the 368th in the Russells Group, and the 369th in New Georgia. By the time these units of the 93rd Division arrived, however, the fighting had moved on to the west, and all three regimental combat teams were relegated to garrison duty that once again included labor.

In March 1944, troops from the 24th Infantry were sent to Bougainville, where they did see combat, beating off a Japanese attack. They proved themselves steady under fire, but patrolling in the unfamiliar jungle was less successful. Soon after, the 25th Infantry arrived on Bougainville and were quickly ordered to advance through dense, wholly unfamiliar tropical forest. The experienced Japanese easily beat them back, inflicting some casualties. Although most of the African Americans withdrew in an orderly fashion, one company panicked, shooting at shadows and running away from the enemy. It was immediately rumored by white soldiers that the entire 93rd Infantry Division had broken under fire. The black soldiers of Company K who had broken under fire in a strange jungle environment were hardly the first or last American troops to do so. On New Georgia, 700 white soldiers developed panic reactions to Japanese fire as a result of what was then called "jungle fever," in which strange tropical forest sounds, fatigue, and lurid tales of almost superhuman Japanese prowess as "jungle fighters" caused inexperienced men to break down in the face of Japanese fire.

Elsewhere in the Pacific, black infantrymen fought courageously and skillfully. On Morotai, black soldiers of the 25th fought well during a number of dangerous patrols sent out to capture Japanese who resolutely refused to surrender. On one such patrol, they captured Colonel Kisou Ouchi, one of the highest-ranking Japanese officers taken alive anywhere during the war before the surrender of Japan.[66] Despite successes in combat like these, most of the 25th's men spent the war unloading ships or engaging in other service duties that rarely fell to white troops. An officer who served in the 93rd Division at that time recalled that his combat-trained troops, who had excelled in fighting against the Japanese, suffered extreme demoralization after they were later ordered to serve as stevedores. Lieutenant Albert Evans, who had led black soldiers in battle, had great admiration for them but none at all for the "Southern so-called aristocracy" that he believed ran the Army and "would sit up nights trying to think of ways to keep the Negro soldier, particularly the officers, 'in their place.'"[67]

As if to confirm Lieutenant Evans' suspicions, when black troops actually did serve in combat in the Pacific, and served well, their achievements received little official recognition and even less media publicity. When white U.S. Marines landed on Saipan, their courage and skill were quite rightly celebrated in the press and newsreels at the time. However, after the initial Marine victories had driven surviving Japanese troops back into rugged and remote portions of the island, the task of hunting down the armed and still defiant Japanese was given largely to the men of the black 24th Regiment, who for over five months engaged in continuous patrolling and combat against the Japanese. The 24th killed or captured 722 Japanese at a loss of only 10 of its own men killed and about 20 wounded, a performance the Inspector General's office concluded was "superior."[68] Still, it was not until after the fighting ended that it was finally decided that these men were eligible for the Combat Infantryman's Badge and a battle star for their theater service ribbon. *Time* magazine briefly took positive notice of the 24th's heroics, but they were not to be seen in the newsreels that played to large audiences in theaters across the nation.

Included in the first large task force sent to the Pacific were two black Engineer Aviation Battalions, the 810th and the 811th. They used heavy equipment to build roads, bridges, fortifications, and airstrips across the Pacific and in Australia while fighting tropical disease and overt racial segregation and discrimination without a loss of discipline or morale. What they accomplished was overshadowed by the heavily publicized conflicts that sometimes broke out between white and black troops. For example, when the men of the 93rd Division, deprived of the company of women for nineteen months, landed in the Philippines, they found many Filipinas—some of them sex workers—to be quite friendly. Not surprisingly, the African American soldiers reciprocated this welcome in ways that profoundly offended the white southern soldiers of the "Dixie" Division, which had been in the Philippines before the 93rd arrived.

Numerous fights between men of the two divisions took place before some unknown occurrence triggered a massive confrontation. Extending for two miles along both sides of a road, men of the "Dixie" Division lined up on one side of the road with the 93rd on the other side. Both sides had fixed bayonets, and their rifles were loaded and ready to fire. It took the best efforts of senior officers from both sides running up and down the road pleading for peace before the potential disaster was finally averted.[69] On Guam, black sailors and white Marines from the South clashed over the same issue: relations with Gaumanian women. After several nonlethal battles, Marines drove through the Navy camp after midnight firing indiscriminately, and more firing continued to be exchanged throughout the following day. A number of men were killed or injured on both sides. As Walter White, who was there and participated in the subsequent trial, wrote, forty-four black sailors were sentenced to prison terms. Only a few white Marines also faced charges and were found guilty.[70]

Despite deadly confrontations like this, and pervasive racial discrimination, several black soldiers in the Pacific theater reported that they had struck up close friendships with white soldiers, some even coming to consider a white man their best friend. When the war ended, so did these friendships. The culture of racial hostility and separation in America was still in power. Some black servicemen were hurt by this, but others shrugged it off as something they fully expected.[71]

Unlike the Pacific Theater, where even Douglas MacArthur, who had no enthusiasm for black troops, had to admit that they had contributed positively to the war effort, in Europe either black soldiers came under intense criticism for their performances in combat, or their contributions were ignored. Black quartermaster troops, for example, took heavy casualties while bravely ferrying supplies to the blood-soaked beachhead at Anzio, in Italy, acts for which little recognition was forthcoming. A little later during the Italian campaign, black soldiers would become the center of unwanted attention.

Just as the performance of the 92nd Division in World War I led to the Army's conviction that black officers were useless and black soldiers inadequate for the demands of combat, in 1944 the 92nd Division once again became the focus of accusations of incompetence and cowardice. Some regiments of the division had many soldiers with little education, but one that would later join it, the 366th, was remarkably well educated. Of its 132 black officers, 128 were college graduates, several had master's degrees, and two had Ph.D.s. Every enlisted man had at least an eighth-grade education. The unit was well trained and had high morale despite experiencing repeated racial insults at camp A. P. Hill in Virginia. However, when it arrived in Italy, it was assigned not to combat but to guarding airbases. Its morale and combat-readiness suffered greatly.

Except for the 366th, the men of the 92nd Division were not well educated, nor were they well trained. Most of their officers were white southerners, and black officers of the division thought many of them were inferior men who had been "dumped" in a black division to rid white units of them. As a black lieutenant in the division scornfully put it, "The Army decided we needed supervision from white Southerners as if war was plantation work and fighting Germans was picking cotton."[72] Their overall commander was Major-General Edward M. ("Ned") Almond, a Virginian married to General George C. Marshall's sister, who soon rejected the men of the 92nd as inferior in every way, a decision that did not surprise other officers, such as Lieutenant-General William P. Ennis, who had long thought Almond a racist.[73] Almond soon after called all of the division's black officers together to insultingly inform them that he did not believe any black officer should be promoted beyond the rank of captain.[74]

When the 366th, by then ill, dispirited, and broken into small units, was called up to join the 92nd as reinforcements, they were in desperate need of more training and better weapons. Instead, they were thrown into the front lines of mountainous Italy, held so doggedly and well by strongly entrenched German forces. As Colonel Howard D. Queen, commander of the 366th, recalled, Almond's welcoming speech was hardly encouraging: "I did not send for you. Your Negro newspapers, Negro politicians and white friends have insisted on you seeing combat and I shall see that you get combat and your share of the casualties."[75] When Colonel Queen objected, saying that his men were neither adequately trained nor adequately equipped, Almond dismissed him, saying that the 366th would go into the line "equipped or not equipped."[76]

The 366th, like the rest of the 92nd, was assigned to a frontage that was, according to textbook principles, far too large for such a limited number of men to hold. Nevertheless, in the early stages of their combat role, the black soldiers of the 92nd held their positions, patrolled when ordered to do so, and stood enemy artillery fire by moving forward to get out of range rather than withdrawing to the rear.[77] Despite low morale brought about in large part by the racist attitudes of their white officers, who among other things would not allow the division's black officers to enter their segregated officers' clubs, they were generally regarded by senior officers as promising soldiers until early in 1945, when they were ordered to attack heavily fortified German mountain positions of the formidable Gothic Line. Repeated assaults were ordered, leading to such heavy casualties that the men came to believe they were being sent on suicide missions, something that Gino Dinelli, an Italian partisan who was there, grimly confirmed: "The Americans were sending their black troops straight into the front of the German lines, instead of to the side. And there was no reason for it. So the Americans sent these soldiers to die."[78] Some men began to drift away from the carnage toward the rear while others simply took cover and refused to advance. Fewer and fewer of their white officers were seen in the front lines, and morale hit bottom. The Germans who opposed the 92nd concluded that they might fight adequately on defense but that they had made poor use of the terrain, were poorly led, and lacked tenacity.[79]

Black Lieutenant Vernon J. Baker tells a radically different story. Insisting that the men of his platoon of the 92nd who attacked the Gothic Line never "melted away," he recounted numerous actions in which black soldiers fought with exceptional skill and valor. Returning to combat after recovering from a wound, Baker led his twenty-five-man platoon into intense German fire that finally pinned them down. His commander, a white captain, decided personally to go to the rear "for reinforcements," a clear act of cowardice in Baker's judgment. Baker and his men fought on alone waiting for the reinforcements that never arrived. Nineteen of the twenty-five were killed. For his bravery, Baker was reluctantly awarded the Distinguished Service Cross by General Almond, but neither he nor any other black soldier received the Medal of Honor, America's highest military honor in World War II or World War I. It was not until 1997 that President Clinton awarded him the Medal of Honor. Four other black soldiers and two black officers received the Medal of Honor posthumously at the same ceremony.[80]

Alarmed and annoyed by his division's inability to break the German Gothic Line, General Almond complained that his black troops' tendency to "melt away" was widespread but that he still hoped that their battle efficiency would improve. As one German attack followed another, the demoralized elements of the 92nd gave ground, and some eventually were routed so badly that the 92nd's units were replaced. A black colonel, commander of an artillery battalion, wrote to Truman Gibson, who had been in Italy and found fault with the 92nd, that he did "not believe the 92nd a complete failure as a combat unit but when I think of what it might have been, I am heart-sick. . . ."[81] The "failure" of the 92nd in Italy became as notorious as that of their predecessors in World War I. As late as 1970, on the occasion of the 92nd's twenty-fifth reunion, *Newsweek* magazine published an article about "the hopeless 92nd," concluding that the Germans had shattered the division "in a head-on collision. The black troops gave ground, then broke and fled the field. Defeat followed hard on defeat as, two months later, the 92nd was routed again."[82] *Newsweek* did not mention that the 92nd often fought well against formidable German positions, taking 3,000 casualties and receiving 12,000 decorations despite often poor leadership.[83]

That the "notorious" failures of the 92nd Division—some real, some exaggerated, others untrue—should have continued to receive the attention of the mainstream news media is remarkable at a time when African American soldiers were fighting courageously in racially integrated units in Vietnam, having previously done the same thing in Korea. Equally difficult to explain is the failure of the same media to have taken more notice of the truly exemplary combat performances of black troops in the bloody and nearly calamitous Battle of the Bulge in

December 1944 and the subsequent Allied drive across Germany in 1945.

As well-hidden German forces surprisingly crashed through American forces in the Ardennes forest, their tanks protected against Allied air strikes by low cloud cover and heavy snowfall, the Americans fell back in disorder, losing 50,000 killed or wounded during the first week of fighting. Several black units, particularly of field artillery, were caught up in the fighting and responded with conspicuous bravery. One of these units, the 333rd Field Artillery Battalion, was instrumental in holding Bastogne, a key road center that was the scene of savage fighting. The 333rd took heavier casualties than any other Allied unit at Bastogne. Another black field artillery battalion, the 996th, fought so well at Bastogne that it became the first black unit in World War II to be awarded a Distinguished Unit Citation. "The battling bastards of Bastogne," as they were called, became household heroes in America, but few knew that many of them were black. After a month of fighting, American casualties mounted to over 125,000.

Desperate for replacements for badly depleted American units, Eisenhower's deputy, General John C. H. Lee, recommended that black troops who were serving in labor battalions but had some infantry training be integrated into decimated white units at the dangerously fluid front. Lee's appeal was sent out to black units, promising that they would be assigned "without regard to color or race to units where assistance is most needed," where they would fight "shoulder to shoulder" with white infantrymen.[84] Thousands of men immediately volunteered. Eisenhower supported this plan, and even General George C. Patton, another southern general not given to ideas of racial equality, agreed. However, General George C. Marshall, Army Chief of Staff, was horrified by the planned integration, ordering that blacks fight in small all-black units attached to white ones. Disappointed but still determined, these poorly trained black soldiers fought so well that many white southern soldiers quickly accepted them, praising their courage and admitting that they had been wrong in their fixed belief that blacks were cowards. Eventually, Eisenhower praised them, too, and so did Patton. When combat veteran General Charles Lanham later awarded medals to several black volunteers, he said, "I have never seen any soldiers who have performed better in combat than you have."[85]

Major-General E. F. Parker of the 78th Division wrote this report about the black volunteer riflemen:

> Morale: excellent. Manner of performance: superior. Men are very eager to close with the enemy and to destroy him. Strict attention to duty, aggressiveness, common sense and judgment under fire has [*sic*] won the admiration of all men in the company. . . . When given a mission they accept it with enthusiasm, and even when losses to their platoon were inflicted the colored boys accepted these losses as part of war, and continued on their mission. Several decorations for bravery are in the process of being awarded to the members of colored platoons.[86]

Black soldiers of a platoon assigned to another white division, the 99th, were described in a report to Corps headquarters as "courageous fighters and never once did they fail to accomplish their assigned mission. They were particularly good in town fighting and [were] often used as the assault platoon with good results."[87] This platoon was credited with killing 100 Germans and capturing 500 with a loss of only 3 killed and 15 wounded. Another white battalion commander, whose black troops had had low scores on the AGCT, wrote that these men were not only on a par with white troops he had known in "courage, coolness, dependability and pride, . . . they were, during combat, possessed with a fierce desire to meet with and kill the enemy, the equal of which I have never witnessed in white troops."[88] The close quarters shared by white and black infantrymen during these crucial battles in the Ardennes often led to a remarkable breakdown in racial prejudice. One white officer reported that there had never been "the slightest sign" of racial prejudice in his battalion: "When men undergo the same privations, face the same dangers before an impartial enemy, there can be no segregation. My men eat, play, work, and sleep as a company of men, with no regard to color."[89]

Black tank and tank destroyer battalions also fought in the Ardennes and later in Germany. A platoon from the 614th Tank Destroyer Battalion beat back a German attack despite losing over half its men, receiving the Distinguished Unit Citation for their actions. The 761st Tank Battalion had fought its way across France, taking casualties but steadily advancing. A company of the battalion was led by Captain David Williams, a white Yale graduate whose men were initially skeptical about him. But before one attack, Williams called his tankers together: "Now look here, ya cats, we gotta hit it down the main drag, and hip some of them unhepped cats on the other side. So let's roll right on down ole Seventh Avenue, and knock 'em, Jack."[90] Williams' goofy talk eased the men's prebattle tension, and the black tankers eventually came to accept Williams as a good officer who surprised them by actually enjoying combat.[91]

Well known for his racist views, General Patton predictably enough had initially rejected the idea of accepting black troops in his 3rd Army, saying that they were incapable of mastering the complex machinery in tanks, but when his losses mounted and he asked for the best tank battalion left in the United States, he was sent the 761st. Keeping his doubts to himself, Patton welcomed the men with his usual gusto, telling them that "he didn't care what color they were" as long as they killed Germans, whom he described in obscene terms as, among other things, men who practiced sexual intercourse with their mothers. Referring to his widely quoted rejection of blacks as tankers, he told them that he wanted them to make a liar out of him.[92]

The 761st quickly did so, fighting admirably across France despite being unable to find trained replacements for its many casualties. During the fighting in the Ardennes and later in Germany, the 761st continued to drive forward no matter how heavy the German resistance. It was the lead battalion to enter several cities such as Coberg, Germany, that official histories later said were taken by white units. And on at least one occasion, officers and NCOs of the 761st had to plead with completely demoralized white infantrymen not to desert under fire. As a black corporal, Horace Evans, remembered, "They just weren't going to fight anymore and they were in tears. I don't ever recall a black soldier in my outfit crying. I've witnessed a lot of cussin', but not crying."[93]

During the climactic Battle of the Bulge, black Staff Sergeant Edward A. Carter, Jr., of Patton's 12th Armored Division, killed six Germans and captured two others in a single desperate battle although he suffered five bullet wounds himself. When the war ended, Carter was awarded the Distinguished Service Cross, the Army's second highest combat award. Carter left the Army after the end of the war, but dissatisfied with his civilian life, he tried to reenlist in 1949. The Army rejected him because of suspicions that he harbored communist sympathies. These suspicions apparently arose because Carter, the son of a black missionary father and an Indian mother, was born in Shanghai, where he learned Mandarin and Hindustani. In 1937, he fought with the Chinese against the Japanese, then served for two full years with the Abraham Lincoln Brigade in Spain. All of this made him suspicious in that time of rabid anticommunism, but his daughter-in-law, who for years fought to have his military files released, told the Associated Press that she placed the primary blame on racism. Although Carter was finally awarded the Medal of Honor posthumously in 1997, it was not until November 10th, 1999–the day before Veteran's Day–that Army Secretary Louis Caldera issued a formal apology and Carter's military records were expunged of all doubts about his loyalty.[94]

In the last days of the war, the 761st's tanks were running out of gas, which was being reserved for two white armored divisions that were ordered to rush ahead and meet the Soviet tankers. Frustrated, a black tanker managed to convince black quartermaster troops, against orders, to provide the 761st with fuel. The 761st met the Russians on the Steyr River in Austria, one of the first American units to do so.[95] This meeting was not publicized in America.

The Navy was far less willing than the Army to accept black recruits, and the idea of racial integration was repugnant. Well after the war, Representative Adam Clayton Powell, Jr., blasted the Navy as a "modernized, Twentieth Century form of slavery."[96] President Roosevelt repeatedly insisted that the Navy enlist more African Americans, but by February 1943, blacks still made up only 2 percent of the Navy's enlisted force. What is more, two-thirds of these were mess attendants and the remainder were excluded from shipboard assignments. Of the Navy's 20,000 officers and warrant officers, not one was black. Following still greater pressure by the president and Secretary of the Navy Frank Knox, who had praised the heroism of the blacks he served with in Cuba, 10 percent of the sailors drafted in 1943 were black. What is more, a small number of naval noncombat ships accepted blacks in a variety of duties other than mess attendants, cooks, and bakers. Still, at war's end, only 5 percent of the Navy's enlisted men were African American, and the only ones to serve on combat ships did so as mess attendants. It should be noted, however, that when these ships went into actual combat, many of these men took on dangerous roles, such as handling ammunition for guns on deck, and most would gladly have taken on greater combat roles if permitted.

The great majority of enlisted men in the Navy served as manual laborers, loading or unloading ships' cargo in the United States or overseas. Most African Americans assigned to stevedore duties resented the work, feeling that they deserved more equal opportunities. Dramatic evidence that such work could be dangerous, and that blacks felt discriminated against, came with an enormous explosion of hundreds of tons of ammunition at Port Chicago, California. One third as large as the force of one of the atomic bombs dropped on Japan, the blast broke windows in San Francisco, thirty-five miles away, and was felt as far away as Nevada. It destroyed two ships, killing 320 men; 250 of them were black stevedores who were loading the ammunition when the explosion took place. Hundreds more were injured. It was the worst domestic loss of life in America during the war. Fifty of the black sailors who survived refused to return to duty, insisting that the work was too dangerous, and pointing out that only blacks were under orders to load ammunition. The fifty blacks were found guilty of mutiny and sentenced to prison. Civil rights organizations joined the black press in attacking the verdict, and the men were eventually returned to duty.[97] In 1944, another ammunition explosion in California killed over 200 ammunition handlers, almost all of them black. This time there was no mutiny. In 1999, Rear Admiral Lillian Fishburne laid a wreath on the Navy Memorial in Washington established to honor the dead. Admiral Fishburne is an African American woman.

As the war continued, the Navy showed more interest in racial integration, mixing whites and blacks on two ships without incident. Another ship was given an all-black crew with white officers and it also did well. The first black officers were not commissioned into the Navy until 1944, when thirteen new officers were commissioned, all of whom had—perhaps by coincidence—very light skin.[98] By war's end, there were seventy-three black naval officers, but none would command a warship until 1962, when Lieutenant-Commander Samuel L. Gravely took command of a destroyer escort. Late in the war, the Navy began to implement a new plan to integrate blacks on all auxiliary ships in the fleet, not to exceed 10 percent of the crew.

The Coast Guard was far more receptive to black enlisted men than the Navy. Although the number accepted was initially small, Coast Guard officers quickly recognized the ability of some to perform more complex duties. One officer, Lieutenant-Commander John Skinner, volunteered to command a weather ship with a racially integrated crew of 4 black officers and 100 enlisted men and a comparable number of white officers and men. The ship's success with its integrated crew led the Coast Guard to integrate a coastal patrol ship fully and to incorporate small numbers of black crewmen on many of its ships. The Coast Guard commissioned a black officer one full year before the Navy did, and some black Coast Guard officers commanded racially mixed crews.[99]

The Marine Corps, unlike the Coast Guard, had been exclusively white since 1798 and strongly resisted pressure to accept black recruits for as long as it could. In April 1941, the Marine Corps Commandant, Major-General Thomas Holcomb, whose racist views were no secret, made this amazing declaration to the Navy Board: "If it were a question of having a Marine Corps of 5,000 whites or 250,000 Negroes, I would rather have the whites."[100] When the Marines were finally forced to accept black enlisted men, despite General Holcomb, most were sent to a camp in North Carolina, where they would be trained in segregated units but to the same standards as white Marines. The commander of their training was Colonel Samuel A. Woods, Jr., from South Carolina, whom the black Marines came to respect, praising him for his "absolute fairness."[101] The training was led by white drill instructors, but although these men demanded perfection, they, too, were said to be fair and were respected. After their rigorous training, many of these new Marines were placed in one of two coastal defense battalions that were eventually sent overseas but saw little combat. When the Marine Corps was forced to take still more black Marines, many were funneled into duties as messmen, truck drivers, stevedores, and other menial, noncombat roles.

Some 8,000 of these men came under Japanese fire in the Pacific as they unloaded ships and then carried ammunition onshore. Armed and trained to fight as infantry, these black Marines went ashore with supplies while under fire on D-Day on both Saipan and Iwo Jima. Some of them also fought bravely after moving inland on Peleliu and Okinawa. Black Marines fought so well on Saipan that General Alexander Vandergrift, the Corps' new commander, said, "The Negro Marines are no longer on trial. They are Marines."[102] Robert Sherrod, *Time* magazine correspondent, wrote that "Negro Marines, under fire for the first time, have rated a universal 4.0 on Saipan."[103] A 4.0 was the highest possible efficiency rating.

Three college graduates entered the Marine Corps Officer Candidate School in April 1945, but none graduated. Black Marines asked questions about these "failures," and perhaps with good reason, because one of these three later became a lawyer, another a physician, and the third a college professor. Three other candidates followed them and also failed before Frederick C. Branch, a former Marine enlisted man, was finally commissioned in November 1945. He would serve with distinction in the Korean War.

The American military services were even more reluctant to enlist black women than they were black men. Although eighteen black women served in the Army Nurses Corps in World War I, and black women offered their services to all branches of the military as soon as World War II broke out, the services were slow to respond. The Navy took no black women until near the end of the war, and the Marines enlisted none until 1949. However, the Army accepted hundreds of black nurses, who served in Liberia and Australia, and sixty-three black nurses were sent to England to care for German prisoners. Many others served in a variety of roles in the Women's Army Auxiliary Corps (WAC) in this country. With rare exceptions, no matter how educated these women were, they were assigned to the most menial, janitorial duties, such as scrubbing walls and floors. A few were sent to cooks' or bakers' school, but the majority greatly resented the "dirty work" they were required to perform. The only WAC unit to serve overseas was the 6888th Central Postal Directory. The 824 enlisted women and 31 officers of this unit were stationed first in England and later in France, where they were responsible for sorting and redirecting mail. When they first arrived, the women inherited sheer chaos. One warehouse alone held 3 million parcels, many of them filled with rotting food. Working around the clock, the women processed 65,000 pieces of mail and restored order in three months. In general, their overseas experience was a positive one, but the women were dismayed when they discovered that black American soldiers much preferred dating white foreign women to black American women. One black soldier hurtfully put it this way: "We want something we can see at night."[104] However, these same black soldiers became outraged if they saw a black woman walking with a white man.

When the war ended, some black combat veterans believed, or at least hoped, that the racial discrimination they had experienced at home before the war would have lessened. Others had no such illusions. Lieutenant Christopher Sturkey won both his commission and a Silver Star for his bravery fighting with a tank battalion in Europe. When he returned home to Detroit after the war in uniform with his medals, battle stars, and campaign ribbons on full display, he stopped at an inexpensive neighborhood White Tower to order a hamburger. The white girl at the counter coldly said, "We don't serve niggers in here."[105]

SIX

*From Humiliation
to Integration*

A humiliating rebuke at a fast-food restaurant in Detroit was anything but an isolated incident for returning war heroes. Black soldiers and officers who returned to their country after World War II were greeted by the same racism that confronted their fathers after World War I. For example, the following is an often-told, if probably apocryphal, story of a conversation overheard between two black soldiers in France after the end of World War I. Speaking thickly accented "black" English, one man asked the other what he planned to do when he returned home to the South. The soldier answered that he would buy a white suit, white tie, white straw hat, and white shoes, then ask a white girl to join him walking arm in arm down the street of his hometown to the ice cream parlor. He paused to ask his friend what he planned to do. "I'm goin' git me a black suit, black fram haid to foot, and black shoes, I'm gwine to walk slow down de street, jes' behin' you—bound fur de cemetery!"[1]

The same conversation might well have been heard after World War II. Some servicemen had high hopes that when they returned home they would find racial discrimination to be a thing of the past. Most had no such illusions. In 1946, southern mobs beat many black veterans, including some who were still in uniform. In a case that would soon become notorious, a black sergeant who was still in his Army uniform boarded a bus in Georgia to take him home to North Carolina. When Sergeant Isaac Woodward apparently took too long to use the "colored only" toilet facilities at a stop on the way north, the bus driver called the local sheriff, who not only beat the sergeant but struck him in the eyes with his nightstick so often and violently that Woodward was permanently blinded.

Incidents like this one often were actually applauded by many white southerners and largely ignored in the North, but Sergeant Woodward was on his way home after fifteen months of honorable service overseas, and the NAACP was determined not to let the country forget it. Thanks to its efforts, the sheriff was brought to trial, but after listening to him swear that Woodward had attacked him, the all-white jury found him not guilty and the all-white courtroom erupted in cheers. When President Harry Truman heard about the Woodward verdict, he said to Walter White, executive secretary of the NAACP, "My God! I had no idea it was as terrible as that. We've got to do something."[2]

Nothing could be done to restore Woodward's sight, and Truman did little or nothing to end police brutality or lynching, but sooner than anyone imagined, he would take action to integrate the armed forces. Truman should not have been surprised by what happened to Woodward. Mobs in the South had already beaten several returning black veterans still in uniform, and in 1946, before Woodward was blinded, six blacks had been lynched. One black veteran was shot while sitting on the porch of his home—it was not a coincidence that he was the only black to vote in the Georgia primary in his district. Two other black veterans were shot and killed along with their wives in rural Georgia. Crosses were burned as warnings by a defiant KKK, and when these warnings were not heeded, houses went up in flames. Jim Crow laws were enforced even more rigorously than before the war, and there were racial brawls throughout the South, many of them inside military installations, among the worst of these being Air Force bases, where blacks were treated as unwanted surplus personnel. At MacDill Army Air Field in Florida, for example, 1,600 black enlisted men and 2 black officers performed nothing more than routine housekeeping duties. Black troops stationed in Europe faced growing, not lessening, racial tensions as well. In Germany, for example, white American soldiers bitterly resented the all-too-public fact that most of the 25,000 black soldiers there had German girlfriends. Fights often resulted, marriage was prohibited by the War Department, and the commanding general, Joseph McNarney, said, "It will be one hundred years before the negro will develop to a point where he will be on a parity with white Americans." *Newsweek* likened McNarney's words to the "shrill hysterics of

Hitler."[3] Thanks to the opposition of General Thomas C. Hardy, commander of the U.S. Army in Europe and segregationist from Virginia, U.S. troops would not be integrated there until 1952.[4]

Far more loudly than during the post–World War I era, African American activists after World War II demanded equal opportunity, and their voices were heard in many political circles including Truman's White House. Although more and more black leaders called for improved conditions for blacks in the military, in reality, the opportunities for black servicemen were markedly worse in 1946 than they had been at the end of the war in 1945. The Army and Navy continued to insist that both segregation and racial "specializations" such as food service or unskilled labor were necessary, and the Marine Corps firmly resisted calls for greater racial integration.

However, in response to increased political pressure, the Army established a board of senior officers led by Lieutenant-General Alvan C. Gillem, Jr., from Tennessee, to reevaluate Army policy toward blacks. The Gillem Board, three of whose members were southerners, took its charge seriously, evaluating a wide array of information before concluding that although blacks had a legitimate right and duty to defend their country, the Army would need to retain many forms of racial segregation. However, the Gillem report did call for greater use of smaller black units that could be integrated into larger white ones. To the surprise of no one, the military services seized upon the Gillem report as a warrant for maintaining their policies of racial segregation. Senator Burnet R. Maybank of South Carolina declared, "The wars of this country have been won by white soldiers. . . . Negro soldiers have rendered their greatest service as cooks, drivers, maintenance men, mechanics and such positions for which they are well qualified."[5] Maybank had apparently not consulted with southern bomber pilots escorted by black pilots of the 332nd or the white officers and men who fought with black soldiers in the Ardennes.

Black leaders were not pleased, nor were they surprised, by the recommendation of the Gillem Board, and much more surprisingly, President Truman was not pleased either. Truman had been raised in Missouri, where racial prejudice had been a part of the fabric of everyday life, and he had not rejected all of that background, often referring to black Americans as "niggers" during private conversations with whites.[6] Nevertheless, he had openly supported equality for all races for some years. Truman listened when black leaders demanded equality in the military, some even threatening mass civil disobedience if military segregation did not end. Truman was sympathetic to these demands, so much so that much of the Democratic Party, already skeptical about his ability to be elected in 1948, split off into the so-called States Rights "Dixiecrats," who chose to support Governor J. Strom Thurmond of South Carolina, a staunch segregationist. To cloud the issue still further, the Republicans nominated Thomas E. Dewey and made continued racial segregation of the armed forces a plank in their political platform.

Truman may have felt that he had little hope of winning the election because the polls showed Dewey far ahead, and one major newspaper embarrassingly declared that Dewey had won the election before the votes had been fully counted. Truman certainly had no hope of victory without "the black vote," as it was known. Faced with probable defeat at the polls, Truman may have felt that he had nothing to lose by ordering the racial integration of the military, but he also believed that it was morally right. In late July 1948, Truman issued his historic Executive Order 9981:

> It is essential that there be maintained in the armed service of the United States the highest standards of democracy, with equality of treatment and opportunity for all those who serve in our country's defense. It is hereby declared to be the policy of the President that there shall be equality of treatment and opportunity for all persons in the armed forces without regard to race, color, religion, or national origin. This policy shall be put into effect as rapidly as possible, having due regard to the time required to effectuate any necessary changes without impairing efficiency or morale.[7]

The "as rapidly as possible" clause raised doubts about the president's intentions, especially in the minds of black activists, but three days later, during a press conference, Truman clarified the order by his succinct and firm answer of "Yes" when asked if his order meant the eventual end of segregation. When Truman was surprisingly elected a few months later, his answer took on added meaning.

With the exception of the Coast Guard, which had already integrated to some extent, the armed forces were anything but sympathetic to the order. No less a trio of Army heavyweights than Mark W. Clark, George C. Marshall, and Dwight D. Eisenhower had all expressed their opposition to integration after World War II. Unaware of Truman's order at the time that he spoke to military instructors at Fort Knox, General Omar N. Bradley, the Army's current chief of staff, declared that segregation would endure in the Army as long as it prevailed in American society. Bradley later apologized to Truman, who told him that he expected full and rapid compliance. Commandant of the Marine Corps General Clifton B. Cates echoed Bradley's views.[8]

Opposition in the Air Force was based on the racist belief that blacks were not capable of competing with whites in Air Force training. This belief persisted despite the urging of General James H. Doolittle–famous for leading the first air raid on Japan during World War II–that the air force should integrate just as American business was doing. Even after Truman's 1948 election, the Air Force resisted Order 9981 until May 11, 1949, when it announced that effective November 11, 1949, there would be complete equality of "treatment and opportunity," pledging that blacks would be eligible for any assignment for which they were qualified. The Air Force immediately disbanded its all-black units, such as the 332nd fighter wing, and by 1950, the Air Force had no racial quotas or restrictions. Moreover, black airmen lived in fully integrated conditions on Air Force bases.

Despite his clearly expressed personal objections to racial integration, Marine Corps Commandant General Clifton B. Cates ordered the institution of racial equality on November 18, 1949, only one week later than the Navy. All-black units were not immediately disbanded, but race was no longer to be a criterion for assigning a Marine to any specialty. The Army proved to be more recalcitrant. Despite Order 9981, and the conclusion of a committee headed by Charles Fahy, Georgia-born former U.S. Solicitor General, that urged rapid implementation of this order, North Carolinian Kenneth C. Royall, Secretary of the Army, vigorously reasserted the Army's cherished belief that blacks had proven to be incompetent combat soldiers in both World Wars, concluding that they were qualified only to serve as laborers. Ignoring the compelling historical evidence to the contrary, he refused to order racial integration. A few weeks later, he was made to see the need to retire, and with the aid of considerable political pressure, his successor convinced the Army to comply. Needless to say, the adoption of official policy to end segregation and inequality did not guarantee the end of racial discrimination in the military. Nor did racism end elsewhere in America as Ralph Ellison showed so poignantly in his 1952 National Book Award novel, *Invisible Man*.

On June 25, 1950, when 100,000 North Korean soldiers, nearly 1,500 large artillery pieces, and 150 heavy, Soviet-made T-34 tanks crossed the 38th parallel to invade South Korea, the armed forces of the United States were as far from being free of racial inequality as they were from being combat-ready. One of the first ground units sent to Korea with orders to halt the North Korean advance was the still all-black 24th Regiment. Like white Army units based in Japan, these troops had no heavy armor and little artillery and, at first, lacked any weapons that could disable a T-34 tank. Outnumbered as well as outgunned by the North Koreans, white and black American troops alike were able to do little to halt the North Korean advance, firing and falling back, sometimes in disorder. Accusations of weak resistance, or none at all, were made against almost all of the American troops, making the phrase "bug out" famous as both white and black soldiers sometimes abandoned their positions at the first sign of the enemy.[9]

For various reasons, including the historical myth of black cowardice, the 24th became the target of most of these accusations. Some of these accusations were true. On one occasion, the 3rd Battalion withdrew so rapidly that almost all of its weapons, including 102 rifles were left behind. On another occasion, L Company of this battalion had 88 of its 165 enlisted men unaccounted for. Soon after, in late July 1950, First Lieutenant Leon A. Gilbert left his outpost line with fifteen of his men. When ordered back by a senior officer, he refused, and a noncommissioned officer had to lead these men back to their positions. Lieutenant Gilbert was court-martialed for cowardice and sentenced to death, but his sentence was commuted in November 1950.[10] A black officer who knew Gilbert somewhat did not defend his character when he later wrote about the war.[11]

But little attention, if any at all, was given to similar reports from white regiments, which sometimes also had poor officers and inadequate weapons and were frequently panicked by the unfamiliar infiltration tactics of the North Koreans or simply overwhelmed by Korean armor. White units were eventually able to replace inadequate officers and enlisted men, but for the 24th there was no ready source of replacements. It is also likely, as several historians have argued, that some white officers were eager to deflect attention from their own failures by pointing accusing fingers at the 24th.[12] For example, the June 16, 1951, issue of the *Saturday Evening Post* quoted Lieutenant-Colonel Melvin R. Blair as saying that three companies of the 24th had "fled like rabbits."

A black warrant officer who served under Colonel Blair accused him of giving orders during this battle "hysterically and incoherently." Blair later denied making the accusations reported by the magazine, but his credibility suffered further when in 1958 he was convicted of an attempted armed robbery at the Bing Crosby golf tournament.[13] As Thurgood Marshall observed, many of the 24th's own white officers were southerners "who had brought their prejudices with them."[14] The reputation of the 24th Regiment was further tarnished when highly regarded and widely read war correspondent Marguerite Higgins wrote a report about the panic and despair of young soldiers in the 24th. In fact, she was writing about the white 24th Division, not the black 24th Regiment, which was assigned to the 25th Division.[15] There would be no correction until many years later.

There was also more than a hint of racial discrimination in the Army's record of courts-martial. Although blacks constituted only 15 percent of the Army's total force in Korea, blacks were court-martialed twice as frequently as whites. Moreover, they were given far more severe sentences. The Army insisted that this was a product of rank cowardice and indiscipline on the part of black soldiers, but others noted that both the Inspector General's Office and the Office of the Judge Advocate were all-white. When some of the black soldiers who were facing life sentences managed to appeal to the NAACP, it sent Thurgood Marshall, future U.S. Supreme Court Justice, to investigate. After five weeks in Japan and Korea, Marshall found that black officers rarely served as members of courts-martial, that accused black soldiers did not cooperate in their own defense because they felt the proceedings were hopelessly stacked against them, and that four of the court cases that had led to life sentences had lasted less than an hour. Marshall concluded that race bias was obvious: "I have seen many miscarriages of justice in my capacity as head of the NAACP legal department. But even in Mississippi a Negro will get a trial longer than 42 minutes," then he added, "if he is fortunate enough to be brought to trial."[16]

The NAACP was successful in obtaining reduced or reversed sentences for most of the thirty-nine men who had sought help from that organization.

But the great majority of black soldiers of the 24th needed no help from lawyers. They fought very well. A white officer who commanded a platoon in the 1st Battalion of the 24th Regiment from the earliest days of the war has written that although some white officers of the regiment were not well trained, the regiment as a whole trained often and hard in Japan before coming to Korea, contradicting the frequently repeated assertion that garrison life in Japan had so softened these men that they were neither mentally nor physically prepared to face the North Koreans. Despite their inadequate weapons and the overwhelming numbers of the North Koreans, this officer, Lieutenant Lyle Rishell, described his black soldiers and sergeants in glowing terms. He reported that despite horrific bombardments and human wave attacks over difficult terrain to defend, his men never left a position they held without his direct order.[17] He prefaced his book by writing that "the black soldier can be very proud of his devotion to duty and the battles he fought in my unit in Korea."[18] Black Lieutenant-Colonel C. M. Bussey, who in 1950 was a captain commanding the all-black 77th Engineer Combat Company that supported the 24th Infantry, wrote about his men in equally positive terms. Although he did not agree with Rishell that training in Japan was at all adequate, his detailed account describes numerous incidents of great courage.[19] What is more, the all-black 3rd Battalion of the 9th Infantry Regiment was so highly regarded that some white soldiers actually volunteered to join it.[20]

Even the worst detractors of the 24th could not deny that there were black heroes in Korea. Several black officers and enlisted men were decorated for bravery, often posthumously. In fact, the first American soldier of any color to win a Congressional Medal of Honor in Korea was black Private William Thompson of the 24th. Another hero of the 24th was Cornelius H. Charlton, from a family of seventeen children. As a twenty-one-year-old sergeant, he took over when his unit's white officer was killed, leading his platoon against heavy enemy fire and killing at least six North Koreans before being badly wounded. After refusing medical treatment for his severe chest wounds, he again led his men up the enemy-held hill, killing its remaining defenders before he died. Like Thompson, he received the Medal of Honor. Its citation read, "The wounds received during his daring exploits resulted in his death, but his indomitable courage, superb leadership, and gallant self-sacrifice reflect the highest credit upon himself, the infantry, and the military service."[21]

These acts of uncommon valor were not duly celebrated, much less publicized, until much later, and in the meantime contagious stories of widespread black cowardice were everywhere. As a result, as early as July 1950, a few commanders began to transfer black soldiers to understrength white units with positive results, but the Army's overall commander, General Douglas MacArthur, had no such inclination. Not a single African American officer or enlisted man served at MacArthur's headquarters, and his chief of staff, Lieutenant-General Edward M. Almond, was even more opposed to black soldiers than MacArthur. Since commanding the all-black 92nd Infantry Division in World War II, his distrust and dislike of black officers and men had grown. It was General Almond who commanded the allied landing at Inchon that broke the North Korean Army's hold on South Korea. When he discovered the presence of black troops among his forces, he rapidly had them shipped to the rear to serve in various noncombat roles. When replacements were needed for depleted combat units, Almond preferred untrained South Koreans to well-trained black Americans.

When MacArthur complained publicly about Truman's policy of confining the war to Korea rather than taking it into China as MacArthur advocated, Truman replaced him with General Matthew B. Ridgway in April 1951. Although a southerner, Ridgway believed intellectually and religiously in the racial integration of the military. He rapidly integrated black troops into previously all-white units and began to disband all-black ones. These steps were so sensitive that the Department of the Army commissioned *Project Clear*, a classified study by scholars at Johns Hopkins University, to interview officers and enlisted men of both races in Korea and the United States. Whites and blacks alike overwhelmingly agreed that black officers and enlisted men had performed as well in combat as their white counterparts.[22]

While steps toward racial integration were taking place, the 24th Regiment remained all-black except for some white officers. By the time that Chinese troops had driven the allies far back into South Korea, the 24th had become a stalwart force in the allied defense. Nevertheless, many of the soldiers in this now-veteran regiment spoke openly about the racial discrimination they had faced at home and wondered aloud why they should fight for "whitey" against the Chinese, who had done nothing to them. As one soldier put it, "Have the communists ever enslaved our people? Have they ever raped our women? Have they ever castrated and hanged our fathers, grandfathers, uncles, or cousins? Hell, blacks couldn't even vote in certain parts of the country we were here fighting and dying for."[23]

Fight is what they did, month after month against seemingly endless attacks by huge numbers of Chinese, who appeared not to value their lives. A young private, Curtis J. Morrow, who, beginning in December 1950, spent nine months in front-line combat with the black 24th, later wrote a revealing account of what combat was like for these men. Surprisingly, Morrow reported that all his officers, black and white alike, were good leaders and that his sergeants were outstanding. He was particularly inspired by a thirty-two-year-old black lieutenant, a World War II veteran, who cheered his men by his personal bravery and by perpetually singing songs like "Didn't It Rain Childrens?"[24] The 24th did occasionally bend under relentless Chinese attack, but it did not break, and that is something that not all white units could claim. In fact, when the Chinese first entered the war, many white American units retreated in pell-mell disorder, as did white troops from some other United Nations units.[25] Morrow's account of the day-to-day combat endured by black men of the 24th leaves little doubt that they were a highly competent fighting force, more than a match, in fact, for the Chinese, who died in terrible numbers trying, and failing, to break their defensive positions.[26]

There were only 1,075 blacks in the Marine Corps in 1950, about half of them mess stewards, but some black Marines fought at the frozen Chosin Reservoir, where the Marines were cut off by overwhelming numbers of Chinese, and a black Marine pilot was shot down and killed there while providing close support to his embattled fellow Marines.[27] As a white Marine officer who was at Chosin wrote, "Color doesn't seem to be any register of guts."[28] By 1953, with the Korean armistice near, there were over 15,000 black Marines, most of them serving in combat units. Major-General O. P. Smith, who commanded a division in Korea containing about 1,000 blacks, reported that they performed as well as white Marines. One black man became a respected sergeant-major of racially integrated forces, and Lieutenant Frederick Branch, the first black Marine officer, also served capably in Korea. Another African American officer, Colonel Daniel James, flew sixty-four combat missions over Korea in 1953, later becoming a general officer. Two other young black officers who were there served in the Marine Corps for over twenty years.[29]

The Navy expanded by 24,000 African Americans from the onset of the Korean War to the armistice in 1953. Some black naval officers flew in combat, and in a complete reversal of past policy, very few of the new enlisted men were cooks or mess attendants. And even though the commanding general of the Far East Air Forces, Lieutenant-General Earle E. Partridge, did not believe that blacks were capable flyers, one shot down the first North Korean jet of the war and another flew daring reconnaissance missions.

Despite all this seemingly compelling evidence of courage and martial skill by blacks in Korea, as late as May 1956 General Mark W. Clark,

Army Commander in Italy during World War II, and former Commander in Chief of the UN Forces in Korea, gave a talk in his new retirement role as president of the Citadel, the Military College of South Carolina. *U.S. News and World Report* carried the talk, headlined "Negro Battalions 'Weakened the Battle Line."[30] Clark informed his audience of Citadel cadets that during the fighting in Italy, "the 92nd gave, in fact, a bad performance. It was the worst division I had."[31] Although he saw nothing firsthand of the fighting in Korea, Clark went on to say that the all-black battalions used in Korea "would not stand dependably against fire; where they were placed in the battle, weakened the battle line."[32] He repeated his opposition to integrated infantry units because he believed too many blacks in a unit would weaken its fighting capacity. The impact of his words on the South Carolina cadets can easily be imagined. The article also quoted General Edward M. Almond's well-known opposition to racial integration of the Army.

But the magazine also went on to describe those portions of the *Project Clear* report that had been made available by the Army. The great majority of officers who responded to its questionnaire about the performance of black troops in Korea on twenty-eight phases of combat behavior rated black soldiers in integrated units as "about on a par" with white soldiers. *Project Clear* concluded: "As sized up by their Negro and white companions, Negroes in racially mixed squads showed 'substantially' the same number of cases of good and bad performance as white soldiers." The final conclusion of the project was "Integration works in the Army."[33] Once again, the entrenched verdicts of high-ranking officers were contradicted by the observations of officers who actually served in combat with integrated units.

After the armistice ending the Korean War in 1953, large numbers of troops remained in the demilitarized zone along the 38th parallel, with many thousands more serving in Germany and elsewhere during the Cold War years of the 1950s and early 1960s. Until America's entry into the Vietnam conflict in 1965, America's military forces were almost entirely at peace, yet this same period, from 1953 to 1965, was one of the most tumultuous in the history of American race relations. What happened during this period would have a profound impact on race relations within the military.

On May 17, 1954, the U.S. Supreme Court concluded, "In the field of education the doctrine of 'separate but equal' has no place. Separate educational facilities are inherently unequal." Although this momentous decision should have shaken the South to its very foundations, the initial reaction of both southern political leaders and the southern press was surprisingly mild. By 1954, white people in the South had grown accustomed to at least some blacks voting in most southern states, as well as to their occasional appearance on juries and school boards, their occupation of some white-collar jobs, and the admission of some of them to formerly all-white colleges. By this time blacks were participating in both collegiate and professional sports, were sometimes able to eat in integrated railroad dining cars, and faced somewhat milder Jim Crow laws, although hotels, restaurants, bathrooms, and drinking fountains were still segregated, and blacks were still required to sit in the back of public buses. Even after the Supreme Court handed down a decree of implementation of its order, which did not come until May 1955, most of the South appeared willing to accept the Court's decision, which pointedly had set no deadline for compliance. School integration progress took place in a number of southern states, with some of them, including Arkansas, Florida, Louisiana, Tennessee, and Texas, voting to overturn their own school segregation state laws.

But this would soon change. Led by Mississippi, at this time a virtual police state of anti-integration, fervent white supremacy organizations began to organize their war against school integration as if once again fighting for their very survival against what they saw as the "Second Reconstruction." Following Mississippi's passionate example, the South rose up in a widespread torrent of anti-integration activities. Many books were banned, with others being purged from libraries, newspapers no longer carried prointegration editorials or articles, and magazines that did so disappeared from newsstands; television programs were censored or withheld altogether, and many motion pictures were banned. Liberal southerners who attempted to support integration were attacked both verbally and physically, and some were forced to leave the South altogether.

By the start of 1956, over 1,000 black students had been admitted to formerly all-white colleges or universities in the South, but on February 6, 1956, a riot took place on the campus of the University of Alabama over the attempted admission of Ms. Autherine Lucy. The climate of resistance to integration had been growing ever more heated, in part due to the fiery calls of politicians like Senator Harry F. Bird, who called for "massive resistance," but also in response to a ground swell of fear and outrage throughout the South over what was increasingly seen there as yet another northern attempt to dictate to the South what should have been their decision to make, in their own way, and at their own pace. Even southern governors who had previously accepted the principle of gradual integration now joined the segregationist resistance. For example, in a striking turnabout, previously moderate Governor Leroy Collins of Florida declared in March of 1956, after the Autherine Lucy riot, "We are just as determined as any other southern state to maintain segregation." Governor Orval Faubus of Arkansas, who had also previously accepted integration, now also took a strong stand against it. Before 1956 had ended, southern states had voted more than 100 prosegregation measures into law. When public schools opened in the fall of that year, violence broke out in several states.

As this change in the southern temper from gradual acceptance of integration to violent resistance to it was taking place, President Eisenhower took no action, repeatedly stating that "laws should not change people's hearts." And after a federal district judge ordered the University of Alabama to reinstate Ms. Lucy, the trustees of the university expelled her that same day. Eisenhower's response was to say, "I would certainly hope that we could avoid any interference."[34] And he could. The federal government took no action, allowing the University of Alabama to remain a segregated institution for seven more years.

In September 1957, as the nation watched on television, Governor Faubus called out the Arkansas National Guard to prevent nine black students from entering the all-white Central High School of Little Rock. When a court ordered the withdrawal of the Guardsmen he complied, allowing nine children to approach the school three weeks later only to be met by a hysterically violent mob that defied police and forced the children to abandon their efforts to enter the school. In response, President Eisenhower finally took action, ordering 1,000 paratroopers to Little Rock and placing some 10,000 Arkansas National Guardsmen on federal service. In response to these actions, the Supreme Court firmly refused to allow any postponement of integration because of the Little Rock violence. Governor Faubus then closed the high schools of Little Rock, insisting that "I will never open the public schools as integrated institutions." His actions made him a southern hero, and he was reelected for an unprecedented third term by an enormous popular vote.

Inspired by Rosa Parks' refusal to give up her seat in the "colored" section of the bus to a white man, there had been a successful 382-day-long boycott of city buses in Montgomery, Alabama, during 1955 and 1956 in protest against bus segregation, and soon after, in addition to passive resistance, a new spirit of confrontation was born. It came in part through the leadership of Dr. Martin Luther King, Jr., and in part by local organizations that came together to develop a coordinated policy of "sit-ins." Inspired by the Student Nonviolent Coordinating Committee (SNCC), sit-in demonstrations spread throughout the entire South, attracting national attention as well as a number of participants from the North, who exposed themselves to police arrest and brutality alongside young black southerners. Some lunch counters and small restaurants throughout the South began to yield to these tactics, opening themselves to black customers, but the sit-ins were not restricted to eating places. They also spread to hotels, public parks, motion picture theaters, swimming pools and beaches, churches, courtrooms, and many other previously segregated places.

Young blacks and whites came together on rented buses to form so-called freedom rides challenging segregation in interstate buses and terminals. On several occasions local mobs attacked these freedom riders, often beating them severely and burning their buses. In Mississippi, more than 300 of these young people were jailed, many of them suffering brutal treatment. Despite this growing violence in response to peaceful protest, and in part because of it, by 1962 the number of black children now attending schools that had been previously segregated had doubled in a number of southern states. But in two states, Mississippi and Alabama, racial attitudes had hardened dramatically. Mississippi was the poorest state in the union and perhaps the most isolated from national life and from public opinion. Less than 2 percent of all blacks over the age of twenty-one in Mississippi were registered voters. In 1955, three blacks were lynched there, one of them a fourteen-year-old boy, Emmitt Till. It came as no surprise that no one was punished for his murder, nor were any of those who lynched another victim in 1959.

In 1962, ABC made Mal Goode the first black network television reporter, seen by many as a hopeful sign of racial integration. But in September 1962, when a federal court ordered James Meredith to be admitted to the University of Mississippi as a student, the response was dramatic. Governor Ross Barnett personally blocked Meredith's registration, and his lieutenant-governor did the same thing the following day. A week later a force of 320 federal marshals entered the university campus and protected Meredith while he was installed in a dormitory. That night President John F. Kennedy spoke to the people of Mississippi on national television, appealing to their honor and that of the university. The response was a violent attack, first by students and then by mobs of citizens throwing stones, bricks, bottles, gasoline bombs, and other missiles while brandishing clubs and firearms. The marshals fought back with tear gas, and when regular Army troops arrived, they joined the battle, also confining their response to tear gas. The fighting lasted throughout the night, and when troops finally drove the mob away by the following morning, two people lay dead—one of them a French journalist—with 375 injured, 166 of them federal marshals. Twenty-nine of the marshals suffered gunshot wounds.

The climate of confrontation was equally intense in Alabama. In January 1963, Governor George C. Wallace gave his inaugural address by declaring, "I draw the line in the dust and toss the gauntlet before the feet of tyranny and I say segregation now, segregation tomorrow, segregation forever." In April of that year Dr. King, along with Reverend Fred Shuttlesworth and Reverend Ralph D. Abernathy, began a campaign for some degree of desegregation in Birmingham, which was generally seen by the black community as the most racist of big cities in the South. The Birmingham police commissioner was Eugene "Bull" Connor, who chose to close all city playgrounds, parks, and golf courses rather than submit to a court order that had declared them open to citizens of all races.

Staging their first march on Good Friday, Dr. King and his associates were arrested, but the demonstrations continued to grow ever larger, with many of the marchers—a substantial number of them mere schoolchildren—being arrested and placed in prison. On May 2 alone, 500 persons were arrested. The following day, after the police had knocked over marchers with fire hoses and attacked them with cattle prods and viciously biting police dogs, some onlookers at the parade threw stones and bottles at the police. The situation became so tense that President Kennedy and members of his cabinet, as well as business leaders from Birmingham, negotiated a kind of settlement that promised fulfillment of the desegregation orders in ninety days. Governor Wallace immediately repudiated it, and on the night of May 11, after a meeting of the Ku Klux Klan, two dynamite explosions devastated the home of Dr. King's brother. Soon after, two more bombs destroyed the headquarters of the black movement, the Gaston Motel. In response, thousands of angry blacks rioted, attacking the police and being attacked in return. A number of stores and buildings belonging to whites were set on fire, as were some homes of blacks. Much of this was seen on television across the country, with the images of unarmed black women and children being attacked by savage police dogs and clubbed by police officers, creating memories that would not soon be forgotten or forgiven.[35]

National opinion was clearly turning against Alabama. When a federal judge ordered the University of Alabama to admit two black students, leading to Governor Wallace's personal intervention of "standing in the school house door," television cameras rolled, and the melodrama reached a climax. Wallace gave in but ordered National Guardsmen to prevent the integration of schools in Birmingham and elsewhere in Alabama. In response, President Kennedy federalized the National Guard and ordered them back to their homes, an action leading to five days of peaceful school integration. But the following Sunday morning at the Birmingham Baptist Church, an enormous blast of dynamite killed four black girls, one aged eleven, the other three aged fourteen. Another fourteen African Americans were injured. When black mobs rallied in protest, a white policeman shot a sixteen-year-old black boy in the head with a shotgun from behind. Another black boy was shot while harmlessly riding a bicycle.

The well-publicized horrors of these events in Birmingham led to demonstrations across the country against this sort of antiblack violence. Matters worsened on June 12, when Medgar Evers, the state secretary of the NAACP in Mississippi, was shot to death in front of his home in Jackson. A white man was charged with the murder but freed after two mistrials. Even more violence continued around the South as well as in northern cities. In August of that year, 200,000 people, many of them white, assembled in front of the Lincoln Memorial to symbolize the peaceful search for interracial decency. Millions of Americans watched, among them President Kennedy, who soon after sent to Congress the most powerful bill demanding civil rights yet put forward in this country, specifying all of the reasons why racial equality was important to the country but ending with these words: "Because it is right."[36] The president's bill called for the abolition of racial barriers in employment, union membership, and voting and the desegregation of public schools as well as the prohibition of discrimination in state programs and public housing. It also banned discrimination in all public places, including hotels, restaurants, and theaters.

After President Kennedy's assassination later in 1963, President Lyndon B. Johnson continued to give priority to this civil rights bill, struggling in many ways to ensure its passage into law as the Civil Rights Act. The attack against the Civil Rights Act was led by the Republican candidate for the presidency in 1964, Barry Goldwater, who predicted that the North would join the South in refusing to recognize this court-imposed racial integration. Perhaps as a result of his rhetoric, the summer of 1964 saw riots in several northern cities, but when the election came, Goldwater was able to carry only six states, five of them in the Deep South, plus his home state of Arizona. Johnson won a landslide victory.

Goldwater's defeat did nothing to end the racial violence in the South. Black servicemen in the South felt that their lives were in danger whenever they left the comparative safety of the military bases. While Goldwater was running for the presidency, black Lieutenant-Colonel Lemuel Penn was shot to death by Ku Klux Klansmen as he drove home from an Army Reserve training exercise.[37] Three young civil rights workers in Mississippi, two of them white, were murdered in December 1964, and as television audiences watched the sneering defiance of local law enforcement officers, the FBI moved in to arrest twenty-one Mississippians as well as the sheriff of the county in which the murders had taken place. Many more students from the North as well as the South, some of them white, responded by serving as volunteers to register Negro voters. Many of these students were beaten, and at least six were murdered.

The civil rights violence would come to a head in Selma, Alabama. For months, black demonstrators had marched to the Selma courthouse attempting to register to vote, only to be prevented by the sheriff, who jailed 2,000 of them. A state trooper shot a black activist to death in a nearby town, leading Martin Luther King, Jr., to organize a march from Selma to Montgomery. While the marchers were gathering in Selma on Sunday morning, March 7, 1965, Alabama state police attacked them with whips, clubs, and tear gas, and a national television audience watched in horror. Demonstrators took to the streets across the country while thousands of people, including several hundred clergymen, rushed to Selma to join the planned march to Montgomery. One of these ministers was beaten to death. Five days later, protected by federal troops ordered there by President Johnson, 20,000 marchers from all over the country arrived in Montgomery. Thanks to the presence of troop protection the march was peaceful until that night, when a Klansman murdered a woman demonstrator on her march back to Selma.[38]

In August 1965, the president signed into law the Voting Rights Act. For once, the president, the Congress, and the Supreme Court were of one mind. The opposition of southern states to integration and to voting rights began to collapse. But only five days after this landmark in the civil rights movement, the United States was horrified by an explosive episode of racial violence. On August 11, 1965, violence erupted in Watts, a largely black district of South Central Los Angeles. For close to a week, thousands of blacks looted stores, set fires, burned cars, and stoned police and firemen, shooting at some of them. Before the National Guard and the police were able to end the violence, 34 people had been killed, 31 of them black. Another 1,000 were injured, some of them seriously, and 4,000 people were under arrest. Property losses were calculated to be in excess of $40 million.[39]

As the rioting wore down, white residents across the city finally emerged from their homes, where many had barricaded themselves, fearing firebombs or drive-by shootings. Many had been prepared to fire back if that had happened. It did not, but the tension generated by the Watts Riots spread across the country, leading to well over 100 major riots in cities throughout the North and a few in the South. Of these, the worst took place in Detroit during the summer of 1967, when a force of 15,000 police and federal troops was needed to control the violence. Even worse than the carnage in Watts, 1,000 people were injured and 43 were dead in Detroit, over fourteen square miles had been completely gutted by fire, and the estimated property loss was greater than it had been in Los Angeles.

President Kennedy had a sincere intellectual commitment to racial equality, and he had made significant steps toward this goal before his death in November 1963. After Kennedy's assassination, President Lyndon B. Johnson displayed a deeply emotional determination to eliminate racism through his planned Great Society. In 1964, he signed the Civil Rights Act initiated by Kennedy, but in that same year, the U.S. Navy bombed targets in North Vietnam, and Johnson sent more military advisers to South Vietnam to join the ones earlier ordered there by Kennedy. In early 1965, Johnson ordered widespread bombing attacks, and the war that would shake America to its core and dangerously strain relations between blacks and whites was under way.

While the racial climate in the United States was changing from the end of the Korean War to the early days of the war in Vietnam, all branches of the military, some more successfully than others, were making sincere efforts to integrate their forces. Yet it is little wonder that the young black and white servicemen who came into this newly integrated military brought with them fears and hopes about racial equality that were continually challenged by events in the world outside their military bases. They could not fail to notice that the military was attempting to bring about advancements in racial integration and equality that the country at large could not seem to achieve.

While race relations in the United States were taking twists and turns, with significant steps toward lessening discrimination leading to great expectations that were challenged and sometimes shattered by racist violence, America's armed forces were undergoing their own tribulations with racial integration. By 1953, all new draftees, regardless of race, lived in the same barracks, ate in the same mess halls, showered together, and stood in lines shoulder to shoulder as doctors carried out frequent, unannounced "short-arm" inspections searching for evidence of venereal disease. Their basic training was integrated as well, with black noncommissioned officers barking orders at white and black trainees alike. But there were few black officers to be seen. In 1962, only 1.6 percent of the officers in all four services were black, and a decade later, the percentage was only 2.3.[40]

Southern draft-boards had not yet divested themselves of Jim Crow practices. In 1961, an Albany, Georgia, all-white draft board ordered Preston King, a black man then a graduate student at the London School of Economics, to appear for a preinduction physical exam. Well aware that white draftees were addressed as "Mister," King refused to appear until he, too, was addressed as "Mister." After his return to Georgia, he was arrested, tried by an all-white jury, and sentenced by a white judge to eighteen months in federal prison. Free on bail, King fled to the United Kingdom, where he went on to become a university professor and his daughter became a member of Britain's House of Commons. King's many requests for a pardon were refused until February 21, 2000, "President's Day," when President Clinton granted him a pardon to attend the funeral of his oldest brother. The Associated Press reported that King, "tears streaming down his face," was met in Atlanta by twenty family members, some of whom he had never met. King told the press, "This is a wonderful homecoming." However, his daughter, the British MP, called the homecoming "bittersweet."[41]

As the Vietnam War demanded more and more draftees, southern draft boards again displayed the racial bias of nearly all-white draft boards. From 1965 to 1970, only 6.6 percent of Americans on draft boards were black, and no blacks served on draft boards in Mississippi. During this period, blacks made up 11 percent of the population but 14.3 percent of all draftees. For example, a black Mississippian was drafted even though he worked two jobs to provide the sole support of his mother, his disabled father, and eight siblings.[42] In addition to the inequities of the draft, college students, most of whom were white, were often able to obtain draft deferments. One observer noted that from 1965 to 1970, Harvard, Princeton, and Yale combined had only two men drafted who were killed in action.[43] Whites also avoided service in Vietnam by joining National Guard units. In Alabama, for example, with 30 percent of its population black, its National Guard of 15,030 included only 10 blacks. Forty-two percent of Mississippi's population was black, but its National Guard of 10,365 included exactly 1 African American.[44] Despite the widely perceived injustices of the draft, not only did most blacks accept being drafted, but many volunteered.

After basic training, black draftees were assigned to combat units, particularly in the Army, where they often served as infantrymen. In the other services, a disproportionate number became cooks, mess attendants, motor pool drivers, repairmen, or maintenance personnel. The explanation given was that these men had such limited education that more technical jobs, such as typing and operating radar equipment, were beyond their ability. There was some racial tension on military bases as blacks and whites tended to prefer their own company, their own music, and their own card or dice games, and when they left their bases, the two races tended to go their own ways. Most of the racial trouble that occurred in the armed forces before the war in Vietnam began took place outside military and naval bases or ships. Housing for dependents was almost always segregated, and in the South, many Jim Crow laws still held sway. What is more, black American servicemen encountered increasing hostility overseas. Urged on by white servicemen, Japanese, South Korean, and German civilians—all of whom had welcomed black Americans in the early post–World War II years—now avoided them, often complaining about their boisterous manner, loud radios, and threatening manner.

When blacks and whites served together in combat zones in Vietnam, not only did they typically cooperate fully, but men of each race often risked their lives for men of the other. It was common for such men to share cigarettes and canteens, seemingly oblivious of racial differences. The shared danger and physical discomfort of fighting a determined, courageous, and often unseen enemy in mud and steaming heat, plagued by insects, and never sure what tomorrow might bring not only made most soldiers "color-blind" but sometimes forged intense friendships between men of different races.[45] A graphic example of racially mixed soldiers' lives in a Vietnamese combat zone is provided by the French National Television film *The Anderson Platoon*. Named after its platoon leader, Lieutenant Joseph B. Anderson, Jr., a black West Pointer, the sixty-minute film won an Oscar and an Emmy. It was shot by Pierre Schoendoerffer, who had been captured by the Vietnamese at Dien Bien Phu ten years earlier.[46]

In addition to black and white friendships forged in the heat of this war, its horror often left lasting and unwanted memories. Arthur E. Woodley, Jr., a black paratrooper with the 5th Special Forces Group, befriended a Ku Klux Klan member from Arkansas, then saved his life after he was badly wounded. Later, Woodley's patrol found a naked white soldier staked to the ground. Much of his skin had been peeled from his body and his face was badly mutilated. He had lain in the sun for three days as dogs, rats, and insects attacked his body, now swarming with maggots. Barely still alive, the soldier pleaded with Woodley to put him out of his misery. Horrified, yet unwilling to kill "another American citizen, another GI," Woodley radioed headquarters asking what should be done.[47] No rescue could be made in time, so Woodley was told that it was "his responsibility." Unable to witness more of the man's agony, Woodley finally put his M-16 to the soldier's head: "I said, 'You sure you want me to do this?' He said, 'Man, kill me. Thank you.'"[48] Twelve years later, Woodley still had a recurring nightmare in which it was he who was staked out in agony:

> I still have the nightmare twelve years later. And I will have the nightmare twelve years from now. Because I don't wanna forget. I don't think I should. I think that I made it back here and am able to sit here and talk because he died for me. And I'm living for him.
>
> I still have the nightmare. I still cry.
>
> I see me in the nightmare. I see me staked out. I see me in the circumstances where I have to be man enough to ask someone to end my suffering as he did.
>
> I can't see the face of the person pointing the gun.

I ask him to pull the trigger. I ask him over and over.
He won't pull the trigger.
I wake up.
Every time.[49]

As black servicemen learned after World War II, the friendships they made with white soldiers seldom survived after the war. As one black soldier recalled his friendships with whites, "Sure, we were buddy-buddy in the Nam. ... There were a couple of guys I was wounded with, crawled around in the mud together, ate out of the same can of beans and drank the same water. But when we got to the stateside hospital they didn't want to know me at all."[50]

As 1965 and 1966 passed into 1967, blacks began to complain that they were assigned to combat duty far more often than whites. In fact, blacks comprised about 10 percent of the Army but, early in the war, took 23 percent of the casualties, not a surprising figure because blacks often comprised 20 percent of combat units and sometimes as much as 50 percent.[51] For the entire war, however, the black casualty rate was 12.1 percent, less than the proportion of blacks in the Army by the war's end.[52] When black soldiers and Marines were rotated out of combat to rear areas, they were surprised and angered to find that these "rear echelon" troops were almost all white. They were also infuriated by the failure of the South Vietnamese Army to go into combat. It was commonplace for black servicemen to fight with South Vietnamese soldiers in rear areas.[53] It was in 1966 that Bobby Seale and Huey Newton founded the Black Panthers, a militant organization that soon attracted Stokeley Carmichael and the attention of the FBI.

Race relations grew noticeably more tense after Dr. Martin Luther King, now a Nobel Peace Laureate, publicly declared his opposition to the war, observing not only that America's long support of French colonialism, like the current denial of political independence to Vietnam, was immoral, but that the war was diverting resources from programs to improve the lives of poor Americans of all races to the support of a brutally repressive government in South Vietnam. He urged all concerned Americans to raise their voices in churches and synagogues for an end to the war. Many others, from Malcolm X to James Baldwin, Eldridge Cleaver, and Julian Bond, joined King in calling for the war's end.[54]

During the 1968 Olympic Games in Mexico City, when African American sprinters Tommy Smith and John Carlos took the victory stand, they did not listen respectfully to the National Anthem while the American flag was raised as other Americans had done during this and previous Olympic Games. Instead, both men lowered their heads while raising a leather-gloved fist high into the air as "a black power salute." The resulting shock went far beyond the Olympics. Their actions were seen as denying that they were Americans, proud of their country. Instead, they portrayed themselves as different, separate, and militant. When photos of the two men were seen around the world, many white Americans were shocked and outraged. When the same salute was given by blacks in Vietnam, whites sometimes reacted violently.

Some white servicemen in rear areas or naval installations in South Vietnam now openly began to question the loyalty of black soldiers. They flew Confederate flags, paraded in Ku Klux Klan robes, and burned crosses. Blacks responded with "Afro" haircuts, "dap" handshakes, more clenched-fist "Black Power" salutes, and black leather "solidarity" wristbands, while tension mounted. In return, black soldiers were assailed by antiblack graffiti and offended when white servicemen would drive past them on the road, often with derisive comments and gestures rather than an offer of a ride. In response, many blacks began to assert their solidarity by avoiding contact with whites unless required by their duties. Most blacks pointedly chose racial separation over integration. Many must have felt as one soldier did when he received a letter with newspaper clippings about the riots that were taking place in America: "They have me confused, the police brutality and all. It makes me wonder whether we're fighting the right war."[55]

After the assassination of Dr. King in 1968, America exploded, with violence breaking out in 110 cities, killing thirty-nine people. It took 75,000 troops finally to restore order. Many black soldiers in Vietnam reacted with expressions of rage, and confrontations, including fights, often took place. The sounds of "redneck" music frequently enraged blacks just as the thought of black men and white women together at social gatherings inflamed many whites. Despite the display of the Confederate flag over the Naval Headquarters Building at Cam Ranh Bay, black NCOs managed to avert deadly violence by enraged black soldiers, but deadly violence did erupt between the races in a military prison in Vietnam, while angry Vietnam-veteran black Marines at Camp Lejeune, North Carolina, killed a white corporal.[56] White Marines retaliated by throwing phosphorus grenades into the home of a retired black sergeant-major, a man who, unbeknownst to them, had bravely exposed himself to enemy fire to save a wounded white Marine in Vietnam, being wounded in the attempt.[57]

Other serious racial incidents occurred on bases far removed from Vietnam, such as Goose Bay, Labrador, as well as on several U.S. Navy ships and on several U.S.S. Air Force bases. One riot at Travis Air Force Base in California lasted four days leaving one dead and thirty injured. There was a racial brawl on the aircraft carrier U.S.S. *Kitty Hawk* that left thirty black seamen facing court-martial charges. No whites were charged. In that same year, 1972, black midshipmen were elected to the top four offices of their sophomore class at the U.S. Naval Academy.[58] However, during that same year, white cadets at the Air Force Academy were permitted to display Confederate flags in their dormitory windows or on their bathrobes, but "black" symbols could not be displayed. Black cadets were openly called "boy," "spook," "snowflake," and "nigger." On one occasion, white upperclassmen forced black cadets to remain in a pushup position for an hour because they had refused to sing "Dixie."[59] Again in 1972, high-ranking black officers in uniform were refused service in southern restaurants so often that General William Westmoreland had to denounce the practice. In Vietnam itself, heroin use soared, and black enlisted men began to refuse to obey white officers.[60] In a shocking number of instances, fragmentation hand grenades were hurled into a disliked officer's quarters as he slept. Several hundred so-called fragging incidents were recorded with seventy-one recorded fatalities.[61] How many of these deaths were inflicted by black servicemen is not known.

As the war in Vietnam dragged on, more and more black servicemen became openly hostile to whites, referring to them as "Chucks," "honkies," "dudes," "pigs," "rabbits," and other opprobrious names. Violence seemed inevitable. As Lieutenant-Colonel Frank Peterson, a black Marine pilot in Vietnam, put it, "You have some very angry blacks who are here who are going to go back and are going to be more angry once they return. There is a hell of a chance that many of the blacks who are being discharged, if they encounter the right set of conditions, will become urban guerrillas."[62] The majority of black servicemen polled in Vietnam said that there would be race violence after they returned home, and 45 percent said that they would join in: "Hell, yes, I'd riot. If they be kicking crackers' asses, I'm going to get in and kick a few myself. I'm just doing what my grandfather wanted to do and couldn't."[63] What is more, by 1968, only three black servicemen in ten reported that they got along better with whites in Vietnam than they had at home, and the majority expected racial violence to worsen.[64] Not all black veterans agreed with the militants. One unemployed Vietnam veteran said, "I don't want to make any trouble. I don't feel I ought to hate Whitey. A lot of my friends in Vietnam were white and we had good times together. I'm not prejudiced against white people."[65] He was in the minority.

In response to the epidemic of racial turmoil surrounding the war in Vietnam, all of the military services instituted major campaigns to eliminate sources of racial antagonism, including the removal of insensitive base commanders.[66] Colin Powell recalled using the film *Brian's Song*, in which star black running back for the Chicago Bears, Gale Sayers, poured out his affection for a dying white teammate, Brian Piccolo, with positive effect on both races in the Army.[67] The most widely controversial of these changes were ordered by Admiral Elmo R. Zumwalt, Jr., the Navy's new Chief of Naval Operations, appointed to this post in 1970 over thirty-three more senior officers. Raised by his physician parents to hate racism, Zumwalt was shocked by the racial hostility he found, swearing to transform what he called the "lily-white racist Navy" into one of racial equality and opportunity. Zumwalt's racial reforms encountered heated political opposition from southern congressmen and much resentment in the Navy, particularly from his Chief of Naval Operations predecessor, Admiral Thomas Moorer of Alabama, who derided him for "blackening" the Navy.[68] Undaunted, he soon made remarkable strides, sending out a spate of "Z-grams," as his memos were known. Sensitivity programs flourished; post exchanges stocked black cosmetics, popular black food items, and black magazines and newspapers; off-base discrimination was combated; and promotions of blacks were encouraged. Enlisted men were allowed to grow beards, sideburns, and mustaches and to wear civilian clothes on post. Admiral Zumwalt insisted, "There is no black Navy, no white Navy, just one Navy–the United States Navy." A new recruiting slogan was also used: "You can be black and Navy too." President Nixon did not share his confidence. Discussing welfare reform with H. R. Haldeman on May 13, 1971, Nixon referred to a "little Negro bastard," then added, "I have the greatest affection for them but I know that they're not going to make it for 500 years."[69]

Signs of goodwill in the military began to replace animosity in the mid-1970s, and by 1980, the military services were not only integrated but remarkably harmonious. As early as 1972, the Marines assigned white female recruits to black women drill instructors.[70] In 1972, the last full year of the draft, blacks made up 12.6 percent of the armed forces enlisted ranks, and with the onset of the all-volunteer force, the numbers of blacks enlisting in the military rose dramatically. Over 30 percent of the Army's enlisted men were black, as were 22 percent of the Marines, 14 percent of the Air Force, and 12 percent of the Navy. Almost 8 percent of the Army's officers were black, compared to some 5 percent of the Air Force's officers, 4 percent of Marines, and just under 3 percent of naval officers. The National Guard and the reserves also enlisted larger numbers of blacks during this first decade after the termination of the draft, and the number of black women expanded from 3.3 percent of the women officers and 14.4 percent of the enlisted women in 1972 to 10.3 percent of the officers and 27.4 percent of the women enlisted personnel a decade later.

During the same decade, race relations in the military improved dramatically with far greater opportunity for promotion of both black men and women as well as far greater racial sensitivity and equality on military stations in the United States and abroad. There could still be tension, to be sure, but the lethal violence and racial separation that characterized the Vietnam War years had slowly evaporated. The first military action seen by this new all-volunteer military took place in the unlikely location of Grenada, toward the southern end of the Windward Islands. Known to the world principally as the source of one-third of all of the nutmeg grown on earth, it had been an obscure member of the British Empire until it was granted dominion status in 1974. Since that time its government had been headed by Sir Eric Gairy, a man who, though highly eccentric, was staunchly pro-West, but his use of gang violence to maintain his power by intimidating the citizenry eventually lost him all popular support.

In 1979, Maurice Bishop, a socialist leader of a reform movement, staged a bloodless coup, promising all Grenadans economic and political reforms while turning the island into a socialist democracy. Bishop's coup had no sooner taken place than Cuban shipments of military weaponry, including some heavy weapons and Russian armored cars, landed. Even more troubling to the United States was Cuba's promise to build a large, potentially military, airfield on the island. Grenada soon received advisers from Russia, North Korea, East Germany, Bulgaria, and Libya not to mention a large number of Cubans, nearly 800 of whom were paramilitary construction workers sent to begin work on the airfield. The administration of President Jimmy Carter paid little heed to these developments, although the United States did send aid to neighboring democracies that expressed concern over the Cuban presence. But with the election of Ronald Reagan in 1982, the attitude of the United States changed dramatically. Grenada was no longer a minor irritant; it became a crucial threat to U.S. national security.

In October 1983, Bernard Coard, who led the communist faction within the government, carried out a coup, placing Bishop under house arrest and, in the eyes of the United States, endangering some 1,000 Americans on the island, 600 of whom were students at the Saint George University School of Medicine. When Bishop's supporters soon after attempted to free him from house arrest, troops from the People's Revolutionary Army drove them away, killing at least fifty and wounding at least that many others. Bishop and three of his most senior supporters were then forced to kneel on a basketball court and were shot to death.

The response of the United States was to mount a large military operation employing Marines, Army Special Forces, airborne battalions, and naval and Air Force personnel. Called Operation Urgent Fury, America's military response was typified by blunders, with landings taking place in the wrong areas, empty barracks being besieged for hours, helicopters crashing into each other, and inexplicable confusion on all sides. Despite this almost comical blundering, the operation secured Grenada in a matter of a few days at the cost of 19 American lives with 116 others wounded. Grenada lost 45 soldiers killed in action with others wounded. Cuban losses amounted to 24 dead, 59 wounded, and 650 captured. Press coverage of the fighting made no mention of the racial composition of the U.S. forces. It was noted, however, that the U.S. Army awarded 8,612 medals, although only about 7,000 troops had actually gone onshore.

In late December 1989, the United States embarked on its largest military mission since Vietnam, an attack on Panama. The purpose of the military action was to capture the country's dictator and one-time U.S. informant, Manuel Noriega, to install the democratically elected government in Panama, and to disarm the Panamanian Defense Force. These aims were accomplished with far greater skill than was demonstrated in Grenada, with men and women in several branches of the service displaying considerable heroism and skill as the Panamanian troops were quickly overcome and disarmed. Called Operation Just Cause, the invasion of Panama cost 23 U.S. lives with 323 men and women wounded. Almost 300 Panamanian soldiers were killed, and another 120 or so were wounded. At least 300 Panamanian civilians were also killed, and many hundreds of others were injured. Significantly, once again American press coverage, including television reporting, which was prominent throughout the action, paid no particular attention to the racial composition of the American forces.

By 1990 it was generally agreed that compared to their draftee predecessors, the men and women of the all-volunteer Army were better educated, more literate technically, better trained, better motivated, and much less likely to abuse alcohol or drugs, or indeed to present any other kind of disciplinary problem.[71] On the other hand, however, compared to the young unmarried white males of the draftee military, the all-volunteer military was composed of an unprecedented proportion of minorities, women, married couples, single parents, and part-time reservists. Much of this changed composition of the military was due to greatly improved pay schedules as well as better housing, better conditions on military facilities, and much better dependent-related benefits as well as postservice educational benefits for the volunteers.

Many commentators were pleased to observe that racial minorities, including women who faced poor civilian employment opportunities, were able to enjoy relatively better economic and social benefits during peacetime military service. That many of these men and women chose to remain in the military by reenlisting was seen as further evidence of their maturity, experience, and continuing skill in the operation of ever more sophisticated military systems. Many of these benefits were enjoyed by black men and women, but it was noted by many concerned observers that should there be serious military action, they would suffer a disproportionately large number of casualties, just as they had in Vietnam.

These fears were put to the test in August 1990, when Iraq invaded and occupied Kuwait. In President George Bush's massive military buildup, 25 percent of the military personnel sent to the Persian Gulf were African American. Over 33,000 women were sent to the Persian Gulf as well, many of them black and many of them in assignments that could place them under enemy fire. As it happened, the fighting was over in a few days and only twenty-seven black soldiers were killed, about 15 percent of the total American deaths. Thirteen American women died, including five who were considered combat fatalities; two others were taken prisoner, one of whom was raped and tortured.[72]

Thanks to the overwhelming technical superiority of the allied forces, British and French as well as American, the ground fighting ended before severe casualties were taken on the allied side, although perhaps 10,000 Iraqis were killed, mostly by allied air attacks. As had happened in Grenada and Panama, the fully integrated American armed forces made comparisons of heroism or skill on the part of the races impossible. Individuals of white, black, and Hispanic backgrounds all received honors for their heroism, and there were no apparent accusations of cowardice on the part of any racial group. In fact, most written accounts of this war make no mention of the racial composition of American forces.[73]

This record of racial integration is remarkable because at that same point in history, one of this country's worst race riots was ignited, first by the 1991 televised police beating of Rodney King in Los Angeles, followed in early 1992 by the rioting that exploded after the acquittal of the police officers who were involved. At least 54 people were killed, some while television cameras captured the violence. Over 2,000 were injured, many seriously, including white truck driver Reginald Denny, whom millions saw being battered and stoned by triumphant black assailants. More than 800 buildings were burned, leaving South Central Los Angeles a fire-gutted wasteland. The Rodney King case changed the Los Angeles police department just as it changed people's perception of police brutality across America.[74] But it did not trigger racial violence in the United States military.

Late in 1992, the role of race in America's military operations would take on a new dimension. Widespread starvation in Somalia, brought about by drought as well as the brutal oppression of competing warlords, brought to Somalia a humanitarian effort by the United Nations that involved black American soldiers, sailors, Marines, and airmen. These men and women found themselves deeply troubled by the opposition to their efforts on the part of the Somalis. Many of the victims of American fire in Grenada were of African ancestry, as were some in Panama. Veterans of those two conflicts left little or no record of their feelings about killing fellow blacks. In Somalia that would change.

Begun in December 1992, Operation Restore Hope was intended to help end the famine in Somalia brought about by interclan warfare and the anarchy that had resulted when all government offices closed, leaving the country without electricity, water, sanitation, postal service, hospitals, schools, or police. Most Somali professionals, merchants, and civil servants fled the country. Warlords ruled their followers by their control over sacks of grain piled up in city warehouses, while clan rivals engaged in banditry, theft, and open warfare.

Along with some 13,000 troops sent by twenty countries under United Nations mandate, 25,000 American servicemen and women were sent to Somalia, where for over a year they established some degree of police security for many of the Somali people, built roads, dug wells and latrines, created water purification systems, vaccinated children, and performed wonders of food distribution under the watchful, and usually hostile, eyes of warlords and their followers. The American forces were racially mixed with about 30 percent being black and still others Hispanic. Among the UN forces, only the American troops included women, 12 percent of the total force committed.[75]

Told that Operation Restore Hope was a humanitarian mission, the Americans expected it to be like the relief action that U.S. forces had carried out so well six months earlier in Florida after Hurricane Andrew devastated a large area. In Florida, they carried no weapons and were welcomed by grateful Americans who had survived the terrible storm but lost their homes. Expecting a similar reception in Somalia, most were shocked to find themselves in the capital city of Mogadishu facing sullen, even hostile, crowds who demanded food even though markets were open and food appeared to be plentiful. Despite all the help the black troops provided, crowds cursed them, called them "nigger" and *adoorn* (slave), threw stones at them, tried to grab the sunglasses off their faces, and stole everything they possibly could. Sometimes, they even sniped at both black and white Americans, who were under strict orders not to return fire unless they knew exactly who had fired the shot and no one else was in the line of a return shot.[76] Other UN troops were under no such orders, often returning fire and killing Somalis.

Many American service people, like those of other countries, came to see the Somalis not as the victims of misfortune, but as ungrateful, lazy, even evil people. White Americans often expressed these sentiments openly and sometimes beat Somalis against orders. Their actions perplexed black soldiers, who were at once appalled by Somali conduct but sympathetic to them as Africans. Black women troops were especially sensitive to white hatred of Somalis. As one woman put it, "There was a lot of hate showed [*sic*] in the beginning from white soldiers toward the Somalians."[77] Another complained that even black male soldiers were too aggressive toward the Somalis: "No women are being heard wanting to beat a kid" (for stealing).[78] Black Americans of both sexes were offended by the frequent anti-Somali tirades by white servicemen, including "jokes" about wanting to shoot them or run them down.

This hostility had a racial basis, but except in rural areas, where American forces were seldom sent, the Somalis often went out of their way to provoke the peacekeepers, and their occasional sniper fire was not meant simply to harass. The Americans suffered a higher percentage of casualties in Somalia than they did in the Gulf War, and the television images of an American soldier's body being dragged through the streets of Mogadishu by exultant Somalis were not easily forgotten by the now furious and bewildered Americans. In an attempt to capture two Somali warlords in Mogadishu, American Rangers mounted a major campaign, surrounding the city and exchanging heavy fire with the Somalis. After days of heavy fighting, the Somali resistance faded away but not until 18 Americans had been killed and 75 wounded. One man was held prisoner for eleven days before being released. Over 500 Somalis were killed, and twice that number were wounded.[79] Except for this battle in Mogadishu, throughout the sixteen months of Operation Restore Hope, Americans killed only 2 Somalis. Troops from other nations killed many more.[80]

Despite all the frustration and confusion that American troops experienced throughout their "humanitarian" mission to Somalia, "the level of discipline and cooperation within the units was strikingly high. Physical conflicts between soldiers were practically unknown," reported two sociologists who lived with troops in Somalia during May 1993 and found the mood in the soldiers' compound "almost mellow."[81] This could not have been said about American troops in Vietnam, but it mirrored the pattern seen in 1991 during the Gulf War, when race relations were not an issue and racial conflict was not reported by military sources or the press.

What is more, the mission to Somalia convinced many black Americans that their commonalities with Africans had been romanticized. A black sergeant-major spoke for many of his comrades when he said: "I deployed as an American and I'll come back as an American. This talk about our ancestors coming from here has it wrong. My people are from East Texas. I learned a lot about race the hard way back home. But in the Army we should all be brothers in the same church."[82]

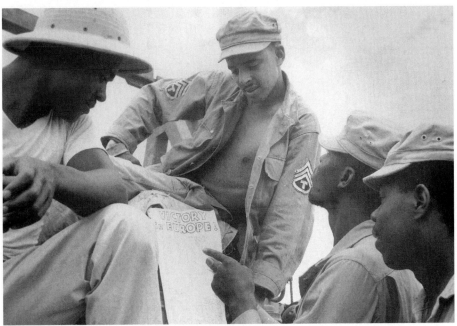

TOP: African American Marines move through the trenches on the beach of Peleliu Island during battle in September 1944. (National Archives). *BOTTOM:* Black troops in Burma stop work to read President Truman's Proclamation of Victory in Europe. (National Archives).

TOP: Pvt. Jonathon Hoag is awarded the croix de guerre by General Alphonse Juin for courage in treating wounded, even though he, himself, was wounded. Pozzuoli area, Italy. (National Archives). *BOTTOM LEFT:* Cautiously advancing through the jungle while on patrol in Japanese territory, this member of the 93rd Infantry Division is among the first African American foot soldiers to go into action in the South Pacific theater, May 1944. (National Archives). *BOTTOM RIGHT:* Troops of a field artillery battery emplace a 155mm howitzer in France, June 1944. (National Archives).

TOP: This African American combat patrol of the allegedly "cowardly" 92nd Division advanced three miles north of the furthermost point occupied by American troops to contact an enemy machine gun nest in Italy, August 1944. (National Archives).
BOTTOM: Marine Corp Pfc. Luther Woodward with the Silver Star awarded to him for "his bravery, initiative and battle-cunning" while fighting in the Pacific. (National Archives).

TOP: Brig. General Benjamin O. Davis in France, August 1944. (National Archives).
BOTTOM: African American soldiers lay a smoke screen to cover bridge-building activities across the Saar River in Germany, December 1944. (National Archives).

TOP: Pilots of the U.S. Army Air Forces fighter squadron, credited with shooting down eight of the twenty-eight German planes destroyed in dogfights over the new Allied beachheads south of Rome, January 1944. (National Archives). *MIDDLE:* Sharing credit for African American fighter pilots' victories are two mechanics. Their squadron shot down twelve German fighter planes in two days early in 1944. (National Archives). *BOTTOM:* Black troops of the 24th Infantry wait to advance behind a tank assault of the Japanese on Bougainville, 1944. (National Archives).

TOP: Enlisted men aboard the USS *Ticonderoga* celebrate the news of Japan's surrender. (National Archives). *BOTTOM:* Men of the 24th Infantry Regiment move up to the firing line in Korea, soon after the Korean War broke out. (National Archives).

Top: Six gunners join hands as a part of 17th Bomb Wing night interdiction teams in Korea. (National Archives). *Bottom:* Sergeant First Class Major Cleveland, weapons squad leader, points out North Korean position to his machine gun crew in 1950. (National Archives).

TOP: Operation "Oregon," a search and destroy mission conducted in Vietnam. An infantryman is lowered into a tunnel by members of the reconnaissance platoon. (National Archives). *MIDDLE:* President Lyndon Johnson meets soldiers stationed at Fort Campbell, Kentucky, in July 1966. (© Bettmann/CORBIS) *BOTTOM:* A female American soldier rests during a United Nations peacekeeping operation in Haiti. (© Peter Turnley/CORBIS)

SEVEN

Black Soldiers in Other Armies

In our effort to understand why black men were so long excluded from America's fighting forces while being subjected to contempt, ridicule, and vilification, it is necessary to examine the roles played by men of African ancestry in the military forces of other societies such as early empires, the Islamic world, and various European colonial powers. What we will find there is radically different from the American experience. In all of these military forces, Africans not only were warriors but were regarded as exceptionally brave. For example, Africans are known to have played a part in Egypt's armies from as early as 2,800 B.C., some of them apparently in roles of authority. They also served in the Roman legions, although their accomplishments are little known and only a few appear to have become officers. Rome's arch-enemy state, Carthage, on the other hand, was led by its famous general Hannibal, who was described at the time as possessing African ancestry, something that the only known portrait of him appears to support. Like the Romans, Greeks disparaged African slaves more than European ones, but just as African slaves served in Roman legions, slaves from Ethiopia and even as far south as East Africa fought well in the armies of Xerxes and Gelon.[1]

A little known but instructive example of Africans serving as highly esteemed warriors comes from the Islamic world. The institution of military slavery was of central importance throughout the Muslim world from Spain in the west all the way east to South Asia. Although slaves sometimes were used as warriors in other parts of the world as different as Mongolia and Venezuela, in the Islamic world slaves were acquired for the sole purpose of serving as full-time professional soldiers. The reasons for reliance on slaves as full-time soldiers in the Islamic world are complex, but there is no doubt that from the earliest times well into the nineteenth century, Muslim dynasties and later, Islamic nations, relied heavily, sometimes even exclusively, on slaves to man their armies.[2]

Purchased or captured in Central Asia, Turkey, Persia, Greece, Africa, the Caucasus, and elsewhere, boys aged eleven or twelve would be inducted into military regiments made up exclusively of slaves. Handsomely uniformed, well fed, and sexually provided for by other male slaves, these young men trained for several years to learn the arts of war, often as elite cavalry. They were taught to develop intense loyalty to their masters and their fellow slave soldiers alike. Later in life, many of these professional slave soldiers took on major political roles, some becoming remarkably wealthy and powerful.[3] From Morocco and Egypt, through parts of West Africa, to Yemen and Pakistan, slave soldiers protected and expanded their leaders' power, wealth, and political control. Their bravery was legendary, just as the intelligence of many led them to great achievements later in life. Berbers, Greeks, Persians, and Slavs all made good military slaves, and Turks were especially sought after as slave soldiers because of their exceptional courage in warfare. But despite the remarkable valor and military skill of the Turks, the most frequently used people as military slaves were Africans, an unmistakable, enduring measure of their heroism and success in battle.[4] One cannot help wondering why for so many hundreds of years their masters never came to see what the Americans did, that they were "natural cowards."

While Islamic armies were relying on African slaves to become their professional soldiers, black armies were growing in strength over much of Africa. The earliest Arab and European visitors to sub-Saharan Africa recorded the presence of huge, heavily armed military forces. Ibn Battuta described an army of 100,000 men with 10,000 cavalry when he visited Mali in 1337. Somewhat later, Europeans such as Vasco de Gama saw armies nearly this large farther south in West Africa. Warfare was commonplace, if not quite universal, in precolonial Africa, and the advent of European trade offering guns and gunpowder for gold, ivory, and especially slaves led to greatly increased combat as the armies of more powerful kingdoms conquered weaker ones to capture prisoners for sale.

It was this world that Portuguese explorers encountered when they sailed along the coast of West Africa in the mid-1500s. But it was not primarily into West Africa, with its formidable armies, that the Portuguese sent troops, but to militarily weak Angola farther south. From the mid-1500s until late in the seventeenth century, Portugal's regular army troops, ably assisted by African soldiers trained to fight loyally and well, were so successful in defeating small, poorly armed tribal forces in Angola that they were eventually able to ship perhaps 8 million slaves from there to Brazil. Later, Portuguese authorities learned to make good use of Angolan men to serve alongside their own soldiers. The same pattern later took place in Mozambique on Africa's East Coast, although the early Portuguese success in conquering African tribal forces in Guiné (now Guinea-Bissau) and Angola was not matched there, where better-armed and better-led African soldiers held them at bay. Also, unlike the New World, where Spanish-borne diseases decimated the Indians, African diseases in Mozambique devastated the Portuguese, whose horses and men died in great numbers.

Not until many years later, when the Portuguese learned to train and rely on African soldiers of their own, were their holdings in Africa reasonably secure.[5] In time, the Portuguese Army recruited so many African soldiers that 50 percent of its force in Mozambique, 42 percent in Angola, and 21 percent in Guiné was African.[6] These men were so loyal that they engaged in no known rebellion or mass desertion. Instead, they earned a reputation among the Portuguese as "fearless soldiers."[7]

The first Europeans to arrive in Africa and the last European colonial power to leave it, the Portuguese have long proclaimed their lack of racial prejudice as a factor promoting their longevity in Africa. In reality, their treatment of slaves was every bit as brutal as that of other European slave-trading nations. For many years, slaves in Brazil were killed and flogged horrendously with utter impunity, even sadistic glee.[8] Slave mistresses could be as cruel as slave masters, especially when a slave woman was suspected of having sexual relations with the master, a common enough occurrence. Such mistresses were known to have slave women's breasts cut off, their fingernails pulled out, and their faces disfigured. One mistress ordered a slave woman's eyes to be gouged out, then served them to her husband for dinner floating in fresh blood in a jelly dish.[9] Slave life was so demanding that the average life of a slave working in Brazilian mines or plantations was only seven to ten years.[10] What is more, a continuing sense of white superiority has been documented in metropolitan Portugal, Brazil, and Africa.[11] Among other things, white Portuguese were racist enough to coin sayings such as "White women were for marriage, mulatto women for sex, and black women for work."[12] However, unlike the Goans, whom the Portuguese ruled in India and described as absolutely useless because "they cannot even defend their own homes," they saw Africans as fearless soldiers.[13]

Maria Luisa Benedita da Silva, the first black woman elected to the Brazilian senate, recently complained that although blacks comprise almost 50 percent of Brazil's population they are underrepresented in business, politics, and the military.[14] That relatively few Brazilians are represented in these aspects of Brazilian society or in elite positions of any kind is beyond dispute, but blacks have long played a major role in Brazil's Army and Navy.[15] They fought alongside white Brazilians against Indians, and later against the Dutch, French, and Paraguayans. Their bravery was "universally acclaimed."[16] Originally they served as a militia—slaves mixed with free blacks—then as racially segregated battalions, but eventually served in integrated army units or navy crews well before integration took place in the U.S. military.[17] Some became officers.[18] In 1910, Georges Clemenceau, who would become the premier of France in World War I, visited Brazil, where he praised the German- and French-trained Brazilian Army, with its large number of *hommes de couleur,* for its efficiency and discipline.[19]

Brazil did attempt to impose a humble, docile "Sambo" role—*Pae João*—on its slaves but it did not take hold. Instead, its slaves remained defiant, frequently escaping and often violently fighting back. Many joined together to form their own societies, called *quilombos*, in remote areas of the country, sometimes remaining free for many years. Some of these slaves were Muslims taken from the Sudan, and as Brazilian historian Arthur Ramos put it, "These courageous, warlike and aggressive blacks refused to become docile slaves in the New World."[20] Over history, the courage of blacks in Brazil's military was not only "universally acclaimed" but attributed to their warlike African heritage.[21] In a complete reversal of the American depiction of its black population as natural cowards, white Brazilians from Portugal, Italy, and elsewhere in Europe agreed that black Brazilians were "natural warriors."

A similar pattern emerged in Mexico under Spanish rule. A free African sailed with Columbus on his second expedition of 1493, and soon after, African slaves were brought to Mexico in significant numbers to replace Indian slaves. As early as 1537, African slaves rebelled in large numbers, fighting hard but eventually being overwhelmed by much better armed Spanish troops. Black slaves in Mexico soon ran away in large numbers. Known as *cimarrones,* they stole muskets, set up their own villages, and often defeated the Spanish troops sent against them. Black slaves were typically described by the Spaniards as "fierce," "bellicose," and "ferocious," and although the Spaniards thought them culturally and, to some extent, racially inferior, they were seen as so warlike that it was imperative to keep firearms away from them.[22] Like Brazilian slaves, they were considered natural warriors.

The next European powers to invade Africa, then train Africans to fight alongside them, were Britain and France, but because their engagement with Africans as warriors was so intensive and so well documented, we will discuss their experiences more fully later in this chapter. The Italians, Belgians, and Germans did not establish much of a military presence in Africa until the 1880s, but the histories of their conflicts with Africans and their utilization of them as soldiers are worth considering. King Leopold of Belgium made what later became known as the Belgian Congo his private treasure trove, killing perhaps 10 million men and women and mutilating others in his utterly ruthless quest for the riches that rubber and ivory could bring him.[23] Even after Leopold's butchery was condemned by the world community, the Congo remained a source of wealth for Belgium and a continuing problem for Belgian troops, who were hard-pressed to protect the interest of Belgian citizens and the Belgian government during the Congo's struggle for independence, which resulted in the creation of Zaire, to this day a terribly troubled state.

Zaire's wealth was far more extensive than King Leopold could have imagined. In addition to being the world's largest producer of cobalt, it is the world's second or third largest producer of industrial diamonds, and the fifth largest of copper, and it has large deposits of zinc, tin, gold, and other minerals. It also has rich oil deposits as well as vast agricultural and hydroelectric potential.[24] To protect and develop these enormous resources, Belgium created the Force Publique of the Congo Free State. Its original recruits were selected from the most warlike ethnic groups in the Congo, and its officers were hired from Turkey, Norway, Canada, the United States, and Belgium, among other nations. This polyglot army performed reasonably well during both World Wars, fighting well in Tanganyika and Italian East Africa, but in 1960, when Belgium refused to Africanize its officer corps, it rebelled, and since that time, it has not been a success in controlling the country's borders with Angola, Uganda, or Rwanda, nor in maintaining internal security.

Despite receiving extensive North Korean and Chinese aid in the 1960s, followed by Belgian, Israeli, and U.S. military aid and training since the 1970s, the Zairian armed forces have continued to be poorly led, trained, armed, fed, and disciplined. Often on the verge of revolution, and more a police force than an army, it has abused the people of Zaire in every way imaginable—rape, theft, forced labor, extortion, arbitrary arrest, murder.[25] Few armies can have rivaled it for corruption and ineptitude, but neither the original Belgian overlords nor recent foreign observers have described the members of this army as "natural" cowards.

"Africans have no fatherland" was an Italian slogan used to justify colonial conquest, especially in Ethiopia and Somalia, prizes that Italy had coveted even before the Berlin Convention in 1885 opened Africa to European expansion. Eritrea was established as an Italian colony in 1890, and Italian forces there grew in strength while Italian diplomacy was combined with military threats in an attempt to convince Ethiopia's emperor, Menelik II, to yield sovereignty to Italy. The Italians recruited large numbers of Eritrean and Tigrean soldiers to their cause while also steadily increasing the number of Italian soldiers and armaments under the command of General Oreste Baratieri. Baratieri boasted that if Menelik did not agree to Italian sovereignty, he would bring the emperor back to Italy in a cage.[26]

Early in 1896, diplomatic negotiations broke down and both sides urgently gathered military strength. The Italian forces crossed into the Central Highlands of Ethiopia, where Baratieri did all he could to entice the Ethiopians to attack the nearly impregnable fortifications his men had thrown up. Although the Ethiopians greatly outnumbered Baratieri's forces, Menelik refused to take the bait, waiting for hunger— brought about by Ethiopian control of supply lines—to drive Baratieri out of his entrenchments. At the same time, Menelik sent agents to convince the Italians that starvation was forcing the Ethiopian army to disperse in search of food. Deceived by these reports and driven to take action by Italian political pressure as well as the growing hunger of his own troops, on March 1, 1896, Baratieri marched out of his fortress to attack what he expected to be the disorganized, fleeing remnants of Menelik's once large and formidable army. Baratieri had 535 Italian officers, nearly 11,000 Italian soldiers, and some 10,000 native African auxiliaries, almost all of them Eritreans. Well armed with modern rifles and artillery, this was a major force, one that Baratieri expected would shatter what he believed to be a demoralized, disorganized, and depleted Ethiopian army.

What followed became what one Italian historian called the "most incredible and absurd battle that has ever taken place in modern history."[27] It was also the bloodiest defeat ever suffered by a colonial power in Africa. Instead of attacking a starving rabble, Baratieri found himself attacked at a place called Adowa by over 100,000 Ethiopians. Although all were barefooted, carrying buffalo-hide shields, and led by officers wearing headdresses shaped like lions' manes, most of them were armed with modern rifles and some with modern artillery. They were led by Menelik himself, riding a mule with a scarlet saddlecloth while one servant held each stirrup for him and another ran alongside shading him with a golden umbrella. This Christianized army was accompanied by hundreds of priests carrying large crosses.[28]

With his forces inexplicably separated, Baratieri's men were quickly overwhelmed. The Italians lost 289 officers and 4,600 soldiers killed, with another 500 men wounded and 1,900 taken prisoner. Their Eritrean allies lost about 4,000 killed, with the rest dispersed or captured when the Italian defeat became a rout. Few of those captured survived, as each prisoner's right hand and left foot were hacked off.[29] Most of the Italian prisoners did survive and were repatriated. The Ethiopian victory was not without a price. Perhaps 7,000 Ethiopian soldiers were killed with an even larger number wounded.[30] Despite these losses, Menelik's army was ready to carry on the fight to free Ethiopian soil of the Italians. When Italy refused an Ethiopian demand that they evacuate their small base on the Red Sea, the Ethiopian army attacked, killing all but a handful of its defenders.[31] The battle of Adowa was the origin of the Ethiopian "fatherland." As an Ethiopian chronicler wrote, "On that day . . . all the army was on fire with devotion for their country and the Nation."[32]

Mussolini's forces returned to Ethiopia in 1935 with modern warplanes, tanks, and poison gas, horrifying the international community by the brutality they used to create "Italian East Africa." As a result of the indiscriminate spraying of poison gas from low-flying airplanes, the loss of Ethiopian civilian life was appalling.[33] World opinion ran strongly against Italy, and Ethiopia became known as a heroic underdog. That half a million people were enslaved by Ethiopian leaders when Italy invaded was not widely known.[34] Italian East Africa would not survive beyond 1941, thanks in large part to the bravery of British-led African troops. Some white British and South African troops did not distinguish themselves, but with a few exceptions, the British African troops did well. What is more, Eritrean soldiers fought more bravely in defense of Italian East Africa than Italian troops did.[35]

German colonial expansion in Africa began as early as 1870 in South West Africa (now Namibia), where the Herero and Hottentot people were fairly easily subdued. By 1904, the Germans had seized all the prime land and almost all the cattle, and most Herero were working as impoverished laborers on German ranches. Togo and Cameroon (Kamerun) were also occupied with little use of force, and German rule there was reasonably benign. But East Africa took a different course. German presence in East Africa was almost single-handedly a product of a frail, racist, utterly vicious scholar-adventurer, Dr. Carl Peters, who over Bismarck's objection, from 1880 to 1891, led sixteen expeditions from the Tanganyikan (later Tanzanian) coast inland to Rwanda. Under the imprimatur of his German East Africa Company, Peters seized land three times the size of Germany. To do so, he ruthlessly whipped, hanged, and shot any African who stood in his way. Although his company planted cotton and rubber along the coast, there were no profits to be had, and Germany's attempts to end the Arab slave trade led to so many attacks by Arab slaves that German officers leading African soldiers from the Sudan had to intervene. Still, Germany chose to spend so little money to modernize ports, coastal facilities, or railroads that by 1901, there were only 2,000 Germans in all of German East Africa, almost all of them living along the coast.[36]

While the Germans were attempting to tighten their hold on the coast and some portions of northern Tanganyika, the south was dominated by some 50,000 Hehe people, who became known to the Germans as "a true warrior people who live only for war."[37] Fearful that the Hehe would extend their raids all the way to the coast, in 1891 the Germans sent a sizable force armed with modern rifles, machine guns, and artillery against them. Almost 3,000 Hehe warriors, only a handful of whom had rifles, waited in ambush. The German commander Zelewski, known as the "hammer" for his brutal style of dealing with Africans, was among the first to die by a thrown spear, followed by 9 other Germans, 3 of them officers, 200 native soldiers, 96 porters, and 23 donkeys.[38] A small German rear-guard escaped. For the next seven years, ever stronger German forces struck at the Hehe until 1898, when, his people exhausted by their struggles against troops with modern weapons, the Hehe chief, Mkwawa, shot himself to death.

A few years later, German Marines established their authority by firing indiscriminately at Africans along the Tanganyikan coast, and German settlers brought the same brutality to East Africa that their counterparts in South West Africa would soon inflict on the Herero. The result was the "Maji-Maji" rebellion of 1904 based on the magical assurance of numerous religious leaders and prophets that their powers would turn bullets into water. When the rebellious leaders had finally been shot or hanged, southern Tanganyika was a burned-out wasteland with at least 100,000 men, women, and children dead of bullets, disease, or famine. The Hehe did not join the Maji-Maji rebellion, preferring to fight with the Germans against their tribal enemies. The Germans came to respect them for their intelligence, loyalty, courage, and discipline. But elsewhere in German East Africa, tribal people continued to put up such brilliant guerrilla-warfare resistance that the German administration chose to rethink its previous white-supremacist, armed-camp approach to its new empire. The worst sadists among the government and civilian population were sent home, and new administrators did all they could both to pacify the East Africans and to convince many to join their government as district administrators and their army—the so-called Schutztruppe—as soldiers. Paid well, given prestige among their fellow tribespeople and German settlers alike, and provided with privileges—each soldier was given a personal manservant—these Africans quickly became loyal, disciplined, and brave soldiers. Their carefully chosen German officers imposed strict discipline but treated them with respect. The new German government of East Africa consciously strove to be more human as well.

At this same time, Herero resistance to German brutality and racism in South West Africa was rising, in large response to the rape of their women, the expropriation of their cattle, and hideous flogging on their stomachs and between their legs when German authorities were displeased. Women as well as men had their intestines torn out, men had their testicles crushed, and women saw their unborn children torn to bits.[39] Growing Herero resistance, along with their search for modern arms, led to deadly German reprisals that killed women and children more often than men.

In 1905, 20,000 elite German soldiers were sent to South West Africa to crush the Herero—"annihilate" was the word their commander used. The Herero fought so courageously against far superior weapons that a German officer admitted that the Germans "had dramatically under-estimated the Hereros . . . the Hereros apparently believe that they can expect no quarter and are therefore fanatically determined."[40] The German commander, General von Trotha, declared that "I know the tribes of Africa, they are all alike. They respond only to force. It was and is my policy to use force with terrorism and even brutality."[41] True to his word, von Trotha ordered an orgy of killing, and despite their lack of modern weapons, the Herero fought back with astonishing courage, which was soon matched by the Hottentots who joined their resistance, winning many battles. When the war ended in 1907, over 1,300 Germans were dead with an equal number wounded. But fully 50,000 Herero men, women, and children had died, many of them intentionally burned alive. The Hottentots also suffered thousands of casualties. Most German soldiers left this campaign with a new respect for African warriors.

This respect would soon be demonstrated in Tanganyika. In 1914, as World War I began, the British sent an expeditionary force to Tanganyika to capture it from the Germans, who proved their new-found faith in African courage by their decision to defend their colony against British invaders with African troops led by only a few hundred German officers. When a British junior officer, who had spent time in East Africa, warned the British commanding general that his force of only partially trained and poorly led Indian troops might not be able to cope with the Germans' Africans, who were well trained, well armed, and well led, the British general dismissed him, saying, "The Indian Army will make short work of a lot of niggers."[42] In the campaign's first battle, the Tanganyikan soldiers routed the Indians, who fled to their ships leaving most of their dead, wounded, and weapons behind. Not for another four years, after an overwhelming British force had been assembled, were these African soldiers and their German officers forced to surrender.

These African soldiers, "askaris" as they were often known, respected their officers, and when World War I came to East Africa in 1914, they fought with uncommon devotion and skill despite terrible disease, hunger, and thirst so intolerable that they often had to drink bird blood or their own urine, holding off and frequently defeating British troops that outnumbered them more than ten to one. Although ferocious in battle, these Africans joined their German officers in extending civil courtesy to British prisoners. More remarkable, when the last remnants of the German East African force under their brilliant and compassionate commander, General Paul von Lettow-Vorbeck, invaded Portuguese East Africa (Mozambique) to escape pursuing British forces, the African population actually welcomed them as saviors![43] The Portuguese were described as being so brutal that they awoke each morning with a gun in one hand and a whip in the other. Although Germans were unaccustomed to passionate welcomes by Africans, they behaved well. The Portuguese did not. They continued to brutalize Africans and seldom fought well against von Lettow's men. On one occasion, a Portuguese sergeant who surrendered was so fearful for his life that he fell to his knees, sobbing and pleading for mercy. A German East African corporal physically caressed and comforted the sergeant as he would a terrified child.[44]

From General von Lettow to the youngest German platoon leader, there was nothing but admiration and praise for the courage and military skills of their African soldiers. Their British adversaries were equally impressed. When Germany signed the armistice ending World War I, von Lettow's men were not only undefeated but determined to fight on. Compelled to surrender by international law, von Lettow's 155 surviving Germans did all they could do to convince their 1,156 African soldiers—all that remained of a force once ten times that number—to surrender their weapons.

Germany would lose its African colonies after World War I, just as Italy would rule only briefly over Eritrea, Ethiopia, and Somalia, but Belgium would retain control of Zaire (formerly the Belgian Congo) until well after World War II, and Portugal would do the same in Mozambique, Angola, and Guiné. Still, it was the British and the French, even more than these other European powers, who would fight first against and then with Africans early in the nineteenth century, and have fought with them since soon after that time until the present day.

We turn first to Britain, whose culture and social institutions are so much like those of the United States, but whose military history with persons of African ancestry took a dramatically different course from the American course. Black men have never played a central role in

Britain's military or naval forces, yet neither have they been subjected to the same degree of racist denigration in terms of military service that black men faced in the United States armed forces. Over time, British attitudes toward persons of African ancestry have varied, ranging from near social equality to outright contempt and police oppression, but the fixed belief that black men were too stupid and cowardly to serve in combat as soldiers or sailors never dominated British military opinion as it did in America.

Throughout their period of intensive slave trading, Britain transported large numbers of slaves primarily to its West Indian colonies such as Jamaica, Barbados, and Trinidad and Tobago, where sugar plantations created previously unimagined wealth, much as oil would do in the latter part of the nineteenth century. Conditions for slaves in the British West Indies were as harsh as those created anywhere in the world. Sugar plantations were run by absentee landowners who, for the most part, had rapid profit as their only goal. As a result, most slaves lived short and miserable lives, dying young before being replaced by another shipment of slaves from Africa until Britain abolished slavery in 1833. Unlike the United States, where slaves were expected and encouraged to reproduce, the demands put upon slave labor in the Caribbean did not lend themselves to reproduction as a means of maintaining the slave population.[45]

Although few slaves were shipped to Britain itself, black people had been known there for centuries. A division of black, so-called Moorish, troops of the Roman legion guarded Hadrian's Wall in the third century, and skeletal remains of what appear to be Africans from centuries past have been found in Scotland. There is also documentary evidence that at least some Britons had been familiar with Africans ever since Roman times.[46] In later years, this familiarity would grow. Henry VII had a famous African trumpeter, and other Africans appeared at court and worked in Britain's great houses. Although they were a mere handful compared to the numbers taken to the United States, some African slaves were taken to Britain itself. Almost all of these slaves were house servants, court entertainers, or sexual partners, not field laborers. By the end of the 1500s, wealthy and titled families, like that of Sir Walter Raleigh, thought it "smart" to have elaborately uniformed black house servants, and so many of them soon appeared in Britain that Queen Elizabeth I urged the deportation of these "blackamoores" because, she said, they were ignorant of Christianity.[47] However, deportation was not systematically carried out, and by the latter half of the seventeenth century, black people were familiar sights in much of the country. By the eighteenth century, there were perhaps 10,000 blacks in Britain, a total that grew after 1784, when many impoverished black Americans who had joined British forces in the Revolutionary War landed in England.[48] Some black men became well-known prize fighters but many others became beggars. Still, racism was seldom apparent. For example, in 1805, a well-dressed black man could walk arm-in-arm in London with a well-dressed white woman and go unnoticed except by American visitors.[49]

Over time, some blacks were shipped away to Sierra Leone, and many others had offspring with white Britons, creating an increasingly light-skinned set of young people while their darker-skinned ancestors grew old and died. But while Britain's indigenous black population was becoming less noticeable, hundreds of black American musicians and entertainers toured British cities. Black dancers, singers, acrobats, comedians, and ventriloquists became well known. One man gave banjo lessons to future King Edward VII, while a former slave, soprano Elizabeth Taylor Greenfield, sang for Queen Victoria. Known as the "Black Swan," she became the most famous black concert artist of her time. The British were so taken by some of the dances the black entertainers introduced to them that they became all the rage, especially the cakewalk, which swept London shortly after the turn of the century.[50] Throughout the nineteenth century, black American visitors to Britain and Ireland, such as Frederick Douglass, were astonished and pleased that the racism they had grown accustomed to in America was nowhere to be seen.[51]

But after the twentieth century began, black visitors and immigrants to Britain dwindled, and by the start of World War II in 1939, there were no more than 7,000 or 8,000 persons of African ancestry in the United Kingdom, and almost all of these were concentrated in port cities such as Cardiff, Liverpool, and London, where black communities had grown largely because black seamen who had served in Britain's wartime merchant navy had decided to settle there. But by that time, there were virtually no persons of African ancestry outside of cities like these, and the great majority of British people, especially those in rural areas, had never met a black person before the influx of large numbers of black American servicemen began in 1942.[52]

As we saw in Chapter 5, despite the best efforts of white American soldiers, sometimes supported by the British government, these newly arrived black American servicemen were quite popular with British people, who treated them extremely well. One British farmer said, perhaps tongue in cheek, "I love the Americans but I don't like them white ones they've brought with them."[53] Those white American servicemen in Britain were outraged by the welcome black soldiers received:

> They vented their fury on blacks, vilified British women who associated with them, and tried to persuade hoteliers and publicans to exclude black customers. Again the reports concur that British people, though disliking black-white contact across the sexes, generally repudiated this kind of overt discrimination and often took the blacks' side in fracas [sic] with whites and even with U.S. military police.[54]

Many British people expressed amazement on meeting African American soldiers that they were ordinary, likable human beings, not the ignorant, subhuman creatures they had so often seen in Hollywood films.[55]

Working-class Britons in particular set no color line. Blacks were often invited into Britons' homes as well as their pubs, and they became especially popular with British women, particularly teenagers, a circumstance leading to great concern as reflected in newspaper stories that appeared on an almost daily basis railing about teenage British girls "running wild." Middle-class white girls rarely dated black soldiers, but working-class teenage girls most certainly did, often being seen in public in relationships that gave every indication of being more than platonic. The British press was certain that these relationships would lead to a flood of mixed-race babies, something that they deplored with increasing vehemence as the war went on. In fact, however, research at the end of the war showed that although illegitimacy rates during the war went up somewhat for women in their late twenties and early thirties, they actually declined for women under the age of twenty-five, the group that was most singled out for criticism. In fact, it was not until 1945, three years after the arrival of large numbers of black and white American servicemen in Britain, that there was a significant rise in the illegitimacy rate. Prior to that time, the illegitimacy rate was actually lower than it had been in prewar years.[56] How many of these illegitimate babies were of mixed race is not known.

Although it was rarely the case that persons of African descent were considered the social equals of middle- or upper-class Britons, racial discrimination against blacks was not highly institutionalized in Britain before the end of World War II. To be sure, there were some vocal racists in Britain who supported the American practice of racial segregation, arguing that it had important implications not only for British racial purity but also for the development of the South African Union. However, many other Britons thought that southern racial segregation was "absurd and doomed to failure."[57] Significant social problems involving persons of African ancestry were infrequent in Britain until just after World War I, in 1919. Some black servicemen, particularly merchant seamen, had found employment in British port cities during the war, and other blacks had come to Britain during the war from the West Indies to work in the war industry. When white British servicemen returned from their wartime service to reclaim the jobs they had lost, trouble ensued. There were numerous race riots in 1919, and in all port cities police began to maintain close surveillance of neighborhoods and places of entertainment that had a significant black presence.

Soon after, the publicly recognized presence in Britain of "half caste" children, as they were called, led to considerable political discussion resulting in immigration controls against persons of African ancestry. And although Jim Crow laws, similar to those in the American South, did not develop in Britain in anything like the same degree, residential segregation arose in large cities, as did some degree of racial exclusion in public places. By the 1950s, West Indian migrants to Britain confronted job discrimination and residential segregation, as well as exclusion from pubs, dance halls, and even churches. Racial slurs were commonplace, as was violence at the hands of so-called Teddy-boys, or young white working-class men.[58] Reinforcement for these measures and attitudes came from many of the thousands of British officers and men who had served in Africa with African soldiers. Few of these men returned to Britain with the belief that large numbers of blacks should take up residence in Britain or become the equals of white Britons, but most respected them as warriors whom they had fought with and against on many occasions during the latter part of the nineteenth century and early years of the twentieth.

The first major British confrontation against an African army came early in the nineteenth century. The British had long coveted the Kingdom of Asante in the Gold Coast, now Ghana, for its gold as well as its slaves. In 1824, they sent a mixed force of British-trained and -armed African soldiers along with British regular Army troops to destroy the

Asante. After a bizarre exchange of music by the bands of both sides, the Asante attacked and routed the British. Fifty years later, in 1874, General Sir Garnet Wolseley, who had fought bravely in the Crimean War against Russia in 1854–1855, where several former West Indian slaves took part in the famous "Charge of the Light Brigade," was given command of a sizable, well-armed force of British regular troops who would again attempt to defeat the Asante.

Before launching his attack against the relatively poorly armed Asante, he distributed a pamphlet to his officers assuring them, "It must never be forgotten by our soldiers that Providence has implanted in the heart of every native of Africa a superstitious awe and dread of the white man that prevents the negro from daring to meet us face to face."[59] This was not quite the "natural cowardice" that American slave owners proclaimed, but the next best thing. Perhaps Wolseley had not heard of the British defeat by these same "negroes" in 1824, or perhaps he was only hoping to encourage his men. In either case, he would soon have to eat his words, because although badly outgunned, the Asante fought so bravely that Wolseley called this campaign the "most horrible" he had ever taken part in (he had fought, and been wounded, in Burma as well as the Crimea). He managed to fight his way into the Asante capital but was then forced to retreat to the coast with heavy losses and little to show for the "triumph" the British press grandly proclaimed.[60]

Only five years later, this time wearing their famous "red coats" and white cork sunhelmets rather than the drab khaki Wolseley's men had worn during their fight against the Asante, a substantial British Army invaded Zululand, in Natal, on the east coast of Southern Africa. Because the Zulus had conquered numerous neighboring African kingdoms and were seen as a threat to British economic and political interests in the area, the time for conquest had come. Armed with modern rifles and powerful artillery, the British expected little difficulty in overcoming the "savage" Zulus—near-naked, bare-footed warriors armed primarily with spears. In the war's first battle, a force of over 50 British officers, 806 British "redcoats," and some 500 African allies were attacked by several thousands of Zulus. Despite withering British fire, the Zulus drove forward until they were able to fight hand-to-hand with the British. When the fighting ended, 52 officers, as well as all 806 British soldiers and all their African allies lay dead. No British battalion had ever lost so many officers in one battle, not even at Waterloo, and for a

British force of that size to be killed virtually to the last man was un-heard of. One transport officer who barely escaped by riding away wrote, "Never has such a disaster happened to the English army."[61]

At least 3,000 Zulus were killed in this first battle, and before the war ended, some six months and several major battles later, at least 10,000 Zulus would die in battle, and a similar number probably died of wounds. In every subsequent battle, Zulu warriors threw themselves at massed British firepower as their troops either fired from behind walls or stood shoulder-to-shoulder in a square formation. Zulu attacks proved nearly suicidal as the British fire from cannon, gatling guns, and rifles was devastating. A British sergeant wrote this: "I confess that I do not think that a braver lot of men than our enemies in point of disre-gard for life, and for their bravery under fire, could be found any-where."[62] An officer wrote, "We all admire the pluck of the Zulus . . . under tremendous fire they never wavered, but came straight at us."[63] Another officer wrote, "There is no doubt that the Zulus fight splen-didly. They rush straight up and don't seem to fear death at all."[64] Fi-nally, the words of this officer: "Talk about pluck! The Zulu has all that. They were shot down one after the other and they still came on in hun-dreds."[65]

In 1883, the British would again send troops against Africans, this time against the so-called Dervishes or fuzzy-wuzzies in the eastern Su-dan, an Arabic word meaning "land of the blacks." The Dervish army had embarked on a holy war—a *jihad*—to cleanse the Sudan of its cor-rupt Egyptian rule, which profited enormously by illegally taking 50,000 slaves a year out of the Sudan. The Dervishes' divine mission to end this outrage was created by a man claiming descent from Muham-mad. As the reincarnation of the prophet, he called himself the Mahdi, "the expected leader." He was a magnificent orator cut from the tradi-tional cloth of the warrior-priest of Islam. He was also a strict Muslim. Europeans who saw him reported that he always smiled benevolently, even when he was ordering torture and death for wrongdoers.

The men who flocked to the Mahdi's cause were almost as diverse as the Sudan itself. The Mahdi's cavalry and most of his officers came from the partly Caucasian Baggara tribe of horse and cattle nomads. Some of these men actually wore medieval helmets, breastplates, and chain mail to battle and swung huge broadswords. These relics of the Crusades found their way to one of the hottest places on earth, where men actually attacked British machine guns wearing fourteenth-century armor. Other Dervishes were Hadendoa tribesmen, who were also partly Caucasian, but mixed with more Negroid peoples. It was their hairstyle—poking upwards like a fright wig—that led the British to call them fuzzy-wuzzies. Most of the infantry in the Dervish army were black Africans such as Dinka, Shilluk, and Nuba from the non-Muslim south. Thousands of these dark-skinned men found their way into the Dervish ranks, where they were usually led by lighter-skinned officers.

Marching to the call of war trumpets made from elephant tusks, the Mahdi's army defeated one garrison of Egyptian soldiers after another, captured modern weapons, and attracted more men to his cause. When the Egyptian government mounted an expedition of nearly 9,000 men led by a British colonel, William Hicks, and other British officers, 50,000 Dervishes attacked them, killing all the British officers including Hicks. Only about 200 Egyptians survived. The Mahdi's army then surrounded the city of Khartoum, where British General Charles Gordon had been set up as the governor-general of Sudan.

After much delay, the British sent a relief column to "save" Gordon, who was besieged by Mahdist soldiers. Once again, General Wolseley led the British force, which included kilted Scottish infantry and black Sudanese soldiers. The Dervishes attacked with astonishing bravery. Twice they broke through the ranks of soldiers manning the British "square," something that had never been done before in history. The idea of African horsemen in suits of armor swinging their broadswords at bayonet-wielding, kilted Scottish infantry in temperatures that reached 165 degrees in the sun is almost too much for the modern imagination, but it happened. To compound their feat of arms, the Dervishes captured some British machine guns before they were driven off.

Their heroism inspired this famous tribute by Kipling (who was not a witness):

> So 'ere's to you, Fuzzy-Wuzzy, at your
>   'ome in the Sowdan;
> You're a pore benighted 'eathen but
>   a first-class fighting man;
> An 'ere's to you Fuzzy-Wuzzy, with
>   your 'ayrick 'ead of 'air—
> You big black bounding beggar—for
>   you bruk a British square.[66]

When word came that Khartoum had fallen and Gordon had been killed, Wolseley's army marched away, leaving Sudan to the Dervishes. A few months later the Mahdi died, but his successor not only held the Mahdist state together but strengthened its army. Thirteen years later, when the British belatedly decided to avenge Gordon's death, the Dervish army numbered more than 100,000 men, most of whom had rifles. They also had some machine guns and nearly 100 modern artillery pieces. In fact, the British decision to march on Khartoum had less to do with avenging Gordon (although vows of revenge had been heard ever since his death) than with the fear that the French were about to extend their domination of the western Sudan to the east by seizing the Upper Nile.

The British Army of 25,000 men included many distinguished regiments, such as the 21st Lancers and Highland Scots (the Camerons and the Seaforths), but only one-third of the Army was British. The rest were Egyptian peasant soldiers and black Sudanese troops, some of whom had previously fought with the Dervishes before they deserted or were captured. This time the British Army was led by Horatio Herbert Kitchener. As a major of intelligence, Kitchener had served in Wolseley's unhappy expedition. He spoke Arabic and despite his appearance (he was a bulky six feet two inches with strikingly blue eyes), he often dressed as an Arab, riding off into the desert in search of information, carrying a bottle of poison in case of capture. Kitchener was cold, ambitious, and thoroughly ruthless. His men would take no prisoners. Along for the ride was a young officer named Winston Churchill. Although Churchill was a serving officer with the 4th Hussars in India, thanks to the influence of his wealthy and beautiful mother, the mistress of several powerful men, including the man who would become King Edward VII, he wangled his way into serving as a lieutenant with the 21st Lancers.

Most of the British officers feared that the Dervishes would not fight, but just in case they did, their soldiers were encouraged to create "dumdums" by cutting an X into the nose of their lead bullets. Despite their large size, standard-issue .45-caliber bullets tended to go through the Dervishes without stopping them, and the wounded black men would stagger and even crawl ahead despite several wounds. Dumdums, which blew a fist-sized hole in a man, were much more effective. Cursing the heat, dust, sand, flies, scorpions, and large tarantulas, the British Army slowly marched toward Omdurman, the Mahdist capital. Each evening, all ranks, including officers, Africans and Britons alike, bathed nude in the refreshing waters of the Nile.[67]

Riding ahead of Kitchener's army, many scouts searched for the Dervishes. As luck would have it, Churchill was one of the first to sight them. "The whole side of the hill seemed to move," he wrote later, "and the sun, glinting on many hostile spear-points spread a sparkling cloud."[68] When he rode back to Kitchener with the information, the general didn't recognize him, which was just as well, since Kitchener heartily disliked Churchill for publishing criticisms of his senior officers (many of the other officers dismissed him simply as a brash, arrogant "twit"). However, another officer, Sir Reginald Wingate, did recognize Churchhill, and in a scene at least as strange as that of nineteenth-century black men wearing medieval armor in the blistering African sun, Churchill was invited to join Wingate for lunch. As the Dervish army "jog-trotted" toward them at a rate that Churchill estimated as four miles per hour, the gentlemen officers chatted politely while they were served lunch on a white linen tablecloth. They drank from crystal and ate with proper silverware, seemingly oblivious of the heat, the flies, or the Mahdist army of 60,000 men or more bearing down on them.[69]

The Dervish cavalry charged the British lines and died to the last man. Not one came closer than thirty yards. Then, the infantry attacked, again and again, dying by the thousands before the intense British fire. A war correspondent for the *Daily Mail*, G. W. Steevens, wrote, "No white troops would have faced that torrent of death for five minutes, but the Baggara and the blacks came on."[70] What is more, those who survived did not run away from the British guns; they walked slowly and disdainfully away "with a haughty stalk of offended dignity."[71] On one flank of the battle, the 21st Lancers rode out in the last great cavalry charge in British history. At the head of a troop of twenty-five men was Churchill, who shot several Dervishes at point-blank range, just missing one man who wore medieval armor. The Lancers fought bravely, as did the British infantry, but their part in the battle was a sideshow. The brunt of the Dervish attack was taken and broken by the black Sudanese soldiers of Colonel Hector Macdonald's 1st Brigade. It was the unyielding courage of those African troops that won the battle, not the heroics of the Lancers or the famous British regiments whose position in the British defense line was not seriously attacked. After the battle, white British troops saluted the heroism of their black comrades with howls of approval. The black Africans howled back with delight.[72]

More than 10,000 dead Dervishes lay on the battleground; 15,000 or so others lay wounded. Most of these were finished off by British, Egyptian, and Sudanese troops, a necessary precaution, Kitchener later argued, because these men would use their last breath to kill any British soldier who tried to help them. As devout Muslims, they believed that a brave death like this would lead them to paradise. In a subsequent battle, British artillery fired high-explosive shells against a Dervish defensive position. The Dervish soldiers could have retreated, but they chose to stay in their trenches, where more than 3,000 of them died.

It was a strange war that pitted Islamic religious zeal against Christian revenge. Perhaps most ironic was the fact that many of the best soldiers on both sides were "pagan" African tribesmen from the southern Sudan. Whether on the side of the Mahdi or the British, those tall, thin-legged black men (they averaged six feet in height) fought with discipline and reckless courage, "utterly fearless," as one British observer called them.[73]

British officers and men would fight against and alongside Africans in numerous subsequent wars in Uganda, Kenya, Nigeria, Southern Rhodesia, and other parts of British Africa. As recently as the 1950s, British Army troops would fight alongside African soldiers in the King's African Rifles to quell the Mau Mau rebellion against British rule in Kenya. The British would also ask Africans to serve Britain overseas. Thousands of black men from the West Indies served in World War I. These men fought against Germans and their African allies in Africa, Egypt, and Palestine. When they routed Turkish troops in the Jordan River Valley, they were commended in dispatches for "steadiness under fire."[74] For their valor and discipline in Palestine, this comment by a commanding officer was typical: "They acquitted themselves most splendidly."[75] After defeating the Germans following hard fighting in the Cameroons, a historian concluded that "the fighting men of West Africa stand high for staunch courage and cheerful endurance."[76] Although they did not serve as combat soldiers in Europe, thousands of black West Indians carried ammunition and supplies to the front-line trenches in Flanders, often under deadly shellfire. They took heavy casualties and performed so valiantly that the British commander, Field Marshal Sir Douglas Haig, praised them with, for him, these strong words: "The West Indian soldier showed himself indifferent to danger and undismayed by heavy casualties."[77] Haig clearly did not share the conviction of American generals that blacks were "natural cowards."

During World War II, 76,000 black Africans served in South African uniforms, while another 500,000 Africans from Ghana, Kenya, Nigeria, and Tanganyika wore British uniforms. Once again, they fought courageously and well, although once again they were not used in combat in Europe. A number of Africans served as officers in these military units, but until 1942 none actually received a commission like those held by regular army white British officers. By the end of World War II, however, there were close to 100 African men holding King's Commissions.[78] During World War II, blacks were integrated into Canadian Army units, leading American General Benjamin O. Davis, who saw them in Britain, to remark, "A border line makes so much difference."[79]

Despite a major presence of Africans in British service during both World Wars, as well as the fact that black men had served in British military forces for over 200 years, the British Army was most often seen by others—and certainly thought of itself—as an army of white men officered by other whites from the "better" social backgrounds. It was often forgotten that by the mid-1700s, every prestigious British regiment marched to powerful martial strains created by black drummers and trumpeters.[80] As we have also seen, during America's Revolutionary War, the British Army made greater use of freedmen and runaway slaves than Washington's forces did. Although the great majority of these black Americans served in noncombat roles, some served as combat infantry, marines, and even cavalry. At least 1,500 black Americans fought in combat against Washington's troops, and one man, Samuel Burke, was credited with killing ten Americans in a battle at Hanging Rock.[81]

Africans of slave ancestry served in combat throughout the British West Indies in almost continual warfare against the French from 1793 to 1815, and some served in Britain's wars outside of the West Indies.[82] As noted earlier, blacks fought in the British campaign against New Orleans in 1815, and others served with distinction in the fighting along the east coast of America earlier in what came to be known as the War of 1812. However, with the exception of some laborers, or "pioneers" as they were known by the British, the British armies that fought against Napoleon were white, as, with a few exceptions, was the British Army that fought in the Crimean War in the mid-nineteenth century.

With very few exceptions, Africans did not fight with the British during the Boer War in Africa, although they served as laborers in all of Britain's African campaigns and sometimes displayed exemplary courage.

Despite the contributions of black soldiers and sailors to Britain's victories in World Wars I and II, at the end of World War II, Britain's Army Council concluded that "colored men" should not hold permanent commissions in the regular army and, indeed, that the army should greatly limit the presence of "West Indian and similar colored people" from its ranks, arguing that it was "undesirable" for British military units serving overseas to contain men of African ancestry. After heated debate, the Army Council was overruled, and British subjects of non-European racial background, including those of African ancestry, were admitted to the Royal Navy and the British Army, but their numbers were strictly limited, just as they had been earlier by government fiat.[83] Perhaps as a result, black military heroes do not have a prominent place in the history of the British Army. In fact, one of the most popular and highly regarded historical surveys of Britain's Army, *Britain and Her Army, 1509–1970*, by Correlli Barnett, makes no mention at all of black soldiers in Britain's military history.[84] And Sir John Fortescue's monumental thirteen-volume *History of the British Army* devotes less than a handful of pages to black soldiers in British service, most of these involving the battle of New Orleans.[85]

The British Commonwealth Division fought with uncommon courage and competence during the Korean War. After a rocky beginning, the Canadians fought superbly, and the veteran Australian infantrymen seemed fearless to the Americans, who often watched them in awe. New Zealand artillerymen were respected, too, and so were British soldiers of the 27th and 29th Brigades, who regularly stood firm against Chinese "human wave" attacks when some American units did not. The Commonwealth Division suffered 1,263 dead and 4,817 wounded while inflicting perhaps 10,000 casualties on the Chinese, but even these losses paled alongside those of the Americans—over 33,000 dead and more than 105,000 wounded.[86] No colonial African units were engaged in the Korean War, and if black Britons served, they were integrated into British regiments and their actions have not been publicized.

The major British military action since the Korean War took place in Argentina in the war over the Falkland Islands in 1982. After three months of often ferocious land, sea, and air combat, the Argentines surrendered with the loss of several major warships, over 100 warplanes, and at least 1,000 men killed in action. Over 11,000 Argentine troops surrendered. British losses included nine aircraft, six ships sunk (with ten others badly damaged), 255 men killed, and nearly 800 wounded.[87] Hundreds of photographs show British troops embarking, exercising aboard ships, or in land combat situations. Except for Ghurkas, who were part of the invasion force, these men from the elite Royal Marines, Parachute Battalions, and Guards Regiments appear to have been entirely made up of white men. The sole exception is a black soldier of the "2 Para," who is pictured in the front row of men ready to leave for the Falklands.[88] No doubt some others of African descent fought in this war, but their numbers would appear to have been small, and British published reports of the fighting did not single them out.[89] The world did learn, however, that Prince Andrew flew a helicopter on dangerous operational missions.[90]

During the 1960s, Britain maintained its 3 percent limit on black enlistments, but it was reported that the numbers of blacks who became noncommissioned officers compared favorably with the number of white soldiers who attained similar rank. Statistics describing the number of blacks in Britain's armed forces in recent years are not obtainable, although an official Ministry of Defense declaration in 1985 stated that there was "no discrimination by race, religion, or color" in the armed forces. However, just a year later, Prince Charles made a public comment on the lack of black soldiers in the Guards Regiments, a matter that was subsequently brought up in the House of Lords. A British historian in the 1980s concluded his review of blacks in Britain's military with these words:

> Compared to the United States Armed Forces . . . the British Army lags far behind. Racial exclusiveness shelters behind often specious arguments about the quality of command, the response of white soldiers to black officers, and also the need to preserve the social milieu of the officer core.[91]

Like Britain, France was active in the Atlantic slave trade, shipping large numbers of slaves to its West Indian colonies such as Saint-Domingue (Haiti), Guadeloupe, and Martinique. Few African slaves found their way to metropolitan France, but France's West Indian colonies were the site of a flourishing and highly lucrative sugar-producing industry. Many of these black West Indians achieved positions of influence after the abolition of slavery. Black West Indians served in constabulary forces, while some slaves and freedmen served in the French Navy. However, the continental armies that fought under Napoleon were almost entirely white, with only a few men of African ancestry serving in the Grande Armée. By the time of the Crimean War in the 1850s, some African cavalrymen led by white French officers fought with distinction against Russian forces, but once again in 1870–1871, when France, then thought by many to be the world's foremost military power, was defeated by Prussia, its army contained few black African soldiers.

However, a few years earlier, France had not hesitated to use African troops in Mexico. Because white French soldiers stationed along the Mexican coast near Vera Cruz were dying of yellow fever in large numbers, in 1862 Emperor Napoleon III sent for a regiment of Sudanese soldiers, all of whom had been emancipated from slavery as a condition of their enlistment. Although their commanding officer was white, their other officers and noncommissioned officers were African. Arriving in Mexico in 1863, immaculately clad in all-white uniforms, these troops exhibited splendid discipline as well as bravery in battle, but they succumbed to yellow fever just as often as France's white soldiers had.[92]

The French have long insisted that they "have never adopted the racial doctrines affirming the superiority of whites over men of color."[93] And it has not been unusual for French government officials to make public proclamations of the same sort as this representative in the United Nations Security Council did: "There are few traditions which are so much a part of the history of my country as the concept of equality between the races."[94] In support of this claim, the French point out that they abolished slavery in metropolitan France in the sixteenth century. The warm welcome that the French extended to both black American and black West African soldiers during both World Wars did much to support the claim that France rejected racism. The color-blind atmosphere of Paris in the 1920s and 1930s reinforced France's reputation for upholding racial equality, inspiring black American novelist Richard Wright to say, "There is more freedom in one square block of Paris than in all of the United States."[95]

Yet, as historian William B. Cohen has shown, throughout much of France's history, her people treated blacks, and thought of them, very much as Britons and other Europeans did. French knowledge of

African-descended people was not as extensive as it was in Britain or Spain, but a few Africans lived in France as early as the thirteenth century, and in the 1520s, Francis I had a young black mistress. By the sixteenth century, blacks became much more numerous in France, and travelers' reports from Africa were beginning to have an impact on French thinking as well. Although nearly half of French adults at this time were illiterate, Pierre Bergeron's 1648 account of famous African travels instructed many French readers that Africans "are so savage that they hardly know how to speak, so dirty that they eat the intestines of animals full with manure without washing them, and so brutal that they resemble more hungry dogs than men who have reason."[96] Traveler's accounts like this one were soon followed by a host of "scholarly" treatises that emphasized the small brains and low intelligence of Africans. And like many other Europeans, for the French, black as a color had deep associations with death, filth, and evil.

The seventeenth century saw the French enslaving both Indians and runaway blacks in Canada, while they treated their West Indian slaves every bit as harshly as the Spaniards, Danes, Dutch, and Britons did. Because there were so few white women in the French West Indies, some miscegenation between white Frenchmen and African women was tolerated in the seventeenth century, but by 1711, interracial marriage was made unlawful in Guadeloupe and, by 1724, in Louisiana. Around this same time, some 5,000 former slaves and stranded black seamen were in France, surviving as jugglers, boxers, servants, and prostitutes, "held in low esteem, ridicule, and fear."[97] Fearful of this influx of black people, the French passed laws restricting interracial marriage and prohibiting black people from entering France.

In the 1740s, Marechal de Saxe raised a black military company in France, but it engendered so much controversy that after his death in 1750 it was disbanded. It has been estimated that there were no more than 1,500 persons of African descent in France at this time, but the French fear of racial mixing was so great that in 1777 the entry of African slaves was forbidden, and in the following year, all blacks were either sent back to French colonies or kept in stockades in France.

It is noteworthy that although there were many times more blacks in Britain at the time, the British did not place similar legal restrictions on them.[98] Social ostracism and prejudice also grew markedly, with lower-class white Frenchmen determined to protect their "whiteness" as a superior racial trait. As early as 1780, there was an ugly race riot in Bordeaux, and in 1794, Napolean reimposed slavery, forbidding the entry of blacks into France and expelling black students from the Ecole Polytechnique in Paris.[99]

The racial climate in West Africa, particularly Senegal, was different. Perhaps because French control there was weak, with few French people actually living in its principal city, Saint-Louis, and because Senegal was seen as being vital to France's imperial interests, the racial atmosphere there was positive. The races respected each other, intermarriage was common, and Africans had legal rights equal to those of white French people.

France attempted to extend her colonial power in West Africa, but African resistance was fierce. In 1857, African soldiers fought so courageously against French troops in the Western Sudan that French General Louis Faidherbe reported, "They march against our fire as if to martyrdom, it is clear that they wish to die."[100] Not exactly, but they did wish to resist. Because Europeans usually had such short life spans in the disease-wracked tropical forests of West Africa, in 1857 French General Faidherbe, who was convinced that Africans were as intelligent as Europeans and equally brave, began to train Senegalese native soldiers to a high level of military efficiency.[101] Known as Tirailleurs Sénégalais, they served as a standing professional army led by French and some African officers, fighting gallantly throughout West Africa.

French native West African military units would continue to be known by this name throughout history, although they would soon consist of men from all over West Africa, with Senegalese often in the minority. In 1892, Tirailleurs Sénégalais, along with French Legionnaires and Marines, developed great respect for the African troops that opposed them in the Kingdom of Dahomey in what is now Benin. Once again, the French had overwhelming firepower including modern machine guns and artillery. But led by their now-famous professional women soldiers known to Europeans as "amazons," the Dahomeans fought so bravely that the French could not praise them highly enough. As a Foreign Legionnaire later wrote of them, "We were attacked by a body of the enemy some thousands strong, and we formed into company squares to resist their onslaught . . . our fire literally mowed down the advancing lines but they came on again and again in the most determined manner."[102]

At this stage of history, the French were much more willing than the British to treat Africans as their social equals and to commission them as officers. The French Revolution had democratized its social institutions, including the military, where men of humble birth were able to receive regular army and navy commissions. So were some men of African parentage. Faidherbe's son by a Senegalese woman attended France's prestigious military academy, Saint-Cyr, was commissioned, and was killed in the Franco-Prussian War. Another who attended Saint-Cyr, and later became a highly decorated colonel of French Marines, was Alfred A. Dodds, born in 1842 in Saint-Louis, the son of a French administrator and a part-Senegalese mother. Despite his mixed race, Dodds led troops in combat for twenty years in Southeast Asia and West Africa before taking command of the French forces, both white and African, that invaded and defeated the Kingdom of Dahomey in a series of hard-fought battles in the early 1890s. These men were commissioned by the French Army almost a century before the first African was commissioned by the much more class-conscious, and somewhat more race-conscious, British. In fact, a few men of African ancestry served as French officers during the *ancien régime*.[103]

The French differed somewhat from the British not only in their willingness to commission black officers but in their insistence that Africans were "born soldiers," as one of their staunch proponents, the famous General Charles Mangin, declared.[104] To underscore this point, Mangin described the bravery of Africans who fought against the French in 1890: "There were instances of magnificent madness, as when a horseman came to plant his banner some twenty paces from the French," and "There were a few horsemen of insane gallantry who paraded under our bullets slowly turning their long rifles."[105] Later, a six-foot, four-inch Bambara sergeant saved Mangin's life, becoming a hero not only in Mangin's eyes but throughout France.[106] So impressed were the French by African gallantry that one French historian recently concluded, "There was not a single opinion advanced by the French on the subject of the valor of the black soldier which has been printed that is not complimentary."[107] Some French officers privately criticized black soldiers for not standing firmly against artillery barrages or poison gas, or even for disliking night fighting—this latter criticism was also made against some of Britain's famed Guard Regiments, among other outstanding white troops.[108] But there was nothing written by French military officials that could add any support to the many "official" American declarations about black cowardice.

During World War I, France conscripted approximately 200,000 West African soldiers, compared to some half million Africans recruited by the British; however, the population from which Britain was able to draw military recruits was more than five times larger than the population of French West Africa. Most of these African conscripts served in France itself, with some 30,000 of them, or approximately 17 percent, killed in action. These troops were not very well trained when the war broke out, and a few did not fight well initially, but most fought bravely, helping to blunt the German drive into France in 1914. By the end of the war, West African troops had earned an enviable reputation for their courage just as we have seen, black American soldiers did who fought with the French at the same time.

For the first time in French history, metropolitan France had experienced the presence of large numbers of Africans. The response by French civilians was extremely welcoming. There was no evidence of a color line and little to suggest discrimination in any form. Like the American soldiers in France at this same time, these men were treated with warm affection, and although intimacy with French women was discouraged, ordinary social interaction was remarkably free of segregation.[109] Beginning in 1928, African troops from France's colonies served tours of duty in France, principally in the south. These soldiers were received extremely well, recreational centers were established throughout southern France specifically for them, and French officials organized welcoming committees to help the soldiers make a positive adjustment to France. When on leave, these African soldiers were taken to various tourist attractions and also enjoyed the use of free railway passes. As World War II approached, much of the French Army integrated itself by bringing African regiments into white French divisions. Various sources, including the diaries of French officers and men, indicate that this dramatic social experiment was well received by the French military and civilian world alike.[110]

Whereas Africans serving in the French Army during World War I constituted only about 3 percent of the French Army, in World War II that percentage would rise to almost 10. At the start of World War II, ten of the eighty French divisions defending France's border with Germany were made up of African or West Indian troops, some 200,000 men in all. Although casualty rates are difficult to ascertain because a significant number of these men became prisoners of war and did not survive their incarceration, it is likely that 12 percent of these black soldiers died during World War II.[111]

When the German invasion struck in May 1940, African infantrymen bore the brunt of the German assault, fighting tenaciously and retreating in an orderly manner even when overwhelmed by German tanks. It is impossible to determine the reality of their very strong perception that they fought far more bravely for France than did many white French units that rapidly became demoralized and surrendered. But it is clear that their resistance was fierce and that it was recognized as such by the Germans, who took brutal retaliatory measures against African soldiers. A German press account confirms this: "The French fought tenaciously; the blacks especially used every resource to the bitter end, defended every house. To break them, we had to use flame throwers, and, to overcome the last Senegalese we had to kill them one by one."[112] One thing is clear: The all-African or racially mixed regiments that fought the Germans in 1940 took far higher casualties than did the all-white French regiments.

Later in the war, black French soldiers fought in the savage Libyan campaign and then in Italy. They also played a critical role in the Free French Army that landed in southern France in August 1944, capturing Toulon. Although these men were among the best troops that General Charles de Gaulle had, when it came time for the French Army to move into Paris at the head of the Allied liberation columns, de Gaulle replaced them with white French soldiers, even though these young Frenchmen had seen relatively little combat. De Gaulle believed it was essential to make France aware that white Frenchmen had brought about the victory, thereby ridding France of its shame of defeat. For the African soldiers, this was a humiliating dismissal. Sent to barracks in southern France or West Africa, they expressed their anger in a number of conflicts brought about by their complaints of poor food, clothing, housing, lack of back pay, bans on the sale of alcohol, and disputes over access to women.

Occasionally, there was deadly conflict resulting from what the African soldiers perceived as interracial insults. In one deadly incident after the war, thirty-five African soldiers were killed and an equal number badly wounded. The African soldiers who were shot down so brutally were former prisoners of war who were angry because back pay, which had long been due them, was continually refused. Believing that they had served France far beyond the call of duty by their heroic ser-

vice on the battlefield and their tremendous suffering in German pris-
oner-of-war camps, they could not understand why France had now rejected them. It was the first of several dramatic illustrations that the
French did not truly regard blacks as their equals any more than they
did Jews or Arabs.[113] A poll taken in Paris in 1967 after an influx of perhaps 200,000 African workers since the end of World War II showed
that 52 percent of Parisians admitted holding antiblack feelings, and
American blacks who visited Paris at this time reported that they felt
French racism strongly.[114]

France sent a single regiment to Korea as a part of the United Nations
force. These troops were highly regarded by their allies, but there is no
information concerning any black soldiers who may have served in this
unit. However, West African soldiers served well during the 1945–1954
war in Indo-China. Americans tend to remember this war primarily in
terms of the ill-fated defense of Dien Bien Phu, where some black para-
troops dropped into the fortress as eleventh-hour reinforcements, while
many others served in artillery batteries whose fire often stopped Vietnamese attacks.[115] Some of these men were among the more than
10,000 who surrendered when further resistance became impossible,
and many others died.[116] The fate of Dien Bien Phu was deemed so important that American forces might well have intervened had the
British not refused to join them, but its defense was only the last act in
a long war that took the lives of over 92,000 French troops, with another 114,000 men wounded and 30,000 captured, losses that dwarfed
those of Americans, who eventually followed them to Vietnamese bat-
tlefields.[117]

And then there was Algeria, where an insurrection by Arab national-
ists led to one of the greatest crises in French history, one that threatened constitutional government and led to the very real possibility that
French troops would take over Paris by force. It can hardly be said that
the Algerian population rose up against France in an overwhelming rejection of French rule. At the end of 1956, there were only 20,000 FLN
(National Liberation Front) rebels out of a population of 9 million.[118]
By that time, France had conscripted so many new soldiers and called
up so many reservists that there were over 300,000 French troops in Algeria, the largest French Army ever sent overseas.[119]

French West African soldiers fought in Morocco in 1908, where one
battalion excelled but another fought so poorly that it had to be withdrawn. Other Tirailleurs Sénégalese fought admirably in Spanish Mo-

rocco in 1924–1925.[120] They also fought in Casablanca in 1947, where they fired on rebellious citizens. At the start of the violent rebellion in Algeria in 1943, West African troops again played an active role in France's efforts to quell the uprising, but as the violence spread and grew more and more vicious, few African soldiers took part. Their absence is strange because when riots occurred in Nice in 1947, it was West African soldiers who were sent to restore law and order.[121]

Whether as professional slave soldiers, warriors in their own African societies, conscripts, or enlistees in European military forces, Africans have achieved a widespread, well-deserved reputation for heroism in battle. Europeans who fought against them marveled at their death-defying bravery, and other white men who fought alongside them came to rely on them as soldiers of steadfast valor. Like other soldiers, they had faults—some real and some imagined—but only in America did military leaders join ordinary people in declaring that they were "natural cowards." A recent extensive review of the history of European racist beliefs about Africans makes no mention of cowardice as an African trait.[122]

EIGHT

Looking Ahead

Explaining the unique yet enduring American conviction that African Americans were unsuited for warfare because of their inherent cowardice is no simple matter. This belief was not only held by many senior American officers but the written policy of the War Department and of many senior officers throughout the military services until well after the end of the Korean War. It is true that at least one battalion of the black 92nd Division faltered during an attack near the end of World War I in France, and black men of this same division sometimes did not distinguish themselves in Italy during World War II. Some members of an all-black regiment avoided battle during the early weeks of the Korean conflict, too. Still, white troops sometimes were guilty of the same behavior in these same wars, and many black troops of the 92nd Division fought with extraordinary skill and courage in both World War I and II, just as other black troops did in Korea. What is more, as we have seen, black soldiers and sailors fought so bravely in America's earlier wars that their willingness to fight and die in battle would seem to have been proven beyond any reasonable doubt. Yet, there was not only doubt about their courage but certainty on the part of many important military and political leaders that they were too cowardly to be used in battle.

That this certainty was rooted in racism is obvious. But it was not inherent in racism everywhere. Only in America did whites steadfastly hold to this belief in black cowardice despite overwhelming evidence of their bravery in battle. The Danes, Spaniards, Belgians, Germans, Portuguese, British, and French all felt superior to Africans in one way or another but rarely if ever imputed cowardice to them. For example, French officers often praised the bravery and discipline of West African soldiers from the Bambara people but then added that they were quite stupid, implying that their lack of intelligence made it easier for them to obey white officers even when their lives were at risk.[1] And French General Charles Mangin, the foremost proponent of Africans as "natural" soldiers, did not believe that they lacked intelligence; nevertheless, he attributed their startling courage to the "fact" that their nervous systems were less developed than those of Europeans, leaving them impervious to the anticipatory fear of battle, and little frightened by combat itself.[2] A French officer agreed: "Injury does not stop him; he scorns it. It is true to say that his nervous sensitivity, very much below ours, does not let him feel pain as violently as we do."[3]

Why, then, did Americans alone among slave-owning people develop their conviction that blacks were inherently cowardly? Perhaps because the Americans had a large black slave population living on their farms and plantations, with other free African Americans living in their towns and cities. The fear of black uprisings drove Americans, especially those in the South, to prevent blacks from obtaining weapons and to keep any possibly rebellious activity under the closest scrutiny. But at the same time, Americans found it comforting to believe that all blacks were cowards and that only the most docile of these people had been sold into slavery in the United States. One can readily imagine how such a belief could have comforted U.S. whites by permitting them to believe that although blacks in Haiti might have staged a successful slave rebellion, U.S. slaves were too cowardly to attempt anything of the sort. Contrived as this belief may seem, it may have been reinforced by the absence of any massive slave rebellion in the United States or even any small ones that led to freedom for the rebels. What is more, generations of slaves learned that the best means of pacifying their owners and avoiding punishment by brutal overseers was to feign meekness and stupidity—the "Sambo" role. "Sambo" was what whites wanted to see, and the more they saw it, the more they could have become convinced that it was reality, not a self-defensive pose.

Over time, the severe punishment of any slave aggression, the rigorous surveillance of slaves' activities, and the palpable rewards for docility created a relatively tranquil slave population that used a façade of docility for its own benefit. And in time, this pattern served to reinforce the cultural stereotype of cowardice. Brazil, with a large slave population, although only about half the size of that of the United States, used similar practices to control them but did not attempt to impose a stereotype of cowardice on its slaves. Brazil's slaves were too bellicose for that. Instead, light-skinned blacks were given social privileges in return for their assistance in controlling dark-skinned slaves. Recall that light-skinned freedmen of African ancestry volunteered to fight for the Confederacy at the start of the Civil War, only to be rejected due to their "natural cowardice." Later, blacks were incorporated into integrated military units that maintained social order. Brazil's slaves were seen as backward but not cowardly.[4] The U.S. dilemma was the occasional need to use blacks in the early wars. Their bravery was ignored in the South until their feats in Cuba received such effusive praise. The reaction was white violence to intimidate them, and political actions to erase their achievements.

One reaction by blacks was to feign docility and incompetence, but blacks in the American South were not unique in adopting the so-called Sambo role of childlike docility and incompetence. During the Roman Empire, over 2 million people were enslaved, including hundreds of thousands of Greeks. Although the Romans had enormous respect for Greek "civilization," they nevertheless treated Greek slaves, some of whom were learned people, with contempt, characterizing them as unstable, irresponsible, untrustworthy, and altogether lacking in self-respect or honor.[5] It should not be surprising that these Greek slaves sometimes behaved as Romans expected them to. During the Middle Ages, Germanic tribes and Norwegians characterized their slaves, or "thralls," as childlike and unintelligent. They also thought them cowardly.[6] For the most part, these thralls were racially the same people as their Nordic masters. It is highly unlikely that only childlike, unintelligent, and cowardly people were enslaved. It is far more probable that the conditions under which slaves lived led them to develop these attributes, whether actual or simulated.

Another telling example of the ways in which slave owners' stereotypes about slaves can change comes from the British West Indies at the end of the eighteenth and the beginning of the nineteenth centuries. Like some slave masters in the American South, slave owners of British Caribbean islands were greatly outnumbered by their slaves. In an effort to control them, these owners not only imposed an especially brutal form of discipline on their African slaves but adopted some of the same stereotypes found in the American South—African slaves were lazy, mentally inferior, and timid.[7] Although such persons would hardly seem to be ideal candidates for military service, when war with France came to the Caribbean late in 1795, disease and repatriation had reduced the population of white Britons so severely that they could not form military units for their own defense. When white troops from Britain were sent to the Caribbean, most of them quickly succumbed to malaria, yellow fever, and alcoholism. The only other potential source of military manpower was African slaves and African freedmen. Most of these black soldiers were slaves, newly arrived from Africa. Few spoke any English, so it was next to impossible for their British officers to communicate with them. To improve matters, some slaves were made noncommissioned officers, a job they performed in such exemplary fashion that some were even given authority over captured white deserters, a truly shocking development in the eyes of slave owners.

The white Jamaicans, who were vastly outnumbered by their slave population, were understandably reluctant to arm slaves, but without an alternative, they did so. In the years of fighting against French forces that followed, the courage and martial skill of these men became universally respected. Their discipline and good conduct were also applauded.[8] White Jamaicans were well aware that these armed black men, most of them slaves themselves, made no attempt to weaken the institution of slavery. Instead, they fought to uphold it. In 1807, all of these black soldiers, some 10,000 men, were granted their freedom, perhaps the largest single act of manumission in the Caribbean before slavery itself was abolished. Unlike Americans, not only did Britons in the West Indies reward their black soldiers for their valor, but most came to think of them as brave men, not cowardly children.[9]

It may be difficult to understand how white Americans, at least in the North, could have failed to acknowledge the well-publicized gallantry of black soldiers during the Civil War or later in Cuba. However, history records many examples of gallant soldiers being thought militarily inept and cowardly not only by their enemies but even by their allies. For example, the Mongols saw nothing to admire in the military performances of eastern Europeans, whom they dominated for centuries. Later, these same Europeans—Russians, Poles, Serbs, Austrians, and Bulgarians—would look askance at the no longer fearsome people of Mongolia, not to mention one another. At the height of the Ottoman Empire, Turkish soldiers outfought men from a dozen countries, seizing their cities and enslaving many of their men and women. They freely expressed their contempt for the military skill and bravery of Greeks, Serbs, Bulgarians, Russians, Armenians, Egyptians, Cossacks, and Caucasian mountain people.

But by the time of the Crimean War in the mid-nineteenth century, the Ottoman Empire, and Turkey's military reputation, had fallen so low that Turkey's British and French allies joined her Russian enemy in scorning the Turkish soldiers as cowards who would only fight, if at all, from behind impregnable fortifications. In reality, the Turks would fight with reckless gallantry in battle after battle, only to receive virtually no credit for doing so from either their allies or their enemies.[10] More recently, when World War II began in the Pacific, most Britons and Americans believed that the Japanese were both inept at warfare and cowardly despite their valiant and victorious battles against Russia in 1904–1905, and again against Germany in 1914, when British troops actually fought alongside them, marveling at their reckless valor. In turn, by the 1930s, the Japanese military scorned what they described as the craven British and Americans while loudly proclaiming their superiority over the despicably timid Chinese.

These few examples, among many others like them, illustrate how easy it is for people with different cultures and religions to develop contempt for one another, especially when racial differences are involved. Even when reality proved that Mongols, Turks, or Japanese were skilled, valiant warriors, the people they conquered could still hate them, disparaging them as warriors, finding them not valiant but instead brutal, and victorious due only to their greater numbers, an advantage in weaponry, or the treachery of a third party. Mechanisms of psychological denial are so numerous and so highly effective that it was quite possible for white Americans, both North and South, to hold to their convictions about inborn black cowardice despite the historical evidence, and many did just that. But others recognized black military valor not only as a reality, but as a constant threat to the southern way of life, and when blacks returned from Cuba as heroes, the threat they posed expanded to include white supremacy itself. If blacks were equal or even superior to whites in battle, how could the doctrine of white supremacy in all things be maintained? From this time on, many southerners, and some northerners as well, were determined to erase black military achievements from history and to ensure the failure of black troops in any future wars. As we have seen, some worked openly toward this end, spreading rumors, weakening black morale, and hiding white failures, whereas others more unconsciously interpreted black achievements and failures by wholly different standards than the ones they applied to white soldiers. Many of these men occupied high places in the American military establishment.

As we have seen, it was not until well into the Korean War that black soldiers began to gain widespread respect, and not until the war in Vietnam that they finally put all questions about their courage to rest. And slowly, racial discrimination in the military was reduced to such an extent that Colin Powell could declare, "Beginning in the fifties, less discrimination, a truer merit system, and leveler playing fields existed inside the gates of our military posts than in any Southern city or Northern corporation."[11] In 1997, retired Air Force Colonel Alan L. Gropman reinforced Powell's views, writing that the U.S. armed services are "the most racially integrated mass organization in the world."[12] He insisted that no organization of anything like comparable size has more harmonious race relations and "none has as many whites being supervised by blacks—as meaningful a proof of racial integration as one could ask for."[13]

Gropman went on to point out that although blacks constitute only 14 percent of the American population, in every year since the Vietnam War 20 percent of the Army's enlistees have been black. This is so, he argued, because they see opportunities in the military services that are unavailable to them in civilian life. Blacks find military service so congenial that they reenlist half again more often than whites, producing an Army that is 30 percent black. The majority of these soldiers are in noncombat roles such as the medical field, where they receive training that is transferable to civilian careers. Gropman noted that blacks constitute 30 percent of the Army's highest-ranking enlisted personnel, sergeants-major; 11 percent of all officers; and 7 percent of all generals. The Navy, Marines, and Air Force have lower percentages of black officers, but all have senior enlisted personnel in proportion to the percentage of blacks in their force.[14]

Colonel Gropman offered this conclusion:

Clearly, African Americans see benefits in military organizations that continually educate all personnel at all ranks on the need to operate in a bias-free atmosphere; that severely penalize those who cause racial friction; that bar promotions for officers and supervisory enlisted who do not maintain a healthy racial climate; that discharge all known active

members of hate groups; that treat all people of the same rank equally in
terms of pay, allowances, housing, and medical care, regardless of race;
and that scrupulously study the results of promotion boards to ensure
freedom from racial (or any kind of ethnic or religious) prejudice.[15]

It should not be overlooked that General Benjamin O. Davis' son,
Benjamin O. Davis, Jr., became a three-star general. Roscoe Robinson,
Jr., who became an Army general in 1973, later became the first black
four-star general in the Army. Frank E. Peterson, who flew thirty-one
combat missions in Korea, became the first black Marine Corps general
in 1979, and Daniel "Chappie" James, Jr., a U.S. Air Force pilot who
flew 101 combat missions, became a four-star general in 1975. Samuel
L. Gravely became the first black admiral in 1976. Hazel W. Johnson became the first black woman general in the Army in 1979, and, of course,
Colin L. Powell became chairman of the Joint Chiefs of Staff in 1989,
the highest military position in the United States. Since the end of
World War II, there have been dozens of black generals and admirals in
the five military services.

The institutional advances in racial equality that Colonel Gropman
points to are real enough, but many members of minority groups in the
Army continue to believe that they face racial discrimination. For example, in a 1995 study not cited by Colonel Gropman, Lieutenant-
Colonel Maurice Buchanan found that 100 percent of black males, 75
percent of white females, and 50 percent of Hispanic males reported
that institutional racism still exists in the Army, whereas only 40 percent of white males agreed. Those least likely to perceive institutionalized racial discrimination were white male officers.[16] In a 1997 Armed
Forces Equal Opportunity Survey, service members of all ethnic groups
said that race relations in the military were better than in the nation
outside the military.

On the day before Thanksgiving 1999, an Associated Press photo-
graph appeared on the front pages of newspapers across the United
States showing a smiling President Clinton surrounded by fourteen
grinning American soldiers in Kosovo. Three of these soldiers were
black, including one who was a high-ranking noncommissioned officer.
Clinton told the soldiers that the example they set of African Americans, whites, Asians, and Latinos working together in the uniform of
the U.S. Army offered a message to the Kosovars and Serbs that different ethnic groups can coexist.

On that same day, Defense Secretary William S. Cohen called a Pentagon press conference to discuss two new reports about racial concerns in the military. One study showed that the percentage of women and minority officers had more than doubled during the previous twenty years. Another large survey, responded to by over 44,000 servicemen and women, found that members of all races believed that race relations were less positive in local civilian communities than they were on military bases and ships. What is more, large majorities of all races reported that they had close personal friendships with people of other races, with more than half reporting that the number of such friendships had increased since they entered the military. Almost half said that they thought race relations had improved in the military during the past five years, an answer that only 30 percent gave for the nation as a whole.

Despite these positive findings, the majority of racial and ethnic minorities reported experiencing racially offensive behavior in the military. Calling for a militarywide review of racial discrimination, Cohen told the press conference, "There is no place for racism in our society. There is certainly no place for it in the military."[17]

Concerns like these should not overshadow the progress that has been made in racial equality in the armed services, but they do call attention to the persistence of racial discrimination, or at least persistence of the belief that it exists. Army General Remo Butler has examined one significant aspect of this issue, the failure of a disproportionately large number of black officers to advance beyond the rank of major. Up to the rank of major, black officers constitute about 12 percent of the Army's officer corps, but only about half of them advance beyond the rank of major. Conversely, as rank increases, the percentage of white officers increases by about 10 percent.[18]

General Butler, himself black, does not believe that "overt racism" is the principal reason why black officers achieve high rank less often than whites. Instead, he points to a series of social and cultural phenomena that combine to disadvantage black Army officers. First, he notes that black officers who graduate from West Point or a predominantly white college succeed in the Army far better than black officers who graduate from ROTC programs in black colleges. He suggests that graduates of these latter programs have often been poorly prepared by black instructors to behave in ways that would allow them to gain the respect of senior white officers who control the promotion process. He then observes that young black officers are less likely than whites to be assigned to career-enhancing positions because whites benefit from what he calls an "old boy network."[19] When an important position is open, a senior commander is most likely to choose a junior officer whom he knows and respects. Most of the time, that junior officer will be white, not black.

What is more, Butler suggests, "Because there are relatively few senior black officers, there are fewer role models for young black officers to emulate, and few black mentors to show them the ropes and the pitfalls."[20] Butler reports that young black officers too often fail to attach themselves to a mentor early in their careers, tending to look for advice or assistance only during crises. When Butler asked senior white officers why they didn't get to know many of their black junior officers, they routinely answered that the black lieutenants either seemed hostile or "gave the impression that they didn't want to be bothered."[21] But when asked about their white junior officers, most white colonels spoke fondly and at length about them.

Although insisting that black and white Americans share "much common ground," Butler argues that there are distinct cultural differences that tend to divide black and white Americans. "And those differences influence the way we in the military interact. In this vibrant multi-cultural society, how much do we actually know about one another? How do we view our differences in dress, music, and attitudes?" His answer is that the Army is dominated by white cultural attributes that many young blacks understand poorly or not at all, and that for a young officer from a black college to enter this world can be an ordeal of culture shock.[22]

Military life, General Butler tells us, can be confusing even for experienced white officers, and young black officers and their spouses frequently do not know what is expected of them. Should they attend a formal "hail and farewell" ceremony for a retiring senior white officer? At informal events, he reports, any officer not wearing "khaki pants, pullover shirts with collars, and loafers" is not merely violating an informal dress code but likely to be perceived as a rebel. Similarly, for a black or Hispanic male officer, a well-groomed mustache may be culturally correct, but white officers see mustaches as indicators of rebellion. Generals, Butler tells us, do not have mustaches: "And there is an old adage in the Army that generals make people who look like themselves generals."[23] According to Butler, at present only West Point provides young officer candidates with formal training in military customs and courtesy.

General Butler believes that the current tensions resulting from military culture shock can be overcome with better education and mentoring. He rejects the idea that these tensions and the failure of most black officers to advance to senior rank are a product of racism. Most analysts of today's military services agree with him. There is need for better socialization of young African American officers, and the challenges of overcoming cultural confusion and conflict will not easily be met, but no matter how difficult it may be to develop a racism-free "one Army," "one Navy," "one Marine Corps," "one Air Force," and "one Coast Guard," the U.S. military services have come a long way from that all-too-recent time when military leaders insisted that blacks were by nature "childlike, unintelligent, and cowardly." Racism may never be eliminated altogether, but the "natural cowards" are gone forever.

Notes

Introduction

1. *Newsweek*, June 7, 1999, p. 30.
2. *Los Angeles Times*, June 4, 1999.
3. *Newsweek*, June 7, 1999.
4. Powell (1995:62).

Chapter 1

1. Quarles (1996:8).
2. Quarles (1996:13–14).
3. Foner (1974:7).
4. Fick (1990).
5. Litwack (1979:16).
6. Ibid.
7. Russell (1863:119).
8. Olmstead (1860).
9. Hofstadter and Wallace (1970:187).
10. Robertson (2000).
11. Frazier (1949:89).
12. Genovese (1979); Kolchin (1983).
13. Thomas (1997:424).
14. Taylor (2000).
15. Fischer (1989:52).
16. Wood (1974).
17. Dirks (1987).
18. Fick (1990:25–26).
19. Mintz (1995:13).
20. Ibid.
21. Furnas (1969:99).
22. Ibid., p. 105.
23. Ibid., p. 117.
24. Nell (1855:216–217).
25. Fischer (1989:389).
26. Wyatt-Brown (1982:16).
27. Fischer (1989:260–261).
28. Berlin (1980:13).
29. Dirks (1987).
30. Litwack (1979:3).
31. Frazier (1949:56).
32. Patterson (1982:65).
33. Tadman (1989:21).
34. Nell (1855:221).
35. Litwack (1979).
36. Weatherly (1923:292).
37. Mazrui (1977).
38. Anonymous (1877).
39. Fiske (1970:62).
40. Nell (1855:12).
41. Quarles (1996:11; see also xxii).
42. Ibid., p. xxiii.
43. Donaldson (1991:15).
44. Quarles (1996:142).
45. Ibid., p. 174.
46. Bennett (1969).
47. Kaplan (1973:47).
48. Lanning (1997:15).
49. Quarles (1996:82).
50. Nell (1855); Gibbs (1975).
51. Bolster (1997).
52. Kaplan (1973:47).
53. Langley (1967).
54. Litwack (1961:162); Frazier (1949:62).
55. Glatthaar (1990:8).
56. Donaldson (1991:29).
57. Ibid., p. 25.
58. McConnell (1968).
59. Ibid.
60. Lanning (1997:26).
61. Nalty (1986:27).
62. Langley (1967).

63. Fleetwood (1895:4).
64. Porter (1996).
65. Peters (1979:12).
66. Foner (1974:30).
67. Mulroy (1993:29).
68. Porter (1996:10).
69. Litwack (1979:37); Cornish (1966:16).
70. Brewer (1969:167).
71. Franklin (1956:84).
72. Bosman (1721).
73. Woodward (1974:16).
74. Frazier (1949).
75. Woodward (1974:20).
76. Litwack (1961:36).
77. Frazier (1949:77).
78. Litwack (1961:155).
79. Hofstadter and Wallace (1970:208).
80. Litwack (1961:224).
81. Basler and Basler (1990:256).
82. Fleetwood (1895:10–11).
83. Furnas (1969:847–850); Hofstadter and Wallace (1970:12–21).
84. Litwack (1979:51).
85. Washington (1903:726).
86. Cornish (1966).
87. Litwack (1979:66).
88. Foner (2000:10–11).
89. Glatthaar (1990:146).
90. Hallowell (1897).
91. Glatthaar (1990:203); Cornish (1966:172).
92. Glatthaar (1990:153).
93. Cornish (1966:86).
94. Palfrey (1863).
95. General's Reports, U.S. Congress, 1863, Vol. 14, p. 133.
96. National Intelligencer, August 24, 1863.
97. Litwack (1979:70).
98. Villard (1903:721).
99. Higginson (1960:30).
100. Ibid., p. 10.
101. McElroy (1879).
102. Higginson (1960:8).
103. Ibid., p. 203.
104. Glatthaar (1990:107).
105. Higginson (1960:43).
106. Ibid., p. 54.
107. Ibid., p. 206.
108. Lanning (1997:54).
109. Emilio (1969).
110. Washington (1903:724).
111. Nalty and MacGregor (1981:32–33).
112. New York Times, March 7, 1864.
113. Nalty and MacGregor (1981:29).
114. U.S. Congress, House Report of the Joint Select Committee on the Conduct of the War, Fort Pillow Massacre, 38th Cong., 1st sess., May 5, 1864, H. Report. no. 65.
115. Lockett (1998); Cimprich and Mainfort (1988).
116. Cornish (1966:173); see also Castle (1974).
117. Wills (1992).
118. Litwack (1979:92).
119. Castle (1974).
120. Cornish (1966:168).
121. Redkey (1992:157).
122. Quarles (1953:38).
123. January 2, 1864, War of Rebellion Records: A Compilation of the Official Records of the Union and Confederate Armies, Washington, DC, 1880–1891.
124. Conrad (1990:110).
125. Franklin and Schweninger (1999).
126. Frederickson (1971:169).
127. Williamson (1965:275–276).
128. Quarles (1953:314).
129. Cornish (1966:147).
130. Miller and Zophy (1978:237).
131. Wills (1906:166–167, 176, 183–184).
132. Fleetwood (1895:12).
133. Ibid., p. 13.
134. Christian Recorder, April 23, 1864.
135. Fox-Genovese (1988:315).

136. Morgan (1966:75).

137. Quarles (1953:331).

Chapter 2

1. Donaldson (1991:46).

2. Woodward (1928:372).

3. Miller and Zophy (1978:240).

4. Donaldson (1991:52).

5. Fox-Genovese (1988:5).

6. Lewinson (1965:20).

7. Ibid., p. 48.

8. Ibid., p. 45.

9. Schurz (1904:303).

10. Hofstadter and Wallace (1970:223).

11. Shapiro (1988:11, 18).

12. Singletary (1984:3).

13. Ibid., p. 47.

14. Ibid., p. 145.

15. Woodward (1974:31).

16. Leckie (1967:99, 235).

17. *Harper's Weekly*, September 7, 1867.

18. *New York Times*, November 20, 1893; Villard (1903:722).

19. Mulroy (1993:116).

20. Ibid., p. 125.

21. Sherman (1877).

22. Woodward (1974:38–40).

23. Hofstadter and Wallace (1970:20).

24. Black and Black (1985:75).

25. Ibid.

26. Donaldson (1991:65).

27. Marszalek (1972).

28. Logan (1965:44).

29. Ibid., p. 100; see also Wells-Barnett (1910).

30. Ibid., p. 99.

31. Congressional Record, 55th Congress, 3rd Session, 1898, p. 342.

32. Logan (1965:244–245).

33. Woodward (1966).

34. Shapiro (1988:71).

35. Graham (1999:12).

36. Ibid.

37. Shapiro (1988:85).

38. Trask (1981:3).

39. Foner (1974:73).

40. Walker (1998:84); Musicant (1990:276).

41. *New York Times*, March 11, 1899, p. 6.

42. Rouse (1898).

43. Post (1960:53).

44. Trask (1981:184).

45. Ibid.

46. Gatewood (1970).

47. "Colored Troops Disembarking," Edison Manufacturing Co., 1898.

48. Trask (1981:214).

49. Walker (1998:183).

50. Musicant (1998:393).

51. Ibid. p. 209.

52. Trask (1981:237).

53. Cashin et al. (1969:163).

54. Ibid., p. 160.

55. Ibid., p. 128.

56. Ibid.

57. Aptheker (1977:Vol. 3, p. 213).

58. Villard (1903:724).

59. Lanning (1997:70).

60. Gatewood (1971:45).

61. Trask (1981:247).

62. Cashin et al. (1969:229).

63. Ibid., p. 160.

64. Ibid., p. xiv.

65. Kennan (1899:144).

66. Ibid.

67. Ibid., p. 264.

68. Musicant (1998:591).

69. Cashin et al. (1969:266).

70. *Savannah Tribune*, March 18, 1899.

71. Lanning (1997:94).

72. Woodward (1974:74).

73. Foner (1974:82).

74. Gatewood (1975:242).

75. Bigelow (1925:283–284).

76. Furnas (1969:854).

77. Ibid.

78. Linn (1997).

79. Gatewood (1975:244).

80. Ibid., p. 282.

81. Robinson and Schubert (1975).

82. *Outlook*, Vol. 70, March 22, 1902, pp. 711–712.

83. Linn (1989:27).

84. Flower (1902:650).

85. Clark (1899:288).

86. Ibid.

87. Ibid.

88. Ibid.

89. Linn (1989).

90. *Outlook*, 1902, p. 711.

91. Gatewood (1975:266).

92. Harrod (1978).

93. *New York Times*, September 7, 1904, p. 3.

94. Weaver (1970).

95. Nalty and MacGregor (1981:63).

96. Pringle (1931:461–462).

97. Weaver (1970:218–219).

98. Roosevelt (1913).

99. Donaldson (1991:78).

100. Foner (1974:103).

101. Baker (1908:17).

102. Ibid., p. 16.

103. Ibid., p. 167.

104. Ibid., p. 28.

105. Aptheker (1975:29).

106. Shapiro (1988:83).

107. Ibid., p. 62.

108. Roberts (1983:108).

109. Ibid.

110. Clendenen (1969:257).

111. Robinson (1947:viii).

112. Ibid., p. 254.

113. Estell (1994:673).

Chapter 3

1. Keegan (1999).

2. Kolata (1999).

3. Furnas (1974:24).

4. Scott (1919: 33).

5. *Crisis*, June-July 1918.

6. Foner (1974:109); Miller (1924:10).

7. *Messenger*, January 1918.

8. Williams (1970:21); Barbeau and Henri (1974:35–37).

9. Foner (1974:111).

10. Heywood (1928:3–4).

11. Barbeau and Henri (1974:34–35).

12. Little (1974:106–107).

13. Coffman (1968:60–61).

14. Barbeau and Henri (1974:47–48).

15. Williams (1970:140–141).

16. Heywood (1928:3–4).

17. Ibid., pp. 4–5.

18. Ibid., pp. 5–6.

19. Ibid., p. 9.

20. *Columbia Record*, April 2, 1918.

21. Little (1974:49).

22. Scott (1919:113).

23. Barbeau and Henri (1974:21).

24. Dowd (1926:58–59).

25. Scott (1919:108).

26. Barbeau and Henri (1974:100).

27. Ibid., p. 101.

28. Scott (1919:108).

29. Ibid., pp. 97–98.

30. Patton (1981:57).

31. Ibid., p. 69.

32. Williams (1970).

33. Patton (1981:81).

34. Wilson (1917).

35. Astor (1998:97).

36. Barbeau and Henri (1974:102).

37. Williams (1970: 63).

38. Delsarte (1919:15).

39. Barbeau and Henri (1974:103).

40. Bliss (1919:28–29).

41. Chandler (1995).

42. Hunton and Johnson (1997:27).

43. Coffman (1968:134–135).

44. Williams (1970:74).

45. Coffman (1968:195).

46. Scott (1919:227–228).

47. Woodson (1921:524).

48. Lanning (1997:138).

49. Heywood (1928:33).

50. Sweeney (1919:142–145).

51. Scott (1919:267).

52. I. S. Cobb, *Saturday Evening Post*, June 1918.

53. Scott (1919:211).

54. Barbeau and Henri (1974:133).

55. Ibid., p. 135.
56. Ibid.
57. Sweeney (1919:155).
58. Ibid., p. 182.
59. Heywood (1928:238–239).
60. Cobb (1918:295).
61. Barbeau and Henri (1974:137).
62. Dowd (1926:102).
63. Mason and Furr (1920:41–42).
64. Hunton and Johnson (1997:43).
65. Lee (1963:9).
66. Bullard (1925:295).
67. Barbeau and Henri (1974:138).
68. Moton (1919).
69. Greer (1918).
70. Millett (1975:429).
71. Ross (1920:114–115).
72. Patton (1981:95).
73. Barbeau and Henri (1974:155).
74. Du Bois (1919:82).
75. Cushing (1936:464).
76. Barbeau and Henri (1974:156).
77. Ibid., p. 157; see also Lee (1963).
78. Patton (1981:95).
79. Barbeau and Henri (1974:161).
80. Ibid.
81. Bullard (1925:296).
82. Ross (1920:5).
83. Ibid., p. 9.
84. Ibid., p. 44.
85. Ibid., p. 64.
86. Ibid., p. 68–69.
87. Ibid., p. 80–81.
88. Williams (1970:166).
89. Millet (1975:429).
90. Bullard (1925:297).
91. Williams (1970:185).
92. Cooley (1919:39).
93. Barbeau and Henri (1974:166).
94. Williams (1970).
95. Little (1974:349).
96. Barbeau and Henri (1974:170).
97. Foner (1974:125).

Chapter 4

1. *The World*, February 18, 1919.
2. Little (1974:361).
3. U.S. Senate (1923:55–59; 494–497, 502–505, 568).
4. Ibid., pp. 473–474.
5. Moton (1919:159).
6. White (1929:28).
7. Ibid., p. 112.
8. Furnas (1974:291).
9. Perrett (1982:88).
10. Wade (1987:203).
11. Ibid., pp. 203–204.
12. Shapiro (1988:154).
13. Grimke (1919:8).
14. Hofstadter and Wallace (1970:247).
15. Perrett (1982:87).
16. Mowry (1963:128–129).
17. *New York Times*, September 30, 1919, p. 5.
18. White (1948:48–49).
19. Ellsworth (1982).
20. Kolker (1999).
21. Shapiro (1988:xvi).
22. Marks (1983:297).
23. Nelson (1970:626).
24. Perrett (1982:83).
25. Farrington (1971:36).
26. Reid (1992).
27. Lindop (1970:56).
28. Farrington (1971:36); Furnas (1974: 319).
29. Erens (1990:131).
30. Cripps (1993:23).
31. Noble (1970:79).
32. Null (1990:76).
33. Noble (1970:57).
34. Furnas (1977:43).
35. Noble (1970:11–12).
36. Buckler (1954)
37. Logan (1965:166).
38. Mowry (1963:136).
39. Furnas (1974:50).
40. Mowry (1963).
41. Overshine (1918).
42. Patton (1981:121).
43. Ibid., p. 120.

44. Myrdal (1944:91).
45. Gropman (1978:3).
46. Ely (1925).
47. Bullard (1925).
48. White (1929:88–89).
49. Patton (1981:147).
50. Lee (1963:45).
51. Ringel (1932:310).
52. Lindop (1970:85).
53. Furnas (1977:189).
54. Kester (1969:59).
55. Frazier (1949:599); Shapiro (1988:263).
56. Allen et al. (2000)
57. Carter (1969).
58. Aptheker (1973:721).
59. Powell (1938:187).
60. Estell (1994).
61. White (1948:67).
62. Ibid., p. 180.
63. Margolick (2000:126).
64. Ibid., p. 117.
65. Baker (1986).
66. Aptheker (1992:195).
67. Astor (1974:169).
68. Foner (1974:131).
69. Houston (1934).
70. Houston (1938).
71. Mershon and Schlossman (1998:25).
72. McGuire (1983:17).
73. Ibid., p. 66.
74. Early (1940:1–2).
75. McGuire (1983:8).
76. White (1948:63).
77. Patton (1981:168–169).
78. Foner (1974:141).
79. Prange (1978:514–515).

Chapter 5

1. Lee (1963:88).
2. Shapiro (1988:340).
3. Dalfiume (1969:122).
4. Hughes, L. "Beaumont to Detroit," *Common Ground*, Fall 1943, p. 104.
5. Lanning (1997:164).
6. Hodgson (1990:248 ff.).
7. Dalfiume (1969:45).
8. Ibid., pp. 56–57.
9. Stimson (1940).
10. McGuire (1983:xxx).
11. Dalfiume (1969:65).
12. Motley (1975:218).
13. *Pittsburgh Courier*, January 10, 1942.
14. McGuire (1983:77).
15. Bennett (1969:415).
16. Terkel (1984:150).
17. Motley (1975:57).
18. Lee (1963:366).
19. Ibid., p. 349.
20. Foner (1974:154).
21. Motley (1975:247).
22. Shapiro (1988:337).
23. Ibid., p. 332.
24. Powell (1945:171–172).
25. Motley (1975:61, 162).
26. Shapiro (1988:308).
27. Robinson and Duckett (1965:44).
28. Motley (1975:76).
29. Ibid., p. 51.
30. Ibid., p. 191.
31. Ibid., p. 257.
32. Lee (1963:440).
33. Palmer (1986).
34. Lee (1963:438).
35. Astor (1998:247).
36. White (1948:225).
37. Shogan and Craig (1964).
38. Cripps and Culbert (1979).
39. Cripps (1993).
40. Lee (1963:387).
41. Ibid., p. 388.
42. Noble (1970:199).
43. Meckiffe and Murray (1998).
44. Cripps (1993:18).
45. Carson (1946); Coffey (1991).
46. Osur (1977).
47. Carisella and Ryan (1972).
48. Blum (1976:192)
49. Hasdorff (1977).
50. McGuire (1983:xvi).

51. Rose (1975).
52. Ibid.
53. Ibid., p. 124.
54. Lee (1963:160).
55. Biggs (1986:19).
56. Hasdorff (1977).
57. Nalty (1997:151).
58. Osur (1977:50).
59. Motley (1975:210).
60. Francis (1955:193–194).
61. Motley (1975:242).
62. Ibid., p. 215.
63. Ibid.
64. Ibid., p. 249.
65. White (1948).
66. Lee (1963:527).
67. Motley (1975:99).
68. Lee (1963:534).
69. Motley (1975:101).
70. White(1948:285).
71. Motley (1975:102, 117).
72. Baker and Olsen (1997:2).
73. Estell (1994:745).
74. Turner (1974).
75. Motley (1975:339).
76. Ibid.
77. Lee (1963:543).
78. Baker and Olsen (1997:151).
79. Lee (1963:555, 573).
80. Baker and Olsen (1997).
81. Lee (1963:589).
82. *Newsweek*, June 8, 1970, p. 45.
83. Hargrove (1985).
84. Lee (1963:689).
85. White (1948:251).
86. Lee (1963:697).
87. Ibid., p. 698.
88. Ibid., p. 702.
89. Ibid.
90. Lee (1963:664).
91. Motley (1975:152).
92. Terkel (1984:263).
93. Motley (1975:159).
94. *Los Angeles Times*, November 11, 1999.
95. Motley (1975:160).
96. Foner (1974:193).
97. MacGregor (1981:92).
98. Stillwell (1993).
99. MacGregor (1981:121–122).
100. Ibid., p. 100.
101. Shaw and Donnelly (1975:2).
102. Ibid., p. 35.
103. *Time*, July 24, 1944.
104. Moore (1996:135).
105. Motley (1975:171).

Chapter 6

1. Levine (1978:341).
2. White (1948:331).
3. *Newsweek*, September 16, 1946, p. 30.
4. Foner (1974:192).
5. Ibid., p. 182.
6. Miller (1973:183).
7. Executive Order 9981, July 26, 1948, item 164.
8. Shaw and Donnelly (1975:54–55).
9. Goulden (1982:125); Bowers et al. (1997).
10. Appleman (1961:194–195).
11. Bussey (1991).
12. Lanning (1997:227).
13. Astor (1998:384).
14. Foner (1974:191).
15. Hastings (1987).
16. Foner (1974:190).
17. Rishell (1993:47).
18. Ibid., p. xiv.
19. Bussey (1991).
20. Bowers et al. (1997).
21. Lanning (1997:229).
22. Bogart (1969:22).
23. Morrow (1997:37).
24. Ibid., p. 29.
25. Goulden (1982).
26. Morrow (1997).
27. Shaw and Donnelly (1975:59).
28. Ibid., p. 61.
29. Ibid., p. 59.
30. *U.S. News and World Report*, May 11, 1956.

31. Ibid.
32. Ibid.
33. Ibid.
34. Woodward (1974:163).
35. Brooks (1974).
36. Woodward (1974:181).
37. Belknap (1987:147–148).
38. Brooks (1974).
39. Conot (1967).
40. Nalty (1997:313).
41. *Los Angeles Times*, February 22, 2000.
42. Baskin and Strauss (1978:98).
43. Westheider (1997:23).
44. Ibid., p. 29.
45. Goff, Sanders, and Smith (1982).
46. Astor (1998:428).
47. Terry (1984:249).
48. Ibid., p. 250.
49. Ibid., p. 265.
50. Taylor (1973:19).
51. Terry (1984:xvi); Goff, Sanders, and Smith (1982).
52. Moskos and Butler (1996:8).
53. Goff, Sanders, and Smith (1982:133).
54. Branch (1988).
55. Taylor (1973:183).
56. Westheider (1997).
57. Terry (1984:157).
58. *Ebony*, January, 1973 pp. 100–106.
59. Westheider (1997:81).
60. Mershon and Schlossman (1998).
61. Hauser (1973:98–102).
62. Taylor (1973:206).
63. Ibid., p. 207.
64. Ibid., p. 209.
65. Stern (1971:215).
66. Hope (1979).
67. Powell (1995:193).
68. Astor (1998:454).
69. *Los Angeles Times*, November 29, 1999, p. B7.
70. *Ebony*, December 1972.
71. Moscos and Butler (1996).
72. Tyson (1998).

73. Gordon and Trainor (1995).
74. Cannon (1997).
75. Miller and Moskos (1995).
76. Ibid., p. 622.
77. Ibid., p. 628.
78. Ibid.
79. Bowden (1999:329).
80. Miller and Moskos (1995:637).
81. Ibid., p. 620.
82. Moskos and Butler (1996:36).

Chapter 7

1. Patterson (1982:177–178).
2. Pipes (1981).
3. Ibid., p. 10.
4. Ibid., p. 183.
5. Newitt (1995).
6. Cann (1997:88).
7. Ibid., pp. 88, 106.
8. Boxer (1963:106–107); Toplin (1981).
9. Freyre (1986:351).
10. Boxer (1963:101).
11. Boxer (1963); Bender (1975); Degler (1971).
12. Bender (1975:112).
13. Boxer (1963:85); Cann (1997:99).
14. Medea (1997).
15. Fernandes (1969); Sodré (1965); Stepan (1971).
16. Ramos (1939).
17. Skidmore (1993:14); de Azevedo (1998).
18. Silva (1993).
19. Nunn (1975:6).
20. Ramos (1939:30).
21. Ibid., p. 151.
22. Palmer (1976).
23. Hochschild (1998).
24. Meditz and Merrill (1994).
25. Callaghy (1984).
26. Packenham (1991).
27. Rubenson (1970:121).
28. Marcus (1975).
29. Packenham (1991:486).
30. Rubenson (1970:126).

31. Ibid., p. 132.
32. Ibid., p. 142.
33. Coffey (1974).
34. Sbacchi (1997).
35. Mockler (1984).
36. Miller (1974:10).
37. Redmayne (1968:409).
38. Ibid., p. 419.
39. Bridgman (1981).
40. Ibid., p. 103.
41. Ibid.
42. Meinertzhagen (1960:105).
43. Miller (1974:308).
44. Ibid., p. 314.
45. Bartl (1995); Fick (1990:26).
46. Fryer (1984).
47. Ibid., p. 9.
48. Ibid., p. 191.
49. Ibid., p. 233.
50. Ibid., pp. 440–444.
51. Douglass (1962).
52. Fryer (1984).
53. Smith (1987:119).
54. Fryer (1984).
55. Noble (1970:10).
56. Rose (1997:147).
57. Rich (1990:51–53).
58. Hiro (1971).
59. Lloyd (1964:88).
60. Edgerton (1995).
61. Emery (1977:92).
62. Edgerton (1988:129).
63. Moodie (1879:281).
64. Ibid., p. 288.
65. Emery (1977:204).
66. Kipling (1899:9)
67. Meredith (1998).
68. Churchill (1987:87).
69. Steevens (1898:264).
70. Ibid.
71. Ziegler (1974:132).
72. Ibid., p. 167.
73. Steevens (1898:17).
74. Lucas (1923:338).
75. Ibid., p.365.

76. Lucas (1924, Vol. 4:117); Johnson (1917).
77. Lucas (1923:339).
78. Killingray (1987:281).
79. Fletcher (1989:104).
80. Fryer (1984:83).
81. Wilson (1976).
82. Buckley (1979).
83. Sherwood (1985).
84. Barnett (1970).
85. Fortescue, (1910–1930, Vol. 10:168).
86. Hastings (1987:329).
87. Hastings and Jenkins (1983:314).
88. Frost (1983).
89. Monaghan (1998).
90. *Washington Times*, May 8, 1984, p. 3.
91. Killingray (1987:284).
92. Hill and Hogg (1995).
93. Cohen (1990:x).
94. Ibid.
95. Ibid., p. 285.
96. Ibid., p. 6.
97. Ibid., p. 64.
98. Ibid., p. 112.
99. Ibid., p. 119.
100. Kanya-Forstner (1969:37).
101. Davis (1934:46).
102. Martyn (1911:207–208).
103. Echenberg (1985:19).
104. Ibid., p. 29.
105. Mangin (1930:71, 82).
106. Echenberg (1985:32).
107. Balesi (1979:33).
108. Higginson (1916:175).
109. Balesi (1979); Echenberg (1985).
110. Echenberg (1985:368).
111. Ibid., p. 365.
112. Ibid., p. 373.
113. Conklin (1997); Bernstein (1990).
114. Cohen (1980:286–288).
115. Simpson (1994).
116. Roy (1965:12).

117. Talbott (1980:6).
118. Ibid., p. 49.
119. Ibid., p. 73.
120. Porch (1991:398).
121. Clayton (1988:154).
122. Jahoda (1999).

Chapter 8

1. Marceau (1911:4).
2. Clayton (1988:338).
3. Marceau (1911:65).
4. Toplin (1981).
5. Petrochitos (1974:40–41).
6. Patterson (1982:249).
7. Braithwaite (1971).
8. Buckley (1979:105).

9. Ibid.
10. Edgerton (1999).
11. Powell (1995:62).
12. Gropman (1997:1).
13. Ibid.
14. Ibid., p. 2.
15. Ibid.
16. Butler (1999:61–62).
17. *Los Angeles Times*, November 24, 1999, p. A5.
18. Butler (1999:54).
19. Ibid., p. 60.
20. Ibid., p. 61.
21. Ibid., p. 62.
22. Ibid., p. 63.
23. Ibid., p. 64.

Bibliography

Abbot, P., and M. R. Rodriguez. *Angola and Mozambique, 1961–1974*. London: Osprey, 1988.

Allen, J., H. Als, J. Lewis, and L. F. Litwack. *Without Sanctuary: Lynching Photography in America*. Santa Fe, NM: Twin Palms, 2000.

Anonymous. "A British Officer in Boston in 1775." *Atlantic Monthly*, 39:389–401, 544–554, 1877.

Appleman, R. E. *South to the Naktong, North to the Yalu*. Washington, DC: Office of the Chief of Military History, Department of the Army, 1961.

Aptheker, H. (ed.). *A Documentary History of the Negro People in the United States, 1910–1932*. Secaucus, NJ: Citadel Press.

Astor, G. *". . . And a Credit to His Race": The Hard Life and Times of Joseph Louis Barrow, a.k.a. Joe Louis*. New York: Saturday Review Press, 1974.

_____. *The Right to Fight: A History of African Americans in the Military*. Novato, CA: Presidio Press, 1998.

Baker, R. S. *Following the Color Line*. New York: Doubleday, Page & Company, 1908.

Baker, V. J., and K. Olsen. *Lasting Valor*. Columbus, MS: Genesis Press, 1997.

Baker, W. J. *Jesse Owens: An American Life*. New York: Free Press, 1986.

Balesi, C. J. *From Adversaries to Comrades-in-Arms: West Africans and the French Military, 1885–1918*. Waltham, MA: Crossroads Press, 1979.

Barbeau, A. E., and F. Henri. *The Unknown Soldiers: Black American Troops in World War I*. Philadelphia: Temple University Press, 1974.

Barnett, C. *Britain and Her Army, 1509–1970: A Military, Political and Social Survey*. London: Penguin Press, 1970.

Barrow, J. L., Jr., and B. Munder. *Joe Louis: 50 Years an American Hero*. New York: McGraw-Hill, 1988.

Bartl, R. "Native American Tribes and Their African Slaves." In S. Palmié (ed.), *Slave Cultures and the Culture of Slavery*. Knoxville: University of Tennessee Press, 1995. Pp. 162–175.

Baskin, L. M., and W. Strauss. *Chance and Circumstance: The Draft, the War, and Vietnam*. New York: Random House, 1978.

Basler, P., and O. Basler (eds.). *The Collected Works of Abraham Lincoln: Second Supplement, 1848–1865*. New Brunswick, NJ: Rutgers University Press, 1990.

Belknap, M. R. *Federal Law and Southern Order*. Athens: University of Georgia Press, 1987.

Bender, G. J. *The Myth and Reality of Portuguese Rule in Angola: A Study of Racial Domination*. Ph.D. Dissertation, UCLA, 1975.

245

Bennett, L., Jr. *Before the Mayflower: A History of Black America*. Chicago: Johnson, 1969.

Berlin, I. "Time, Space, and the Evolution of Afro-American Society on British Mainland North America." *American Historical Review*, 85:44–78, 1980.

Bernstein, R. *Fragile Glory: A Portrait of France and the French*. New York: Knopf, 1990.

Bigelow, P. *Seventy Summers*, 2 vols. New York: Longmans, Green, 1925.

Biggs, B. *The Triple Nickels: America's First All-Black Paratroop Unit*. Hamden, CT: Archon, 1986.

Binkin, M. "The New Face of American Military: The Volunteer Force and the Persian Gulf War." *Brookings Review*, 9:7–13, 1991.

Black, L. D., and S. H. Black. *An Officer and a Gentleman: The Military Career of Lieutenant Henry O. Flipper*. Dayton, OH: Lora, 1985.

Blackwelder, J. K. "Quiet Suffering: Atlanta Women in the 1930's." *Georgia Historical Quarterly*. 61:53–65, 1977.

Blassingame, J. W. *Black New Orleans: 1860–1880*. Chicago: University of Chicago Press, 1973.

Bliss, J. G. *History of the 805th Pioneer Infantry*. St. Paul, MN: Privately published, 1919.

Blum, J. M. *V Was for Victory: Politics and American Culture During World War II*. New York: Harcourt, Brace, Jovanovich, 1976.

Bogart, L. *Social Research and the Desegregation of the U.S. Army*. Chicago: Markham, 1969.

Boles, J. B., and E. T. Nolen (eds.). *Interpreting Southern History: Historiographical Essays in Honor of Sanford W. Higginbotham*. Baton Rouge: Louisiana State University Press, 1987.

Bolster, W. J. *Black Jacks: African American Seamen in the Age of Sail*. Cambridge: Harvard University Press, 1997.

Bosman, W. *A New and Accurate Description of the Coast of Guinea, Divided into the Gold, the Slave, and the Ivory Coast*, 2nd ed. London: Knapton, 1721.

Bowden, M. *Black Hawk Down: A Story of Modern War*. New York: Atlantic Monthly Press, 1999.

Bowers, W. T., W. M. Hammond, and G. MacGarrigle. *Black Soldier, White Army: The 24th Infantry Regiment in Korea*. Washington: U.S. Army Center of Military History, 1997.

Boxer, C. R. *Race Relations in the Portuguese Colonial Empire, 1415–1825*. Oxford: Clarendon, 1963.

Braithwaite, E. *The Development of Creole Society in Jamaica, 1770–1820*. Oxford: Clarendon, 1971.

Branch, T. *Parting the Waters: America in the King Years, 1954–1963*. New York: Touchstone, 1988.

Brewer, J. H. *The Confederate Negro: Virginia's Craftsmen and Military Laborers, 1861–1865*. Durham, NC: Duke University Press, 1969.

Bridgman, J. M. *The Revolt of the Hereros*. Berkeley: University of California Press, 1981.

Brooks, T. R. *Walls Came Tumbling Down: A History of the Civil Rights Movement, 1940–1970*. Englewood Cliffs, NJ: Prentice-Hall, 1974.

Bruge, R. *Juin 1940: Le Mois Maudit*. Paris: Fayard, 1980.

Buckler, H. *Daniel Hale Williams: Negro Surgeon*. New York: Pitman, 1954.

Buckley, R. N. *Slaves in Red Coats: The British West India Regiments, 1795–1815.* New Haven: Yale University Press, 1979.

Bullard, R. L. *Personalities and Reminiscences of the War.* New York: Doubleday, Page, 1925.

Bussey, C. M. *Firefight at Yechon.* MacLean, VA: Brassey's, 1991.

Butler, J. S. *Inequality in the Military: The Black Experience.* Saratoga, CA: Century Twenty One, 1980.

_____. "Race Relations in the Military." In C. C. Moskos and F. R. Wood (eds.), *The Military: More Than Just a Job?* New York: Pergamon, 1988. Pp. 115–127.

Butler, R. "Why Black Officers Fail." *Parameters,* Autumn, 54–69, 1999.

Callaghy, T. M. *The State-Society Struggle: Zaire in Comparative Perspective.* New York: Columbia University Press, 1984.

Cann, J. P. *Counterinsurgency in Africa: The Portuguese Way of War, 1961–1974.* Westport, CT: Greenwood Press, 1997.

Cannon, L. *Official Negligence: How Rodney King and the Riots Changed Los Angeles and the LAPD.* New York: Random House, 1997.

Carisella, P. J., and J. W. Ryan. *The Black Swallow of Death.* Boston: Marlborough House, 1972.

Carson, J. M. H. *Home Away from Home: The Story of the USO.* New York: Harper, 1946.

Carter, D. T. *Scottsboro: A Tragedy of the American South.* Baton Rouge: Louisiana State University Press, 1969.

Carter, P. A. *Another Part of the Twenties.* New York: Columbia University Press, 1977.

Cashin, H. V., and others. *Under Fire with the Tenth U.S. Cavalry.* Salem, NH: Ayer, 1969. (Orig. 1899.)

Castle, A. "Fort Pillow: Victory or Massacre?" *American History Illustrated,* 9:5–10, 46–48, 1974.

Chadbourn, J. H. *Lynching and the Law.* Chapel Hill: University of North Carolina Press, 1933.

Challener, R. D. *The French Theology of the Nation in Arms, 1866–1939.* New York: Columbia University Press, 1955.

Chandler, S. K. "'That Biting, Stinging Thing Which Ever Shadows Us.' African-American Social Workers in France During World War I." *Social Service Review,* 69:498–514, 1995.

Churchill, W. S. *The River War: The Sudan, 1898.* London: Sceptre, 1987. (Orig. 1899.)

Cimprich, J., and R. C. Mainfort, Jr. "Fort Pillow Revisited: New Evidence About an Old Controversy." *Civil War History,* 28:293–306, 1982.

Clark, E. P. "Our Savage War 'for the Cause of Humanity.'" *The Nation,* 68:288, 1899.

Clayton, A. *France, Soldiers and Africa.* London: Brassey's Defense, 1988.

Cleburne, P. R. "Memorial . . . to the Army of Tennessee, 2 January, 1864." *War of Rebellion Records: A Compilation of the Official records of the Union and Confederate Armies.* Washington, DC: 1864.

Clendenen, C. C. *Blood on the Border: The United States Army and the Mexican Irregulars.* New York: Macmillan, 1969.

Cobb, I. S. *The Glory of the Coming.* New York: George H. Doran, 1918.

Coffey, F. *Fifty Years in the USO: Always Home.* Washington, DC: Brassey's, 1991.

Coffey, T. M. *Lion by the Tail: The Story of the Italian Ethiopian War.* New York: Viking, 1974.

Coffman, E. M. *The War to End All Wars: The American Military Experience in World War I.* New York: Oxford University Press, 1968.

Cohen, W. B. *The French Encounter with Africans: White Response to Blacks, 1530–1880.* Bloomington: Indiana University Press, 1980.

Conklin, A. L. *A Mission to Civilize: The Republican Idea of Empire in France and West Africa, 1895–1930.* Stanford, CA: Stanford University Press, 1997.

Conot, R. *Rivers of Blood, Years of Darkness.* New York: Bantam Books, 1967.

Conrad, E. *General Harriet Tubman.* Washington, DC: Associated Publishers, 1990.

Cooke, J. J. *100 Miles from Baghdad: With the French in Desert Storm.* Westport, CT: Praeger, 1993.

Cooley, R. B. "Is There an Explanation?" *Outlook,* 121, September 10, 1919.

Cornevin, R. "The Germans in Africa Before 1918." In L. H. Gann and P. Duignan (eds.), *Colonialism in Africa 1870–1960,* Vol. 1. Cambridge: Cambridge University Press, 1969.

Cornish, D. T. *The Sable Arm: Negro Troops in the Union Army, 1861–1865.* New York: W. W. Norton, 1966.

Cripps, T. *Making Movies Black: The Hollywood Message Movie from World War II to the Civil Rights Era.* New York: Oxford University Press, 1993.

Cripps, T., and D. Culbert, "*The Negro Soldier* (1944): Film Propaganda in Black and White." *American Quarterly,* 31:616–640, 1979.

Cushing, H. *From a Surgeon's Journal.* Boston: Little, Brown, 1936.

Cutler, J. E. *Lynch Law: An Investigation into the History of Lynching in the United States.* New York: Longmans, Green, 1905.

Dalfiume, R. M. *Desegregation of the U.S. Armed Forces: Fighting on Two Fronts.* Columbia: University of Missouri Press, 1969.

Davies, R. W. *Service in the Roman Army.* Edinburgh: Edinburgh University Press, 1989.

Davis, S. C. *Reservoirs of Men: A History of the Black Troops of French West Africa.* Westport, CT: Negro Universities Press, 1934.

De Azevedo, T. *The Colored Elite in a Brazilian City.* New Haven, CT: Human Relations Area Files, 1998.

Degler, C. N. *Neither Black nor White: Slavery and Race Relations in Brazil and the United States.* New York: Macmillan, 1971.

De Gobineau, H. *Noblesse d'Afrique.* Paris: Fasquelle, 1946. (Gabineau in original.)

DeLong, K., and S. Tuckey. *Mogadishu: Heroism and Tragedy.* Westport, CT: Praeger, 1994.

Delsarte, W. *The Negro, Democracy, and the War.* Detroit: Wolverine, 1919.

Dierks, J. C. *A Leap to Arms: The Cuban Campaign of 1898.* Philadelphia: Lippincott, 1970.

Dirks, R. *The Black Saturnalia: Conflict and its Ritual Expression on British West Indian Slave Plantations.* Gainesville: University of Florida Monographs in Social Science, Number 72, 1987.

Donaldson, G. *The History of African-Americans in the Military.* Malabar, FL: Krieger, 1991.

Douglass, F. *Life and Times of Frederick Douglass.* New York: Macmillan, 1962.

Dowd, J. *The Negro in American Life.* New York: Century Company, 1926.

DuBois, W. E. B. "The History of the Black Man." *The Crisis,* June, 63–89, 1919.

Early, S. "Negro Soldiers." *Scholastic*, 37:1–2, 1940.

Echenberg, M. "'Morts pour la France'; The African Soldier in France During the Second World War." *Journal of African History*, 26: 363–380, 1985.

Edgerton, R. B. *Like Lions They Fought: The Zulu War and the Last Black Empire in Africa*. New York: Free Press, 1988.

———. *The Fall of the Asante Empire*. New York: Free Press, 1995.

———. *Death or Glory: The Legacy of the Crimean War*. Boulder: Westview, 1999.

———. *Warrior Women: The Amazons of Dahomey and the Nature of War*. Boulder: Westview, 2000.

Elting, J. R. *Swords Around a Throne: Napoleon's Grande Armée*. New York: Free Press, 1988.

Ely, H. E. *The Use of Negro Manpower in War*, U.S. Army War College, October 30, 1925, Reference C, The Negro Officer, MHRC, CBP.

Emery, F. *The Red Soldier: Letters from the Zulu War, 1879*. London: Hodder & Stoughton, 1977.

Emilio, L. F. *A Brave Black Regiment: History of the Fifty-Fourth Regiment of Massachusetts Volunteer Infantry*. New York: Arno Press, 1969.

Erens, P. "The Flapper: Hollywood's First Liberated Woman." In L. R. Broer and J. D. Walther (eds.), *Dancing Fools and Weary Blues: The Great Escape of the Twenties*. Bowling Green, OH: Bowling Green State University Popular Press, 1990. Pp. 130–139.

Estell, K. *African America: Portrait of a People*. Detroit: Visible Ink Press, 1994.

Farrington, J. *America Awakes: A New Appraisal of the Twenties*. Richmond, VA: Westover, 1971.

Ferguson, N. *The Pity of War*. New York: Basic Books, 1999.

Fernandes, F. *The Negro in Brazilian Society*. (Translated by J. D. Skiles, A. Brunel, and A. Rothwell.) New York: Columbia University Press, 1969.

Feuer, A. B. *The Santiago Campaign of 1898: A Soldier's View of the Spanish-American War*. Westport, CT: Praeger, 1993.

Fick, C. E. *The Making of Haiti: Saint Domingue Revolution from Below*. Knoxville: University of Tennessee Press, 1990.

Fischer, D. H. *Albion's Seed: Four British Folkways in America*. New York: Oxford University Press, 1989.

Fiske, J. "Crispus Attucks." *Negro History Bulletin*, 333: 58–68, 1970.

Fleetwood, C. A. *The Negro as Soldier*. Washington, DC: Howard University, 1895.

Fletcher, M. E. *America's First Black General: Benjamin O. Davis, Sr., 1880–1970*. Lawrence: University Press of Kansas, 1989.

Flower, B. O. "Some Dead Sea Fruit of Our War of Subjugation." *The Arena*, 27: 647–653, 1902.

Foner, E. *America's Black Past: A Reader in Afro-American History*, 1st ed. New York: Harper & Row, 1970.

———. "Was Abraham Lincoln a Racist?" *Los Angeles Times, Book Review*, April 9, 2000.

Foner, J. D. *Blacks and the Military in American History: A New Perspective*. New York: Praeger, 1974.

Fortescue, J. W. *A History of the British Army*, 13 vols. London: Macmillan, 1910–1930.

Fox-Genovese, E. *Within the Plantation Household: Black and White Women of the Old South*. Chapel Hill: University of North Carolina Press, 1988.

Francis, C. E. *The Tuskegee Airmen: The Story of the Negro in the U.S. Air Force.* Boston: Bruce Humphries, 1955.

Franklin, J. H. *The Militant South, 1800–1861.* Cambridge: Belknap Press of Harvard University Press, 1956.

Franklin, J. H., and L. Schweninger. *Runaway Slaves: Rebels on the Plantation, 1790–1860.* New York: Oxford University Press, 1999.

Frazier, E. F. *The Negro in the United States.* New York: Macmillan, 1949.

Frederickson, G. M. *The Black Image in the White Mind: The Debate on Afro-American Character and Destiny, 1817–1914.* Middletown, CT: Wesleyan University Press, 1971.

Freyre, G. *The Masters and the Slaves: A Study in the Development of Brazilian Civilization.* Los Angeles: University of California Press, 1986.

Frost, J. *2 Para Falklands: The Battalion at War.* London: Sphere Books, 1983.

Fryer, P. *Staying Power: The History of Black People in Britain.* London: Pluto Press, 1984.

Fullinwider, S. P. *The Mind and Mood of Black America: 20th Century Thought.* Homewood, IL: Dorsey Press, 1969.

Furnas, J. C. *Goodbye to Uncle Tom.* London: Secker & Warburg, 1956.

_____. *The Americans: A Social History of the United States, 1587–1914.* New York: Putnam, 1969.

_____. *Great Times: An Informed Social History of the United States.* New York: Putnam, 1974.

_____. *Stormy Weather: Crosslights on the Nineteen Thirties, an Informal Social History of the U.S., 1929–1941.* New York: Putnam, 1977.

Gatewood, W. B., Jr. "Negro Troops in Florida, 1898." *Florida Historical Quarterly,* 49:4–9, 1970.

_____. *"Smoked Yankees" and the Struggle for Empire: Letters from Negro Soldiers, 1898–1902.* Urbana: University of Illinois Press, 1971.

_____. *Black Americans and the White Man's Burden, 1898–1903.* Urbana: University of Illinois Press, 1975.

General's Reports of Service, War of the Rebellion, Adjutant General's Office, Returns Division. National Archives, Washington, DC.

Genovese, E. D. *Roll, Jordan, Roll: The World the Slaves Made.* New York: Random House, 1974.

_____. *From Rebellion to Revolution: Afro-American Slave Revolts in the Modern World.* Baton Rouge: Louisiana State University Press, 1979.

Gibbs, C. R. "The First Black Army Officer." *Armed Forces Journal International,* June 1975, p. 24.

Glatthaar, J. T. *Forged in Battle: The Civil War Alliance of Black Soldiers and White Officers.* New York: Free Press, 1990.

Goff, S., and R. Sanders, with C. Smith. *Brothers: Black Soldiers in the Nam.* Novato, CA: Presidio Press, 1982.

Goldstein, D. "Interracial Sex and Racial Democracy in Brazil: Twin Concepts." *American Anthropologist,* 101:563–578, 1999.

Gordon, M. R., and B. E. Trainor. *The General's War: The Inside Story of the Conflict in the Gulf.* Boston: Little, Brown, 1995.

Goulden, J. C. *Korea: The Untold Story of the War.* New York: McGraw-Hill, 1982

Graham, L. O. *Our Kind of People: Inside America's Black Upper Class.* New York: Harper-Collins, 1999.

Grant, M. *The Army of the Caesars.* London: Weidenfeld & Nicolson, 1974.

Gray, J. H. *The Roar of the Twenties.* Toronto: Macmillan, 1975.

Greene, R. E. *Black Defenders of the Persian Gulf War, Desert Shield–Desert Storm: A Reference and Pictorial History.* Fort Washington, MD: R. E. Greene, 1991.

Greer, A. C. *Scott Papers* 113–115; Greer to McKellar, December 6, 1918.

Grimke, F. J. *The Race Problem.* Washington, DC: np, 1919.

Gropman, A. L. *The Air Force Integrates, 1945–1964.* Washington, DC: Office of Air Force History, 1978.

Grundlingh, L. "Aspects of the Second World War on the Lives of Black South African and British Colonial Soldiers." *Transafrican Journal of History,* 21:19–35, 1992.

Haines, G. K. *The Americanization of Brazil: A Study of U.S. Cold War Diplomacy in the Third World, 1945–1954.* Wilmington, DE: SR Books, 1989.

Hallowell, N. P. *The Negro as Soldier in the War of the Rebellion.* Boston: Little, Brown, 1897.

Hargreaves, R. *The Bloodybacks: The British Serviceman in North America and the Caribbean, 1655–1783.* London: Rupert Hart-Davis, 1968.

Hargrove, H. B. *Buffalo Soldiers in Italy: Black Americans in World War II.* Jefferson, NC: McFarland, 1985.

Harrington, P., and F. A. Sharf (eds.). *Omdurman 1898: The Eyewitnesses Speak.* London: Greenhill Books, 1998.

Harrod, F. S. *Manning the New Navy: The Development of a Modern Naval Enlisted Force, 1899–1940.* Westport, CT: Greenwood Press, 1978.

Hasdorff, J. C. "Reflections on the Tuskegee Experiment: An Interview with Brigadier General Noel F. Parrish, USAF (ret.)." *Aerospace Historian,* 24:175–176, 1977, Hastings, M. *The Korean War.* New York: Simon & Schuster, 1987.

Hastings, M., and S. Jenkins. *The Battle for the Falklands.* New York: W. W. Norton, 1983.

Hauser, W. L. *America's Army in Crisis: A Study in Civil-Military Relations.* Baltimore: Johns Hopkins University Press, 1973.

Heywood, C. D. *Negro Combat Troops in the World War: The Story of the 371st Infantry.* Worcester, MA: Commonwealth Press, 1928.

Higginson, G. *Seventy-one Years of a Guardsman Life.* London: Smith, Elder, 1916.

Higginson, T. W. *Army Life in a Black Regiment.* East Lansing: Michigan State University Press, 1960.

Hill, R., and P. Hogg. *A Black Corps d' Elite: An Egyptian Sudanese Conscript Battalion with the French Army in Mexico, 1863–1867, and Its Survivors in Subsequent African History.* East Lansing: Michigan State University, 1995.

Hiro, D. *Black British, White British.* London: Eyre & Spottiswoode, 1971.

Hochschild, A. *King Leopold's Ghost.* Boston: Houghton Mifflin, 1998.

Hodgson, G. *The Colonel: The Life and Wars of Henry Stimson, 1867–1950.* New York: Knopf, 1990.

Hofstadter, R., and M. Wallace. *American Violence: A Documentary History.* New York: Knopf, 1970.

Hope, R. O. *Racial Strife in the Military: Toward the Elimination of Discrimination.* New York: Praeger, 1979.

Hopkins, K. *Conquerors and Slaves: Sociological Studies in Roman History,* Vol. 1. Cambridge: Cambridge University Press, 1978.

Houston, C. H. Letter to General Douglas MacArthur (August 29, 1934), NAACP AF-Military, LCMD.

_____. Letter to Editor, *New York Times,* NAACP AF-Military, LCMD, March 9, 1938.

Hunton, A. W., and K. M. Johnson. *Two Colored Women with the American Expeditionary Forces.* New York: G. K. Hall, 1997. (Orig. Brooklyn: Brooklyn Eagle Press, 1920.)

Israel, A. M. "Measuring the War Experience: Ghanaian Soldiers in World War II." *Journal of Modern African Studies,* 25:159–168, 1987.

Jackson, A. "General Orders, 7th Military District, January 21, 1815." *Niles Weekly Register,* February 25, 1815.

Jahoda, G. *Images of Savages: Ancient Roots of Modern Prejudice in Western Culture.* London: Routledge, 1999.

Jordan, W. *White Over Black: American Attitudes Toward the Negro.* Chapel Hill: University of North Carolina Press, 1968.

Kanya-Forstner, A. S. *The Conquest of the Western Sudan: A Study in French Military Imperialism.* Cambridge: Cambridge University Press, 1969.

Kaplan, S. *The Black Presence in the Era of the American Revolution, 1770–1800.* Greenwich, CT: New York Graphic Society, 1973.

Keegan, J. *The First World War.* New York: Knopf, 1999.

Keil, C. *Urban Blues.* Chicago: University of Chicago Press, 1966.

Kenan, R. *Walking on Water: Black American Lives at the Turn of the Twenty-First Century.* New York: Knopf, 1999.

Kennan, G. *Campaigning in Cuba.* New York: Century Company, 1899.

Kester, H. *Revolt Among the Sharecroppers.* New York: Arno Press, 1969.

Killingray, D. "Race and Rank in the British Army in the Twentieth Century." *Ethnic and Racial Studies,* 10:276–290, 1987.

Kinevan, M. E. *Frontier Cavalryman: Lieutenant John Bigelow with the Buffalo Soldiers in Texas.* El Paso: Texas Western Press, 1998.

Kipling, R. *Barrack Room Ballads and Other Poems.* New York: T. Y. Crowell, 1899.

Kolata, G. *Flu: The Story of the Great Influenza Pandemic of 1918 and the Search for the Virus That Caused It.* New York: Farrar, Strauss & Giroux, 1999.

Kolchin, P. "Reevaluating the Antebellum Slave Community: A Comparative Perspective." *Journal of American History,* 70:579–601, 1983.

Kolker, C. "A City's Buried Shame." *Los Angeles Times,* pp. 1, 16, October 23, 1999.

La Gorce, P-M. *The French Army: A Military-Political History.* New York: Braziller, 1963.

Langley, H. D. *Social Reform in the United States Navy, 1798–1862.* Urbana: University of Illinois Press, 1967.

Lanning, M. L. *The African-American Soldier: From Crispus Attucks to Colin Powell.* Secaucus, NJ: Birch Lane Press, 1997.

Lawley, N. E. *Soldiers of Misfortune: The Tirailleurs Sénégalais of the Côte d'Ivoire in World War II,* 3 vols. Ph.D. Dissertation, Northwestern University, 1988.

Leckie, W. H. *The Buffalo Soldiers.* Norman: University of Oklahoma Press, 1967.

Lee, U. *The Employment of Negro Troops.* Washington, DC: Center of Military History, U.S. Army, 1963.

Levine, L. W. *Black Culture and Black Consciousness*. New York: Oxford University Press, 1978.

Lewinson, P. *Race, Class and Party: A History of Negro Suffrage and Negro Suffrage in the South*. New York: The Universal Library, 1965. (Orig. 1932.)

Lindop, E. *Modern America: The Dazzling Twenties*. New York: Franklin Watts, 1970.

Linn, B. M. *The U.S. Army and Counterinsurgency in the Philippine War, 1899–1902*. Chapel Hill: University of North Carolina Press, 1989.

———. *Guardians of Empire: The U.S. Army and the Pacific, 1902–1940*. Chapel Hill: University of North Carolina Press, 1997.

Little, A. W. *From Harlem to the Rhine: The Story of New York's Colored Volunteers*. New York: Haskell House, 1974.

Litwack, L. F. *North of Slavery: The Negro in the Free States, 1790–1850*. Chicago: University of Chicago Press, 1961.

———. *Been in the Storm So Long: The Aftermath of Slavery*. New York: Knopf, 1979.

Lloyd, A. *The Drums of Kumasi: The Story of the Ashanti Wars*. London: Longmans, 1964.

Lockett, J. D. "The Lynching Massacre of Black and White Soldiers at Fort Pillow, Tennessee, April 12, 1864." *Western Journal of Black Studies*, 22:84–98, 1998.

Logan, R. W. *The Betrayal of the Negro*. London: Collier Books, 1965.

Lucas, C. P. *The Empire at War*, Vol. 2. London, New York: H. Milford, Oxford University Press, 1923.

———. *The Empire at War*, Vol. 4. London, New York: H. Milford, Oxford University Press, 1924.

MacGregor, M. J., Jr. *Integration of the Armed Forces*. Washington, DC: Center of Military History, United States Army, 1981.

Maness, L. E. "The Fort Pillow Massacre: Fact or Fiction." *Tennessee Historical Quarterly*, 45:287–315, 1986.

Mangin, C. (Général). *Lettres du Soudan*. Paris: Editions des Portiques, 1930.

Marceau, (Capitain). *Le Tirailleur Soudanais*. Paris: Berger-Levrault, 1911.

Marcus, H. G. *The Life and Times of Menelik II, Ethiopia 1844–1913*. Oxford: Oxford University Press, 1975.

Margolick, D. *Strange Fruit: Billie Holiday, Café Society, and an Early Cry for Civil Rights*. Philadelphia: Running Press, 2000.

Marks, S. "Black Watch on the Rhine: A Study in Propaganda, Prejudice and Prurience." *European Studies Review*, 13: 297–334, 1983.

Marszalek, J. F., Jr. *Court Martial: The Army vs. Johnson Whittaker, an Account of the Ordeal of a Black Cadet at West Point*. New York: Scribners, 1972.

Martin, F. *Life in the Legion from a Soldier's Point of View*. New York: Scribners, 1911.

Mason, M., and A. Furr. *The American Negro Soldier with the Red Hand of France*. Boston: Cornhill, 1920.

McConnell, R. *Negro Troops of Antebellum Louisiana: A History of the Battalion of Free Men of Color*. Baton Rouge: Louisiana State University Press, 1968.

McElroy, J. *Andersonville: A Story of Rebel Military Prisons, Fifteen Months a Guest of the So-Called Southern Confederacy. A Private Soldier's Experience in Richmond, Andersonville, Savannah, Millen, Blackshear and Florence*. Toledo: D. R. Locke, 1879.

McGregor, M. J., Jr. *Integration of the Armed Forces, 1940–1965*. Washington, DC: Center of Military History, United States Army, 1981.

McGuire, P. *Taps for a Jim Crow Army*. Santa Barbara, CA: ABC-Clio, 1983.

_____. *He, Too, Spoke for Democracy: Judge Hastie, World War II, and the Black Soldier*. Westport, CT: Greenwood, 1988.

McPherson, J. M. *The Negro's Civil War: How American Negroes Felt and Acted During the War for the Union*. New York: Pantheon, 1965.

Meckiffe, D., and M. Murray. "Radio and the Black Soldier During World War II." *Critical Studies in Mass Communication*, 15:337–356, 1998.

Medea, B. "Interview with Benedita da Silva, Community Activist and Senator." *NACLA Report on the Americas*, 31:13–17, 1997.

Meditz, S. W., and T. Merrill (eds.). *Zaire: A Country Study*. Washington, DC: Library of Congress, 1994.

Meinertzhagen, R. *Army Diary, 1899–1926*. London: Oliver & Boyd, 1960.

Meredith, J. (ed.). *Omdurman Diaries 1898: Eye Witness Accounts of the Legendary Campaign*. Barnsley, UK: Leo Cooper, 1998.

Mershon, S., and S. Schlossman. *Foxholes & Color Lines: Desegregating the U.S. Armed Forces*. Baltimore: Johns Hopkins University Press, 1998.

Michel, M. *L'appel à l'Afrique: Contributions et réactions à l'effort de guerre en A.O.F. (1914–1919)*. Paris: Publications de la Sorbonne, 1983.

Miers, S., and I. Kopytoff (eds.). *Slavery in Africa: Historical and Anthropological Perspectives*. Madison: University of Wisconsin Press, 1977.

Miller, C. *Battle for the Bundu: The First World War in East Africa*. New York: Macmillan, 1974.

Miller, K. *The Everlasting Stain*. Washington, DC: Associated Publishers, 1924.

Miller, L. L., and C. Moskos. "Humanitarians or Warriors?: Race, Gender and Status in Operation Restore Hope." *Armed Forces and Society*, 21:615–637, 1995.

Miller, M. *Plain Speaking: An Oral Biography of Harry S. Truman*. New York: Berkeley/ Putnam, 1973.

Miller, R. M., and J. W. Zophy. "Unwelcome Allies: Billy Yank and the Black Soldier." *Phylon*, 39:234–240, 1978.

Millett, A. R. *The General: Robert L. Bullard and Officership in the United States Army, 1881–1925*. Westport, CT: Greenwood Press, 1975.

Mintz, S. W. "Slave Life on Caribbean Sugar Plantations: Some Unanswered Questions." In S. Palmié (ed.), *Slave Cultures and the Culture of Slavery*. Knoxville: University of Tennessee Press, 1995. Pp.12–22.

Mockler, A. *Haile Selassie's War*. London: Oxford University Press, 1984.

Monaghan, D. *The Falklands War: Myth and Countermyth*. London: Macmillan, 1998.

Moodie, D. C. F. *The History of the Battles and Adventures of the British, Boers, and the Zulus in Southern Africa*, Vol. 1. Adelaide: George Robertson, 1879.

Moore, B. L. *To Serve My Country, to Serve My Race: The Story of the Only African American WACs Stationed Overseas During World War II*. New York: New York University Press, 1996.

Morgan, K. L. "Caddy Buffers: Legends of a Middle-Class Negro Family in Philadelphia." *Keystone Folklore Quarterly*, 11:67–88, 1966.

Morison, E. E. *Turmoil and Tradition: A Study of the Life and Times of Henry L. Stimson*. Boston: Houghton Mifflin, 1960.

Morrow, C. J. *What's a Commie Ever Done to Black People? A Korean War Memoir of Fighting in the U.S. Army's Last All Negro Unit*. Jefferson, North Carolina: McFarland, 1997.

Moskos, C. C., and J. S. Butler. *All That We Can Be: Black Leadership and Racial Integration the Army Way*. New York: Basic Books, 1996.

Motley, M. P. *The Invisible Soldier: The Experience of the Black Soldier in World War II*. Detroit: Wayne State University Press, 1975.

Moton, R. R. "The Lynchings Record for 1918." *Outlook*, 121, p. 159, January 22, 1919.

_____. "Negro Troops in France." *Southern Workman*, 48:220–221, 1919.

Mowry, G. E. (ed.). *The Twenties: Fords, Flappers & Fanatics*. Englewood Cliffs, NJ: Prentice-Hall, 1963.

Mulroy, K. *Freedom on the Border: The Seminole Maroons in Florida, the Indian Territory, Coahuila, and Texas*. Lubbock: Texas Tech University Press, 1993.

Murdock, G. P. *Africa: Its Peoples and Their Cultural History*. New York: McGraw-Hill, 1959.

Musicant, I. *The Banana Wars: A History of United States Military Intervention in Latin America from the Spanish-American War to the Invasion of Panama*. New York: Macmillan, 1990.

_____. *Empire by Default: The Spanish-American War and the Dawn of the American Century*. New York: Henry Holt, 1998.

Myrdal, G. *An American Dilemma*, Vol. 1. New York: Harper, 1944.

Nalty, B. C. *Strength for the Fight: A History of Black Americans in the Military*. New York: Free Press, 1986.

Nalty, B. C., and M. J. MacGregor (eds.). *Blacks in the Military: Essential Documents*. Wilmington, DE: Scholarly Resources, 1981.

Nell, W. C. *The Colored Patriots of the American Revolution, with Sketches of Several Distinguished Colored Persons*. Boston: Robert F. Wallcut, 1855.

Nelson, K. L. "The 'Black Horror on the Rhine': Race as a Factor in Post-World War I Diplomacy." *Journal of Modern History*, 42:606–627, 1970.

Newitt, M. *A History of Mozambique*. London: Hurst, 1995.

Noble, P. *The Negro in Films*. New York: Arno Press, 1970.

Null, G. *Black Hollywood: The Black Performer in Motion Pictures*. New York: Citadel Press, 1990.

Nunn, F. M. "Effects of European Military Training in Latin America: The Origins and Nature of Professional Militarism in Argentina, Brazil, Chile and Peru." *Military Affairs*, 39:1–7, 1975.

Olmstead, C. *A Journey in the Back Country*. New York: Mason Brothers, 1860.

Osur, A. M. *Blacks in the Army Air Forces During World War II*. Washington, DC: Office of Air Force History, 1977.

Overshine, A. T. Subject–Investigation of Colored Officers in the 370th Infantry and 372nd Infantry, to Inspector General, AEF, July 20, 1918, RG 120, NARS.

Owens, J., with P. G. Neimark. *Blackthink: My Life as Black Man and White Man*. New York: William Morrow, 1970.

Packenham, T. *The Scramble for Africa: The White Man's Conquest of the Dark Continent from 1876 to 1912*. New York: Random House, 1991.

Palfry, J. C. *Military Society of Massachusetts*, June 27, 1863.

Palmer, A. "Black American Soldiers in Trinidad, 1942–44: Wartime Politics in a Colonial Society." *Journal of Imperial and Commonwealth History*, 14: 203–218, 1986.

Palmer, C. A. *Slaves of the White God: Blacks in Mexico, 1570–1650.* Cambridge: Harvard University Press, 1976.

Palmié, S. (ed.). *Slave Cultures and the Culture of Slavery.* Knoxville: University of Tennessee Press, 1995.

Patterson, O. *Slavery and Social Death: A Comparative Study.* Cambridge: Harvard University Press, 1982.

Patton, G. W. *War and Peace: The Black Officer in the American Military, 1915–1941.* Westport, CT: Greenwood, 1981.

Perrett, G. *America in the Twenties: A History.* New York: Touchstone, 1982.

Person, Y. "Samori and Resistance to the French." In R. I. Rotberg and A. A. Mazrui (eds.), *Protest and Power in Black Africa.* New York: Oxford University Press, 1970. Pp. 80–112.

Peters, V. B. *The Florida Wars.* Hamden, CT: Archon, 1979.

Petrochitos, N. *Roman Attitudes to the Greeks.* Athens: University of Athens, 1974.

Pipes, D. *Slave Soldiers and Islam: The Genesis of a Military System.* New Haven: Yale University Press, 1981.

Porch, D. *The French Foreign Legion: A Complete History of the Legendary Fighting Force.* New York: HarperCollins, 1991.

Porter, K. W. *The Black Seminoles: History of a Freedom-Seeking People.* (Revised and edited by A. M. Amos and T. P. Senter.) Gainesville: University Press of Florida, 1996.

Post, C. J. *The Little War of Private Post.* Boston: Little, Brown, 1960.

Powell, A. C., Jr. *Marching Blacks.* New York: Dial Press, 1945.

Powell, A. C., Sr. *Against the Tide: An Autobiography.* New York: Richard Smith, 1938.

Powell, C. *My American Journey.* New York: Random House, 1995.

Prange, G. W., with D. M. Goldstein and K. V. Dillon. *At Dawn We Slept: The Untold Story of Pearl Harbor.* New York: Penguin, 1978.

Pringle, H. F. *Theodore Roosevelt: A Biography.* New York: Harcourt, Brace, 1931.

Quarles, B. *The Negro in the Civil War.* Boston: Little, Brown, 1953.

_____. *The Negro in the American Revolution.* Chapel Hill: Published for the Institute of Early American History and Culture, Williamsburg, VA, by the University of North Carolina Press, 1996. (First published in 1961 by the University of North Carolina Press.)

Rainey, T. A. "Buffalo Soldiers in Africa: The U.S. Army and the Liberian Frontier Force, 1912–1927–An Overview." *Librarian Studies Journal,* 21:203–238, 1996.

Ramos, A. *The Negro in Brazil.* (Translated from Portuguese by R. Pattee.) Washington, DC: Associated Publishers, 1939.

Redkey, E. S. (ed.). *A Grand Army of Black Men: Letters from African-American Soldiers in the Union Army, 1861–1865.* New York: Cambridge University Press, 1992.

Redmayne, A. "Mkwawa and the Hehe Wars." *Journal of African History,* 9:409–436, 1968.

Reynolds, P. "The Churchill Government and the Black American Troops in Britain During World War II." *Transactions of the Royal Historical Society,* 35:113–133, 1985.

Rich, P. B. *Race and Empire in British Politics,* 2nd ed. Cambridge: Cambridge University Press, 1990.

Richards, J. "Some Experiences with Colored Soldiers." *Atlantic Monthly,* 124:184–190, 1919.

Ringel, F. J. *America as Americans See It*. New York: Harcourt, Brace, 1932.

Rishell, L. *With a Black Platoon in Combat: A Year in Korea*. College Station: Texas A&M University Press, 1993.

Roberts, R. *Papa Jack: Jack Johnson and the Era of White Hopes*. New York: Free Press, 1983.

Robertson, D. *Denmark Vesey*. New York: Knopf, 2000.

Robinson, B. *Dark Companion*. New York: National Travel Club, 1947.

Robinson, J., and A. Duckett. *Breakthrough to the Big Leagues: The Story of Jackie Robinson*. New York: Harper & Row, 1965.

Robinson, M. C., and F. N. Schubert. "David Fagen: An Afro-American Rebel in the Philippines, 1899–1901." *Pacific Historical Review*, 44:68:83, 1975.

Roosevelt, T. "The Rough Riders." *Scribner's Magazine*, April 25, 1899.

_____. *Theodore Roosevelt: An Autobiography*. New York: Scribner, 1913.

Rose, R. A. "The Lonely Eagles." *Journal of the American Aviation Historical Society*, 10:118–127, 240–252, 1975.

Rose, S. O. "Girls and GIs: Race, Sex, and Diplomacy in Second World War Britain." *International History Review*, 19:146–160, 1997.

Ross, W. A. *My Colored Battalion*. Chicago: Warner A. Ross, 1920.

Rouse, W. J. "The United States Colored Regulars." *New York Times–Illustrated Magazine*, pp. 4–5, June 5, 1898.

Roy, J. *The Battle of Dien Bien Phu*. New York: Harper & Row, 1965.

Rubenson, S. "Adowa 1896: The Resounding Protest." In R. I. Rotberg and A. A. Mazrui (eds.), *Protest and Power in Black Africa*. New York: Oxford University Press, 1970. Pp. 113–142.

Russell, W. H. *My Diary North and South*. Boston: T.O.H.P. Burnham, 1863.

Sbacchi, A. *Legacy of Bitterness: Ethiopia and Fascist Italy, 1935–1941*. Lawrenceville, NJ: Red Sea Press, 1997.

Schneider, W. H. *An Empire for the Masses: The French Popular Image of Africa, 1870–1900*. Westport, CT: Greenwood, 1982.

Schoenfeld, S. J. *The Negro in the Armed Forces: His Value and Status–Past, Present and Potential*. Washington, DC: Associated Publishers, 1945.

Schubert, F. N. *Black Valor: Buffalo Soldiers and the Medal of Honor, 1870–1898*. Wilmington, DE: Scholarly Resources Books, 1997.

Schurz, C. "Carl Schurz on the Negro Crisis." *Current Literature*, 36:302–304, 1904.

Scott, E. J. *Scott's Official History of the American Negro in the World War*. Chicago: Homewood Press, 1919.

Scott, S. F. *From Yorktown to Valmy: The Transformation of the French Army in an Age of Revolution*. Niwot: University Press of Colorado, 1998.

Seligmann, H. J. *The Negro Faces America*. New York: Harper, 1920.

Shapiro, H. *White Violence and Black Response: From Reconstruction to Montgomery*. Amherst: University of Massachusetts Press, 1988.

Shaw, H. I., Jr., and R. W. Donnelly. *Blacks in the Marine Corps*. Washington, DC: History and Museums Division, Headquarters, U.S. Marine Corps., 1975.

Sherman, W. T. Endorsement by General William Tecumseh Sherman to letter, Secretary of War J. D. Cameron to Benjamin F. Butler, January 20, 1877, item 25.

Sherwood, M. A. *Many Struggles: West Indian Workers and Service Personnel in Britain (1939–1945)*. London: Karia Press, 1985.

Shipman, P. *The Evolution of Racism: Human Differences and the Use and Abuse of Science.* New York: Simon & Schuster, 1994.

Shogan, R., and T. Craig. *The Detroit Race Riot: A Study in Violence.* New York: Chilton Books, 1964.

Silva, E. *Prince of the People: The Life and Times of a Brazilian Free Man of Color.* (Translated by Moyra Ashford.) London: Verso, 1993.

Simpson, H. R. *Dien Bien Phu: The Epic Battle America Forgot.* Washington, DC: Brassley's, 1994.

Singletary, O. *Negro Militia and Deconstruction.* Westport, CT: Greenwood Press, 1984.

Skidmore, T. E. *Black Into White: Race and Nationality in Brazilian Thought.* Durham, NC: Duke University Press, 1993.

Smith, G. A. *When Jim Crow Met John Bull: Black American Soldiers in World War II Britain.* London: I. B. Tauris, 1987.

Sodré, N. W. *História Militar do Brasil.* Rio de Janeiro: Editora Civilizaçâo Brasileira, 1965.

Stallings, L. *The Doughboys: The Story of the AEF, 1917–1918.* New York: Harper & Row, 1963.

Steevens, G. W. *With Kitchener to Khartoum.* New York: Dodd, Mead, 1898.

Stepan, A. *The Military in Politics: Changing Patterns in Brazil.* Princeton: Princeton University Press, 1971.

Stern, S. "When the Black GI Comes Home from Vietnam." In J. David and E. Crane (eds.), *The Black Soldier: From the American Revolution to Vietnam.* New York: William Morrow, 1971. Pp. 215–227.

Stillwell, P. (ed.). *The Golden Thirteen: Recollections of the First Black Naval Officers.* Annapolis, MD: Naval Institute Press, 1993.

Stimson, H. L. *Henry L. Stimson Diary.* New Haven: Yale University Press, 1940.

Stouffer, S. A., et al. *The American Soldier: Adjustment During Army Life,* 2 vols. New York: Wiley, 1949.

Suret-Canale, J. *French Colonialism in Tropical Africa, 1900–1945.* New York: Pica Press, 1971.

Sweeney, A. W. *History of the American Negro in the Great World War.* New York: G. G. Sapp, 1919.

Tadman, M. *Speculators and Slaves: Masters, Traders, and Slaves in the Old South.* Madison: University of Wisconsin Press, 1989.

Talbott, J. *The War Without a Name: France in Algeria, 1954–1962.* New York: Knopf, 1980.

Taylor, C. (ed.). *Vietnam and Black America: An Anthology of Protest and Resistance.* Garden City, NY: Anchor Books, 1973.

Taylor, E. R. *"If We Must Die:" A History of Shipboard Insurrections During the Slave Trade.* Ph.D. Dissertation, University of California, Los Angeles, 2000.

Terkel, S. *"The Good War": An Oral History of World War Two.* New York: Ballantine, 1984.

Terry, W. *Bloods: An Oral History of the Vietnam War by Black Veterans.* New York: Random House, 1984.

Thomas, H. *The Slave Trade: The Story of the Atlantic Slave Trade, 1440–1870.* New York: Simon & Schuster, 1997.

Thompson, J. M. "Colonial Policy and the Family Life of Black Troops in French West Africa, 1817–1904." *The International Journal of African Historical Studies*, 23: 423–453, 1990.

Toplin, R. B. *Freedom and Prejudice: The Legacy of Slavery in the United States and Brazil.* Westport, CT: Greenwood Press, 1981.

Trask, D. F. *The War in Spain in 1898.* New York: Free Press, 1981.

Turner, B. "Foreword." In A. E. Barbeau and F. Henri (eds.), *The Unknown Soldiers: Black American Troops in World War I.* Philadelphia: Temple University Press, 1974. pp. xi–xiii.

Tyson, A. S. "A Few Good Women." *Christian Science Monitor*, pp. 9–12, May 20, 1998.

U.S. Congress, Senate. *Alleged Executions Without Trial in France.* Washington, DC: U.S. Government Printing Office, 1923.

Van Deburg, W. L. *The Slave Drivers: Black Agricultural Labor Supervisors in the Antebellum South.* Westport, CT: Greenwood Press, 1979.

Villard, O. G. "The Negro in the Regular Army." *Atlantic Monthly*, 91:721–729, 1903.

Wade, W. C. *The Fiery Cross: The Ku Klux Klan in America.* New York: Simon & Schuster, 1987.

Walker, D. L. *The Boys of '98: Theodore Roosevelt and the Rough Riders.* New York: Tom Doherty Associates, 1998.

Washington, B. T. "Heroes in Black Skins." *Century Magazine*, 66:724–729, 1903.

Washington, V. F. *Eagles on Their Buttons: A Black Infantry Regiment in the Civil War.* Columbia: University of Missouri Press, 1999.

Weatherly, U. G. "The West Indies as a Sociological Laboratory." *American Journal of Sociology*, 29:290–304, 1923.

Weaver, J. D. *The Brownsville Raid.* New York: W. W. Norton, 1970.

Wells-Barnett, I. B. "How Enfranchisement Stops Voting." *Original Rights Magazine*, pp. 42–53, June 1910.

Westheider, J. E. *Fighting on Two Fronts: African Americans and the Vietnam War.* New York: New York University Press, 1997.

White, W. F. *Rope and Faggot.* New York: Knopf, 1929.

_____. *A Man Called White: The Autobiography of Walter White.* New York: Viking Press, 1948.

_____. "Its Our Country, Too." *Saturday Evening Post*, 213, pp. 23–27, December 14, 1940.

Wiley, B. I. *The Life of Johnny Rob: The Common Soldier of the Confederacy.* Garden City, NY: Doubleday, 1971.

Williams, C. H. *Negro Soldiers in World War I: The Human Side.* New York: AMS Press, 1970. (Orig. 1923.)

Williams, F. A. *Just Before the Dawn: A Doctor's Experiences in Vietnam.* New York: Exposition Press, 1971.

Williams, W. L. "The 'Sambo' Deception: The Experience of John McElroy in Andersonville Prison." *Phylon*, 39:261–263, 1978.

Williamson, J. *After Slavery: The Negro in South Carolina During Reconstruction, 1861–1877.* Chapel Hill: University of North Carolina Press, 1965.

Wills, B. S. *A Battle from the Start: The Life of Nathan Bedford Forrest.* New York: HarperCollins, 1992.

Wills, C. W. *Army Life of an Illinois Soldier*. Washington, DC: Globe Printing Company, 1906.

Wilson, E. G. *The Loyal Blacks*. New York: Capricorn Books, 1976.

Wilson, W. Letter to Secretary of War, Newton D. Baker, June 25, 1917. Manuscripts Division, Library of Congress, Washington, DC.

Wood, P. H. *Black Majority: Negroes in Colonial South Carolina, from 1670 Through the Stono Rebellion*. New York: W. W. Norton, 1974.

Woodson, C. G. *The Negro in Our History*. Washington, DC: Associated Publishers, 1921.

Woodward, C.V. *The Strange Career of Jim Crow*. New York: Oxford University Press, 1974.

Woodward, W. E. *Meet General Grant*. New York: Horace Liveright, 1928.

Wyatt-Brown, B. *Southern Honor*. New York: Oxford University Press, 1982.

Ziegler, P. *Omdurman*. New York: Knopf, 1974.

Index